American
Politics
and Government

HUGH DAVIS GRAHAM, Editor
University of Maryland Baltimore County

American Politics and Government:
Party, Ideology, and Reform in American History

Harper & Row, Publishers
New York, Evanston, San Francisco, London

Sponsoring Editor: John Greenman
Project Editor: Karla B. Philip
Designer: Jared Pratt
Production Supervisor: Will C. Jomarrón

AMERICAN POLITICS AND GOVERNMENT:
Party, Ideology, and Reform in American History

Library of Congress Cataloging in Publication Data

Graham, Hugh Davis, comp.
    American politics and government.

    Bibliography: p.
    1.   Political parties—United States—History—
Addresses, essays, lectures.   2.   United States—
Politics and government—Addresses, essays, lectures.
3.   Political science—History—United States—
Addresses, essays, lectures.   I.   Title.
JK2261.G76   329'.02   74-28921
ISBN 0-06-042442-7

CONTENTS

PREFACE

$\mathcal{U}$ntil recently most American historians were agreed on the general direction of American history. A sense of America's purpose and progress enabled them to relate, with some assurance, what had happened in the past to what was happening in the present. In the last few years, however, these assumed linkages between past and present have come apart, eroded by our contemporary confusion. By losing our guiding sense of where our American civilization is going, our confidence in where we have been has been shaken.

This text is designed to help restore these broken linkages in the crucial arena of American politics and government. It focuses less on the institutional structure of American government than on the complex relationship between party, ideology, and reform in American political life as it has evolved in the two centuries since gaining Independence. By relating past and present in a deliberate effort to enlarge the meaning of both, this book is intended to give students the experience of using history to orient themselves and to provide them with a broadened perspective with which to face major contemporary problems.

I am especially indebted to Gordon S. Wood, John G. Ryden, and John Higham for sharpening the questions that promise to shed the most light on the relationship between the past and present and on the efficacy of historical analysis in illuminating contemporary concerns. I also acknowledge with gratitude the permission of the authors and publishers cited herein to reprint the articles that constitute the bulk of the volume; they share no blame for any errors or biases contained in the introductory essay, the headnotes, or the conclusion.

H.D.G.

American
Politics
and Government

INTRODUCTION:
PARTY, IDEOLOGY, AND REFORM

*T*his volume explores American politics and government through a triangular focus that is likely to seem novel to students entering college. Most have learned from civics textbooks the origin and function of the executive, legislative, and judicial branches of government at the national, state, and local levels, and from American history textbooks how these institutions have evolved. Given such a base, it is a challenging and difficult task to assess the complex relationships among party, ideology, and reform in American political life. What is meant by these three broad terms?

Party is the chief instrument of political competition, the point where democratic theory (the elective process) and constitutional structure (the public institutions of government) come together. It is used here in the theoretical, neutral sense as opposed to the generic sense of Democrats and Republicans or Whigs and Free-Soilers, labels that rarely evoke neutrality. *Ideology* refers to the overarching set of principles that most Americans have historically shared and that underpin the governmental system by endowing it with legitimacy. Ideology is also used here in a more familiar sense to locate particular political parties along the customary (but problematical) left-to-right political spectrum.

Reform is the thorniest term of the three because it connotes a value judgment. In the lexicon of politics, reformers have been popularly regarded as morally superior individuals or groups intent upon rooting out evil. Here reformers are regarded as any group of like-minded citizens who engage in political action in order to advance their notion of civic virtue. As such, the term would properly apply, for example, both to prohibitionists seeking to purge society of the evil of alcohol, and to antiprohibitionists seeking to purge society of the evil of gangsterism, which prohibition allegedly fostered. Thus we are dealing with the continuing triangular relationship between (1) party as the primary *instrument* of competition for political power; (2) ideology as a set of theoretically cohesive *principles* that both establishes the boundary of this competition and gives form to the programs that compete for public allegiance; and (3) reform as the political *process* of adjustment to historical change—usually, but not always, within a two-party format with the "outs" attempting to oust the "ins."

Today's party system is a good place to begin because the issues are alive and because political parties with names, constituencies, programs, and histories are more tangible than ideologies and reform movements, which often cut across party lines. Part I contains essays by two contemporary political scientists, Walter Dean Burnham and James MacGregor Burns, whose historical sensitivity is unusually keen and whose analyses transcend the limitations of studies of specific parties by focusing on the larger comparative dimension of party *system.* Although they do this in different ways, Burnham and Burns arrive at a common critical conclusion that may be fairly summarized by the assertion that the roots of our present troubles may be traced to the Founding Fathers. Students are familiar with the institutional system of separation of powers and internal checks and balances established by the founders, a system that is customarily attributed to their genius. But Burnham and Burns are highly critical of their political legacy, which they criticize as too conducive to governmental obstruction and paralysis and as hostile to the wielding of power that is essential to meaningful reform.

Part II deals with the founding generation. It turns from party to ideology, not only because questions of ideology must come before questions of party, but also because the concept of party as we know it was then hardly born. Indeed, one of the paradoxes of American political history is that although its government has functioned largely through political parties, the men who designed it were uniformly contemptuous and fearful of the notion of party, which they equated with selfish and destructive factionalism that might doom the new republic. Part II includes selections from classic primary sources, such as Thomas Jefferson, Thomas Paine, and James Madison, as well as recent pathbreaking analyses by Louis Hartz and Richard Hofstadter. Part II eventually leads us from ideology back to party again, through Madison's ingenious argument in *The Federalist No. 10* that a large republic would mitigate the threat of faction, and through Hofstadter's ironical analysis of the painful evolution of an effective party system within the framework of a constitution that was based upon quite contrary assumptions. Part II concludes with a bit of a chronological cheat: Andrew Jackson's first presidential address to Congress in 1829. True enough, when one thinks of the founders one does not customarily include Jackson, although he was born in 1767 and had become a United States senator before the turn of the nineteenth century. But Jackson's address provides important continuity, first, in the ideological sense by ringing so true to the tone set in Jefferson's first inaugural; and second, because Jackson symbolizes the world's first truly modern party system.

Part III concentrates on a disaster that is unique in our national history: the Civil War and Reconstruction. Readers may be puzzled by the allusion to the Civil War and Reconstruction as a disaster, for of course the war prevented disunion and the Reconstruction destroyed the cancer of chattel slavery and brought the eleven rebellious states back into the Union. These were no small triumphs. But consider the Civil War epoch from the perspectives of ideology, party, and reform. The war pinpointed a near-fatal ambiguity in the ideological legacy of the founders, an ambiguity that was reflected at the founding in the stark contrast between the soaring tribute to liberty and equality in the Declaration of Independence and the implicit sanction of slavery in the Constitution. In the succeeding decades the fundamental structures of society that evolved in the North and the South differed enormously, yet each society repaired to the same Constitution when criticizing the other (excluding, importantly, the Garrisonian abolitionists, who damned the Constitution as "a covenant with death and an agreement with hell"). And when the Confederacy broke away and adopted its own constitution, it was very nearly a mirror image of the original. To a large extent the basic problem was the original failure of the founders to infuse the constitutional structure with the revolutionary spirit of the Declaration. But even when slavely was at last destroyed, the unwillingness of whites to grant and guarantee equal rights of citizenship to blacks made the American egalitarian creed a celebrated abstraction that failed to square with practice.

At the level of party too the epoch was a disaster. A party system whose chief function was to accommodate conflicting interests through peaceful democratic change disintegrated into chaos, and in the ensuing war 618,000 men died—a carnage that exceeds the deaths caused by all other American wars combined, from the Revolution through Vietnam. In the first selection in Part

III David M. Potter describes and analyses the rapid disintegration of the party system, with particular attention to the collapse of the Whigs, leaving the South with a one-party system (which amounted essentially to a no-party system). But party competition between the Democrats and the newly formed Republicans continued vigorously in the North, and Eric McKitrick, in the second selection, takes advange of this unique opportunity to compare the effects of party competition as an independent variable in determining the outcome of the Union and Confederate war efforts.

Finally, at the level of reform, the Republican coalition that emerged victorious from the war was concerned with a broad range of reforms that included the disposition of western lands, railroad construction, education, banking and currency and the national debt, taxation and the tariff, the civil service, and soldiers' pensions. But the dominant concern of the Reconstruction era remained race relations. It is here that the complicated interplay of party, ideology, and reform can be best observed as it bears on one crucial and highly emotional issue that elicits at once the most noble and most sordid of our instincts. In this volatile context Lincoln's Emancipation Proclamation is a classic—first because it signaled to the world the glorious American antislavery commitment, so powerfully embodied in Julia Ward Howe's moving anthem, "As he died to make men holy, let us die to make men free," and second, because Lincoln couched it in an extraordinarily cautious, secular, and almost mockingly limited phraseology that betrays the harsh political realities that Lincoln so shrewdly, if less nobly, perceived.

The final selection in Part III is C. Vann Woodward's perceptive and yet essentially sad analysis of the tragic failure of the Reconstruction to establish a new and more equitable social order in American race relations. Whatever light it may throw on the specific achievements and failures of Reconstruction is all to the good, but the purpose of its inclusion here is less to explain what happened during that period than to illustrate, by example, the interrelationships of the power and the limitations of ideological commitment, party politics, and an attempt at radical reform in America.

Part IV examines party, ideology, and reform in a somewhat more normal context. Such an extraordinary event as the Civil War presents the historian with an invaluable kind of experimental situation in which the basic properties of social and political systems can be tested under extreme but otherwise unlikely conditions. There are no iron laws of social science, but there are legitimate and useful generalizations about social life that help us to understand its rhythms. During the twentieth century we have witnessed three major waves of political ferment: (1) the Progressive era; (2) the New Deal; and (3) the turbulence of the 1960s, whatever we shall some day come to call it. Referring to these three as more normal periods of reformist activity does not minimize the sense of crisis that fueled their very real anxieties. Indeed, their differences are, in the short run, more revealing. Since Burnham and Burns wrote within the context of the third wave of political ferment, Part IV will concentrate upon the first two. The leaders of the progressive movement of the early twentieth century were largely middle- and upper-class citizens who, in a period of rising real wages for industrializing America, were responding to a revolutionary transition in which America was rapidly moving from the farm to the city. The chief dangers seemed to be plutocracy on the right and radical socialism on the left. The principal challenge to historians has been the explanation of why, during a period of industrial expansion from which they stood to benefit, middle-class Americans responded with such alarm.

The New Deal is, at first encounter, much easier to explain. The depression followed the crash, and the classical distinction between the numerous but impoverished left and the wealthy and entrenched right seems neatly appropriate. Yet the crisis of depression was worldwide, at least among the industrialized nations. In such desperate circumstances the standard European rallying cry on the left was socialism and communism, and on the right, facism. Yet in the United States during the Great Depression, socialism and facism never seriously competed for public allegiance. How can we explain such a curious phenomenon; what does it tell us about ourselves?

The reformist ferment of the 1960s involved such apparent paradoxes as a war on poverty in an affluent society, a victory for desegregation that made most of its gains in the South and that was greeted in the North and West less by celebration than by black rioting, and American warfare in Southeast Asia that was successfully throttled by an unlikely coalition in public opinion of left-wing opponents of victory and right-wing opponents of participation. We shall shortly plunge headlong into that, in the context of party systems analysis. But the differences that distinguish these three twentieth-century bursts of reform should not obscure their more fundamental similarities. These include, first, at the level of ideology, the requirement that modern liberal reformers come to grips with a legacy of classical liberal ideology designed to shackle the very power necessary to endow the reforms with meaningful impact. That is, as Herbert Croly perceived in *The Promise of American Life* (1909), in order to fulfill the dreams of Jefferson, it was necessary to repudiate him and embrace the interventionist methods, though not the toryism, of Hamilton. Then, at the level of the functioning of party within the reform impulse, we must abandon the simple dualism that pits the good party, interest, or coalition against the bad one. We must seek to understand, in their own terms, what impelled like-minded groups of Americans to attempt to change the direction of society; and we must examine the advantages they enjoyed, the inner contradictions they faced, and the formidable odds they confronted—as Otis L. Graham, Jr. has done in his essays on the Progressive era and the New Deal. Finally, the Conclusion seeks to assess in broad terms the impact of party and ideology on reform in American history.

PART I

The American Party Systems

Historians have long been in the habit of personalizing political history by focusing on its leading figures, especially, in America, on the president. This has led to textbooks dominated by candidates and issues (customarily locked into the dreary quadrennial format of presidential history), and based upon an assumption that voters were reasonably well informed and basically rational. Because the historical evidence tended to be heavily external and elitist (e.g., party platforms, candidate speeches, campaign tracts) and the aggregate nature of the popular vote, even when analyzed geographically, as by ward or county, often concealed more than it revealed, historians had no access to a more systematic psychosocial profile of the American voter until the post-World War II evolution of scientific survey research.

Modern public-opinion polling produced a portrait of the American voter that was shocking in its implications. Analyzed most notably in *The American Voter*,[1] this hapless

[1] Angus Campbell, Philip E. Converse, Warren E. Miller, and Donald E. Stokes, *The American Voter*, New York: Wiley, 1960. See generally the publications of the Survey Research Center, and Campbell et al., *Elections and the Political Order*, New York: Wiley, 1966.

bulwark of the democratic faith was pictured as being poorly informed to an astonishing degree and innocent of even the most basic ideology or logical consistency along the liberal-conservative spectrum. This has led to a continuing, highly emotional debate that the reader is invited to pursue elsewhere.[2] What concerns us here is the revelation, generally conceded all around, of remarkably stable patterns of partisan loyalty. These tenacious party affiliations apparently stemmed far less from specific voter responses to issues and candidates than from basic underlying preferences largely inherited from parents and culture through the normal socialization of the child. Upon the bedrock of this stability, in turn, was predicated the concept of the "normal" vote—the customary partisan distribution of the vote in the absence of unusual external forces. And from this stable distribution there followed the concept of the normal majority, which in the post-New Deal era involved a national partisan distribution fluctuating just under one-half Democratic, slightly more than one-quarter Republican, and about one-quarter inde-

[2]Early in 1952 the political scientist V. O. Key, Jr. urged upon the staff of the Survey Research Center the concept of party identification, and he pioneered in the theory of critical elections; but he remained hostile to the socioeconomic determinism implicit in the sociological origins of survey research, to its psychological focus on the voter rather than the vote, and to its dismal portrait of the irrational electorate. See Key, "The Politically Relevant in Surveys," *Public Opinion Quarterly* 24 (1960), 54–61; and *The Responsible Electorate,* Cambridge: Harvard University Press, 1966, the latter published posthumously.

pendent or apolitical.[3] This pattern in turn suggested the construction of a basic three-fold typology of partisan elections: maintaining, deviating, and realigning.[4] In *maintaining* elections, in which the normal majority prevails (e.g., the presidential elections from 1936 through 1948), the preceding pattern of partisan majorities persists and is the primary influence governing the vote. In a *deviating* election, this basic or normal division of partisan loyalties is not seriously disturbed, but short-term forces, such as the popularity of Eisenhower in 1952 and 1956, bring about the defeat of the majority party (resulting in a subcategory of the maintaining election known as a *reinstating* election, such as that of 1960, in which the basic partisan loyalties of the normal majority are reasserted). The third type of election, relatively rare but of major

[3]See Campbell et al., *The American Voter,* chap. 5; and Angus Campbell, "Voters and Elections: Past and Present," *Journal of Politics* 26 (November 1964), 745–757.

[4]See *The American Voter,* chap. 16. Gerald Pomper in "The Classification of Presidential Elections," *Journal of Politics 29* (August 1967), 535–566, has convincingly argued that a fourth category, the *converting* election, should be added to this trilogy on the grounds that the realigning category as explicated in *The American Voter* does not distinguish between critical elections that produce a new majority, as in 1928–1932, and those that produce a fundamental rearrangement of the partisan base of a majority party that maintains its hegemony, as in the crucial realignment of 1894–1896. Hence the following four-cell table:

| | | *Majority Party* | |
		VICTORY	DEFEAT
Electoral	CONTINUITY	Maintaining	Deviating
Cleavage	CHANGE	Converting	Realigning

impact, is the *realigning* election, in which the popular excitement associated with politics is sufficiently intense and durable to basically transform the electorate's loyalties and thereby create a new normal partisan majority,[5] as in the critical realignment of 1928–1936, when the Republican majority of the post-McKinley era was overturned by the stock market crash and depression and a new Democratic majority was installed under Franklin Roosevelt's New Deal. In response to this new mode of analysis, political scientists and historians have recently employed the model of *critical realignment* to reconstruct our understanding of the entire evolution of American political life, focusing less on ephemeral candidates, issues, and individual parties than on party *systems,* of which, by rough consensus, there have been five: (1) the experimental system, 1789–1824; (2) the democratizing system, 1828–1854; (3) the Civil War system, 1860–1892; the industrial system, 1894–1932; and (5) the New Deal system, 1932–?[6]

The two essays that follow differ in their perspectives. The first is built squarely upon the party system mode of analysis just described, with its focus on critical realignments and their consequences. The second analysis is more structural and institutional, particularly in its comparison of the presidency and Congress. But both analyses share a broad historical base, they are primarily concerned with the function of

[5]See V. O. Key, Jr. "A Theory of Critical Elections," *Journal of Politics* 17 (February 1955), 3–18.

[6]A valuable collection of essays bearing on the evolution of the American party systems is William Nesbit Chambers and Walter Dean Burnham, eds., *The American Party Systems,* New York: Oxford University Press, 1967.

political parties as the primary instruments mediating between the structure of government and its democratic constituency, and both are heavily critical of a perceived failure in this fundamental relationship.

INTRODUCTORY NOTE

In the essay that follows, political scientist Walter Dean Burnham employs the critical realignment model in a forceful analysis that amounts to a damning indictment. American critical realignments, Burnham argues, particularly the McKinley realignment of 1896, have been accompanied by and have contributed to the accelerating decomposition of party. Burnham argues that the American political system has been effectively and deliberately loaded against the losers in American social and economic life, and that party, as a potentially effective instrument of collective purpose, has been systematically hamstrung by dominant elites. Historically the United States has been dynamic and inventive in her socioeconomic life but politically moribund since the 1860s, Burnham concludes, and her polity has fundamentally lacked the sovereignty that party majorities have possessed in the parliamentary European democracies. The result is accelerating electoral decomposition and party decay to such an extent that Burnham seems to anticipate less another critical realignment than party disintegration—the triumph of nonrule and antiparties—and a quadrennial selling of the president in elections wherein emotional issues are manipulated in a neo-Bourbon fashion to achieve victory rather than to serve a collective purpose. Published in 1969, on the eve of Watergate and the nation's bicentennial celebration, Burnham's indictment is sobering.

The End of American Party Politics

WALTER DEAN BURNHAM

American politics has clearly been falling apart in the past decade. We don't have to look hard for the evidence. Mr. Nixon is having as much difficulty controlling his fellow party members in Congress as any of his Democratic predecessors had in controlling theirs. John V. Lindsay, a year after he helped make Spiro Agnew a household word, had to run for mayor as a Liberal and an Independent with the aid of nationally prominent Democrats. Chicago in July of 1968 showed that for large numbers of its activists a major political party can become not just a disappointment, but positively repellant. Ticket-splitting has become widespread as never before, especially among the young; and George C. Wallace, whose third-party movement is the largest in recent American history, continues to demonstrate an unusually stable measure of support.

Vietnam and racial polarization have played large roles in this breakdown, to be sure; but the ultimate causes are rooted much deeper in our history. For some time we have been saying that we live in a "pluralist democracy." And no text on American politics would be complete without a few key code words such as "consensus," "incrementalism," "bargaining" and "process." Behind it all is a rather benign view of our politics, one that assumes that the complex diversity of the American social structure is filtered through the two major parties and buttressed by a consensus of middle-class values which produces an electoral politics of low intensity and gradual change. The interplay of interest groups and public officials determines policy in detail. The voter has some leverage on policy, but only in a most diffuse way; and, anyway, he tends to be a pretty apolitical animal, dominated either by familial or local tradition, on one hand, or by the charisma of attractive candidates on the other. All of this is a good thing, of course, since in an affluent time the politics of consensus rules out violence and polarization. It pulls together and supports the existing order of things.

There is no doubt that this description fits "politics as usual," in the United States, but to assume that it fits the whole of American electoral politics is a radical oversimplification. Yet even after these past years of turmoil few efforts have been made to appraise the peculiar rhythms of American politics in a more realistic way. This article is an attempt to do so by focusing upon two very important and little celebrated aspects of the dynamics of our politics: the phenomena of critical realignments of the electorate and of decomposition of the party in our electoral politics.

As a whole and across time, the reality of American politics appears quite different from a simple vision of pluralist democracy. It is shot through with escalating tensions, periodic electoral convulsions and repeated redefinitions of the rules and general outcomes of the political game. It has also been marked repeatedly by redefinitions—by no means always broadening ones —of those who are permitted to play. And one other very basic characteristic of American party politics that emerges from an historical overview is the profound incapacity of established political leadership to adapt itself to the political demands produced by the losers in America's stormy socioeconomic life. As is well known, American political parties are not instruments of collective purpose, but of electoral success. One major implication of this is that, as organizations, parties are interested in control of offices but not of government in any larger sense. It follows that once successful routines are established or reestablished for office-winning, very little motivation exists among party leaders to disturb the routines of the game. These routines are periodically upset, to be sure, but not by adaptive change within the party system. They are upset by overwhelming external force.

It has been recognized, at least since the publication of V. O. Key's "A Theory of Critical Elections" in 1955, that some elections in our history have been far more important than most in their long-range consequences for the political system. Such elections seem to "decide" clusters of substantive issues in a more clear-cut way than do most of the ordinary varieties.

There is even a consensus among historians as to when these turning points in electoral politics took place. The first came in 1800 when Thomas Jefferson overthrew the Federalist hegemony established by Washington, Adams and Hamilton. The second came in 1828 and in the years afterward, with the election of Andrew Jackson and the democratization of the presidency. The third, of course, was the election of Abraham Lincoln in 1860, an election that culminated a catastrophic polarization of the society as a whole and resulted in civil war. The fourth critical election was that of William McKinley in 1896; this brought to a close the "Civil War" party system and inaugurated a political alignment congenial to the dominance of industrial capitalism over the American political economy. Created in the crucible of one massive depression, this "System of 1896" endured until the collapse of the economy in a second. The election of Franklin D. Roosevelt in 1932 came last in this series, and brought a major realignment of electoral politics and policy-making structures into the now familiar "welfare-pluralist" mode.

1896

Now that the country appears to have entered another period of political upheaval, it seems particularly important not only to identify the phenomena of periodic critical realignments in our electoral politics, but to integrate them into a larger—if still very modest—theory of stasis and movement in American politics. For the realignments focus attention on the dark side of our politics, those moments of tremendous stress and abrupt transformation that remind us that "politics as usual" in the United States is not politics as always, and that American political institutions and leadership, once defined or redefined in a "normal phase" seem *themselves* to contribute to the building of conditions that threaten their overthrow.

To underscore the relevance of critical elections to our own day, one has only to recall that in the past, fundamental realignments in voting behavior have always been signalled by the rise of significant third parties: the Anti-Masons in the 1820s, the Free Soilers in the 1840s and 1850s, the Populists in the 1890s and the LaFollette Progressives in the 1920s. We cannot know whether George Wallace's American Independent Party of 1968 fits into this series, but it is certain—as we shall see below—that the very foundations of American electoral politics have become quite suddenly fluid in the past few years, and that the mass base of our politics has become volatile to a degree unknown in the experience of all but the very oldest living Americans. The Wallace uprising is a major sign of this recent fluidity; but it hardly stands alone.

Third-party protests, perhaps by contrast with major-party bolts, point up the interplay in American politics between the inertia of "normal" established political routines and the pressures arising from the rapidity, unevenness and uncontrolled character of change in the country's dynamic socioeconomic system. All of the third parties prior to and including the 1968 Wallace movement constituted attacks by outsiders, who felt they were outsiders, against an elite frequently viewed in conspiratorial terms. The attacks were made under the banner of high moralistic universals against an established political structure seen as corrupt, undemocratic and manipulated by insiders for their own benefit and that of their supporters. All these parties were perceived by their activists as "movements" that would not only purify the corruption of the current political regime, but replace some of its most important parts. Moreover, they all telegraphed the basic clusters of issues that would dominate politics in the next electoral era: the completion of political democratization in the 1830s, slavery and sectionalism in the late 1840s and 1850s, the struggle between the industrialized and the colonial regions in the 1890s, and welfare liberalism vs. laissez-faire in the 1920s and 1930s. One may well view the American Independent Party in such a context.

The periodic recurrence of third-part forerunners of realignment—and realignments themselves, for that matter—are significantly related to dominant peculiarities of polity and society in the United States. They point to an electorate especially vulnerable to breaking apart, and to a political system in which the sense of common nationhood may be much more nearly skin-deep than is usually appreciated. If there is any evolutionary scale of political modernization at all, the persistence of deep fault lines in our electoral politics suggests pretty strongly that the United States remains a "new nation" to this day in some important political respects. The periodic recurrence of these tensions may also imply that—as dynamically developed as our economic system is—no convincing evidence of *political* development in the United States can be found after the 1860s.

Nationwide critical realignments can only take place around clusters of issues of the most fundamental importance. The

most profound of these issues have been cast up in the course
of the transition of our Lockeian-liberal commonwealth from an
agrarian to an industrial state. The last two major realignments
—those of 1893–96 and 1928–36—involved the two great transitional crises of American industrial capitalism, the economic
collapses of 1893 and 1929. The second of these modern realignments produced, of course, the broad coalition on which
the New Deal's welfarist-pluralist policy was ultimately based.
But the first is of immediate concern to us here. For the 1896
adaptation of electoral politics to the imperatives of industrial-
capitalism involved a set of developments that stand in the
sharpest possible contrast to those occurring elsewhere in the
Western world at about the same time. Moreover, they set in
motion new patterns of behavior in electoral politics that were
never entirely overcome even during the New Deal period, and
which, as we shall see, have resumed their forward march
during the past decade.

As a case in point, let me briefly sketch the political evolution of Pennsylvania—one of the most industrially developed
areas on earth—during the 1890–1932 period. There was in
this state a preexisting, indeed, preindustrial, pattern of two-
party competition, one that had been forged in the Jacksonian
era and decisively amended, though not abolished, during the
Civil War. Then came the realignment of the 1890s, which,
like those of earlier times, was an abrupt process. In the five
annual elections from 1888 through November 1892, the Democrats' mean percentage of the total two-party vote was 46.7
percent, while for the five elections beginning in February 1894
it dropped to a mean of 37.8 percent. Moreover, the greatest
and most permanent Republican gains during this depression
decade occurred where they counted most, numerically: in the
metropolitan areas of Philadelphia and Pittsburgh.

The cumulative effect of this realignment and its aftermath
was to convert Pennsylvania into a thoroughly one-party state,
in which conflict over the basic political issues was duly transferred to the Republican primary after it was established in
1908. By the 1920s this peculiar process had been completed
and the Democratic party had become so weakened that, as
often as not, the party's nominees for major office were selected
by the Republican leadership. But whether so selected or not,
their general-election prospects were dismal: of the 80 statewide

contests held from 1894 through 1931, a candidate running with
Democratic party endorsement won just one. Moreover, with
the highly ephermeral exception of Theodore Roosevelt's bolt
from the Republican party in 1912, no third parties emerged as
general-election substitutes for the ruined Democrats.

The political simplicity which had thus emerged in this
industrial heartland of the Northeast by the 1920s was the
more extraordinary in that it occurred in an area whose socioeconomic division of labor was as complex and its level of
development as high as any in the world. In most other regions
of advanced industrialization the emergence of corporate capitalism was associated with the development of mass political
parties with high structural cohesion and explicit collective purposes with respect to the control of policy and government.
These parties expressed deep conflicts over the direction of
public policy, but they also brought about the democratic revolution of Europe, for electoral participation tended to rise along
with them. Precisely the opposite occurred in Pennsylvania and,
with marginal and short-lived exceptions, the nation. It is no
exaggeration to say that the political response to the collectiviz-
ing thrust of industrialism in this American state was the
elimination of organized partisan combat, an extremely severe
decline in electoral participation, the emergence of a Republican
"coalition of the whole" and—by no means coincidentally—a
highly efficient insulation of the controlling industrial-financial
elite from effective or sustained countervailing pressures.

IRRELEVANT RADICALISM

The reasons for the increasing solidity of this "system of 1896"
in Pennsylvania are no doubt complex. Clearly, for example,
the introduction of the direct primary as an alternative to the
general election, which was thereby emptied of any but ritual-
istic significance, helped to undermine the minority Democrats
more and more decisively by destroying their monopoly of opposition. But nationally as well the Democratic party in and
after the 1890s was virtually invisible to Pennsylvania voters
as a usable opposition. For with the ascendency of the agrarian
Populist William Jennings Bryan, the Democratic party was
transformed into a vehicle for colonial, periphery-oriented dissent against the industrial-metropolitan center, leaving the Republicans as sole spokesmen for the latter.

This is a paradox that pervades American political history, but it was sharpest in the years around the turn of this century. The United States was so vast that it had little need of economic colonies abroad; in fact it had two major colonial regions within its own borders, the postbellum South and the West. The only kinds of attacks that could be made effective on a *nationwide* basis against the emergent industrialist hegemony —the only attacks that, given the ethnic heterogeneity and extremely rudimentary political socialization of much of the country's industrial working class, could come within striking distance of achieving a popular majority—came out of these colonial areas. Thus "radical" protest in major-party terms came to be associated with the neo-Jacksonian demands of agrarian smallholders and smalltown society already confronted by obsolescence. The Democratic party from 1896 to 1932, and in many respects much later, was the national vehicle for these struggles.

The net effect of this was to produce a condition in which —especially, but not entirely on the presidential level—the more economically advanced a state was, the more heavy were its normal Republican majorities likely to be. The nostalgic agrarian-individualist appeals of the national Democratic leadership tended to present the voters of this industrial state with a choice that was not a choice: between an essentially backward-looking provincial party articulating interests in opposition to those of the industrial North and East as a whole, and a "modernizing" party whose doctrines included enthusiastic acceptance of and cooperation with the dominant economic interests of region and nation. Not only did this partitioning of the political universe entail normal and often huge Republican majorities in an economically advanced state like Pennsylvania; the survival of national two-party competition on such a basis helped to ensure that no local reorganization of electoral politics along class lines could effectively occur even within such a state. Such a voting universe had a tendency toward both enormous inbuilt stability and increasing entrenchment in the decades after its creation. Probably no force less overwhelming than the post-1929 collapse of the national economic system would have sufficed to dislodge it. Without such a shock, who can say how, or indeed whether, the "System of 1896" would have come to an end in Pennsylvania and the nation? To ask such a question is to raise yet another. For there is no doubt that in Pennsylvania, as elsewhere, the combination of trauma in 1929–33 and Roosevelt's creative leadership provided the means for overthrowing the old order and for reversing dramatically the depoliticization of electoral politics which had come close to perfection under it. Yet might it not be the case that the dominant pattern of political adaptation to industrialism in the United States has worked to eliminate, by one means or another, the links provided by political parties between voters and rulers? In other words, was the post-1929 reversal permanent or only a transitory phase in our political evolution? And if transitory, what bearing would this fact have on the possible recurrence of critical realignments in the future?

WITHERING AWAY OF THE PARTIES

The question requires us to turn our attention to the second major dynamic of American electoral politics during this century: the phenomenon of electoral disaggregation, of the breakdown of party loyalty, which in many respects must be seen as the permanent legacy of the fourth party system of 1896–1932. One of the most conspicuous developments of this era, most notably during the 1900–1920 period, was a whole network of changes in the rules of the political game. This is not the place for a thorough treatment and documentation of these peculiarities. One can only mention here some major changes in the rules of the game, and note that one would have no difficulty in arguing that their primary latent function was to ease the transition from a preindustrial universe of competitive, highly organized mass politics to a depoliticized world marked by drastic shrinkage in participation or political leverage by the lower orders of the population. The major changes surely include the following:

- The introduction of the Australian ballot, which was designed to purify elections but also eliminated a significant function of the older political machines, the printing and distribution of ballots, and eased a transition from party voting to candidate voting.
- The introduction of the direct primary, which at once stripped the minority party of its monopoly of opposition and weakened the control of party leaders over nominating processes, and

again hastened preoccupation of the electorate with candidates rather than parties.

■ The movement toward nonpartisan local elections, often accompanied by a drive to eliminate local bases of representation such as wards in favor of at-large elections, which produced —as Samuel Hays points out—a shift of political power from the grass roots to citywide cosmopolitan elites.

■ The expulsion of almost all blacks, and a very large part of the poor-white population as well, from the southern electorate by a series of legal and extralegal measures such as the poll tax.

■ The introduction of personal registration requirements the burden of which, in faithful compliance with dominant middle-class values, was placed on the individual rather than on public authority, but which effectively disenfranchised large numbers of the poor.

BREAKDOWN OF PARTY LOYALTY

Associated with these and other changes in the rules of the game was a profound transformation in voting behavior. There was an impressive growth in the numbers of political independents and ticket-splitters, a growth accompanied by a sea-change among party elites from what Richard Jensen has termed the "militarist" (or ward boss) campaign style to the "mercantilist" (or advertising-packaging) style. Aside from noting that the transition was largely completed as early as 1916, and hence that the practice of "the selling of the president" goes back far earlier than we usually think, these changes too must be left for fuller exposition elsewhere.

Critical realignments, as we have argued, are an indispensable part of a stability-disruption dialectic which has the deepest roots in American political history. Realigning sequences are associated with all sorts of aberrations from the normal workings of American party politics, both in the events leading up to nominations, the nature and style of election campaigning and the final outcome at the polls. This is not surprising, since they arise out of the collision of profound transitional crisis in the socioeconomic system with the immobility of a nondeveloped political system.

At the same time, it seems clear that for realignment to fulfill some of its most essential tension-management functions, for it to be a forum by which the electorate can participate in durable "constitution making," it is essential that political parties not fall below a certain level of coherence and appeal in the electorate. It is obvious that the greater the electoral disaggregation the less effective will be "normal" party politics as an instrument of countervailing influence in an industrial order. Thus, a number of indices of disaggregation significantly declined during the 1930s as the Democratic Party remobilized parts of American society under the stimulus of the New Deal. In view of the fact that political parties during the 1930s and 1940s were once again called upon to assist in a redrawing of the map of American politics and policy-making, this regeneration of partisan voting in the 1932–52 era is hardly surprising. More than that, regeneration was necessary if even the limited collective purposes of the new majority coalition were to be realized.

Even so, the New Deal realignment was far more diffuse, protracted and incomplete than any of its predecessors, a fact of which the more advanced New Dealers were only too keenly aware. It is hard to avoid the impression that one contributing element in this peculiarity of our last realignment was the much higher level of electoral disaggregation in the 1930s and 1940s than had existed at any time prior to the realignment of the 1890s. If one assumes that the end result of a long-term trend toward electoral disaggregation is the complete elimination of political parties as foci that shape voting behavior, then the possibility of critical realignment would, by definition, be eliminated as well. Every election would be dominated by TV packaging, candidate charisma, real or manufactured, and short-term, ad hoc influences. Every election, therefore, would have become deviating or realigning by definition, and American national politics would come to resemble the formless gubernatorial primaries that V. O. Key described in his classic *Southern Politics*.

The New Deal clearly arrested and reversed, to a degree, the march toward electoral disaggregation. But it did so only for the period in which the issues generated by economic scarcity remained central, and the generation traumatized by the collapse of 1929 remained numerically preponderant in the electorate. Since 1952, electoral disaggregation has resumed, in many measurable dimensions, and with redoubled force. The data on this point are overwhelming. Let us examine a few of them.

A primary aspect of electoral disaggregation, of course, is the "pulling apart" over time of the percentages for the same party but at different levels of election: this is the phenomenon of split-ticket voting. Recombining and reorganizing the data found in two tables of Milton Cummings' excellent study *Congressmen and the Electorate,* and extending the series back and forward in time, we may examine the relationship between presidential and congressional elections during this century.

Such an array captures both the initial upward thrust of disaggregation in the second decade of this century, the peaking in the middle to late 1920s, the recession beginning in 1932, and especially the post-1952 resumption of the upward trend.

Other evidence points precisely in the same direction. It has generally been accepted in survey-research work that generalized partisan identification shows far more stability over time than does actual voting behavior, since the latter is subject to short-term factors associated with each election. What is not so widely understood is that this glacial measure of party identification has suddenly become quite volatile during the 1960s, and particularly during the last half of the decade. In the first place, as both Gallup and Survey Research Center data confirm, the proportion of independents underwent a sudden shift upwards around 1966: while from 1940 to 1965 independents constituted about 20 percent to 22 percent of the electorate, they increased to 29 percent in 1966. At the present time, they outnumber Republicans by 30 percent to 28 percent.

Second, there is a clear unbroken progression in the share that independents have of the total vote along age lines. The younger the age group, the larger the number of independents in it, so that among the 21–29 year olds, according to the most recent Gallup findings this year, 42 percent are independents —an increase of about 10 percent over the first half of the decade, and representing greater numbers of people than identify with either major party. When one reviews the June 1969 Gallup survey of college students, the share is larger still—44 percent. Associated with this quantitative increase in independents seems to be a major qualitative change as well. Examining the data for the 1950s, the authors of *The American Voter* could well argue that independents tended to have lower political

awareness and political involvement in general than did identifiers (particularly strong identifiers) of either major party.
But the current concentration of independents in the population
suggests that this may no longer be the case. They are clearly
and disproportionately found not only among the young, and
especially among the college young, but also among men, those
adults with a college background, people in the professional-
managerial strata and, of course, among those with higher
incomes. Such groups tend to include those people whose sense
of political involvement and efficacy is far higher than that of
the population as a whole. Even in the case of the two most
conspicuous exceptions to this—the pile-up of independent
identifiers in the youngest age group and in the South—it can
be persuasively argued that this distribution does not reflect
low political awareness and involvement but the reverse: a
sudden, in some instances almost violent, increase in both
awareness and involvement among southerners and young
adults, with the former being associated both with the heavy
increase in southern turnout in 1968 and the large Wallace
vote polled there.

Third, one can turn to two sets of evidence found in the
Survey Research Center's election studies. If the proportion of
strong party identifiers over time is examined, the same pattern
of long-term inertial stability and recent abrupt change can be
seen. From 1952 through 1964, the proportion of strong Democratic and Republican party identifiers fluctuated in a narrow
range between 36 percent and 40 percent, with a steep downward trend in strong Republican identifiers between 1960 and
1964 being matched by a moderate increase in strong Democratic identifiers. Then in 1966 the proportion of strong identifiers abruptly declines to 28 percent, with the defectors overwhelmingly concentrated among former Democrats. This is almost certainly connected, as is the increase of independent
identifiers, with the Vietnam fiasco. While we do not as yet
have the 1968 SRC data, the distribution of identifications reported by Gallup suggests the strong probability that this abrupt
decline in party loyalty has not been reversed very much since.
It is enough here to observe that while the ratio between strong
identifiers and independents prior to 1966 was pretty stably
fixed at between 1.6 to 1 and 2 to 1 in favor of the former, it is
now evidently less than 1 to 1. Both Chicago and Wallace last

year were the acting out of these changes in the arena of "popular theater."

Finally, both survey and election data reveal a decline in two other major indices of the relevance of party to voting behavior: split-ticket voting and the choice of the same party's candidates for President across time.

It is evident that the 1960s have been an era of increasingly rapid liquidation of pre-existing party commitments by individual voters. There is no evidence anywhere to support Kevin Phillips' hypothesis regarding an emergent Republican majority—assuming that such a majority would involve increases in voter identification with the party. More than that, one might well ask whether, if this process of liquidation is indeed a preliminary to realignment, the latter may not take the form of a third-party movement of truly massive and durable proportions.

The evidence lends some credence to the view that American electoral politics is undergoing a long-term transition into routines designed only to fill offices and symbolically affirm "the American way." There also seem to be tendencies for our political parties gradually to evaporate as broad and active intermediaries between the people and their rulers, even as they may well continue to maintain enough organizational strength to screen out the unacceptable or the radical at the nominating stage. It is certain that the significance of party as link between government and the governed has now come once again into serious question. Bathed in the warm glow of diffused affluence, vexed in spirit but enriched economically by our imperial military and space commitments, confronted by the gradually unfolding consequences of social change as vast as it is unplanned, what need have Americans of political parties? More precisely, why do they need parties whose structures, processes and leadership cadres seem to grow more remote and irrelevant to each new crisis?

FUTURE POLITICS

It seems evident enough that if this long-term trend toward a politics without parties continues, the policy consequences must be profound. One can put the matter with the utmost simplicity: political parties, with all their well-known human and structural shortcomings, are the only devices thus far invented by the wit of Western man that can, with some effectiveness, generate countervailing collective power on behalf of the many individually powerless against the relatively few who are individually or organizationally powerful. Their disappearance as active intermediaries, if not as preliminary screening devices, would only entail the unchallenged ascendancy of the already powerful, unless new structures of collective power were somehow developed to replace them, and unless conditions in America's social structure and political culture came to be such that they could be effectively used. Yet *neither* of these contingencies, despite recent publicity for the term "participatory democracy," is likely to occur under immediately conceivable circumstances in the United States. It is much more probable that the next chapter of our political history will resemble the metapolitical world of the 1920s.

But, it may be asked, may not a future realignment serve to recrystallize and revitalize political parties in the American system?

The present condition of America contains a number of what Marxists call "internal contradictions," some of which might provide the leverage for a future critical realignment if sufficiently sharp dislocations in everyday life should occur. One of the most important of these, surely, is the conversion—largely through technological change—of the American social stratification system from the older capitalist mixture of upper or "owning" classes, dependent white-collar middle classes and proletarians into a mixture described recently by David Apter: the technologically competent, the technologically obsolescent and the technologically superfluous. It is arguable, in fact, that the history of the Kennedy-Johnson Administrations on the domestic front could be written in terms of a coalition of the top and bottom of this Apter-ite mix against the middle, and the 1968 election as the first stage of a "counterrevolution" of these middle strata against the pressures from both of the other two. Yet the inchoate results of 1968 raise some doubts, to say the least, that it can yet be described as part of a realigning sequence: there was great volatility in this election, but also a remarkable and unexpectedly large element of continuity and voter stability.

It is not hard to find evidence of cumulative social disaster in our metropolitan areas. We went to war with Japan in

1941 over a destruction inflicted on us far less devastating in scope and intensity than that endured by any large American city today. But the destruction came suddenly, as a sharp blow, from a foreign power; while the urban destruction of today has matured as a result of our own internal social and political processes, and it has been unfolding gradually for decades. We have consequently learned somehow to adapt to it piecemeal, as best we can, without changing our lives or our values very greatly. Critical realignments, however, also seem to require sharp, sudden blows as a precondition for their emergence. If we think of realignment as arising from the spreading internal disarray in this country, we should also probably attempt to imagine what kinds of events could produce a sudden, sharp and general escalation in social tensions and threatened deprivations of property, status or values.

Conceivably, ghetto and student upheavals could prove enough in an age of mass communications to create a true critical realignment, but one may doubt it. Student and ghetto rebellions appear to be too narrowly defined socially to have a *direct* impact on the daily lives of the "vast middle," and thus produce transformations in voting behavior that would be both sweeping and permanent. For what happens in times of critical realignment is nothing less than an intense, if temporary, quasi revolutionizing of the vast middle class, a class normally content to be traditionalists or passive-participants in electoral politics.

Yet, even if students and ghetto blacks could do the trick, if they could even begin, with the aid of elements of the technological elite, a process of electoral realignment leftward, what would be the likely consequences? What would the quasi revolutionizing of an insecure, largely urban middle class caught in a brutal squeeze from the top and the bottom of the social system look like? There are already premonitory evidences: the Wallace vote in both southern and nonsouthern areas, as well as an unexpected durability in his *postelection* appeal; the mayoral elections in Los Angeles and Minneapolis this year, and not least, Lindsay's narrow squeak into a second term as mayor of New York City. To the extent that the "great middle" becomes politically mobilized and self-conscious, it moves toward what has been called "urban populism," a stance of organized hostility to blacks, student radicals and cosmopolitan liberal elites. The "great middle" remains, after all, the chief defender of the old-time Lockeian faith; both its material and cultural interests are bound up in this defense. If it should become at all mobilized as a major and cohesive political force in today's conditions, it would do so in the name of a restoration of the ancient truths by force if necessary. A realignment that directly involved this kind of mobilization—as it surely would, should it occur—would very likely have sinister overtones unprecedented in our political history.

Are we left, then, with a choice between the stagnation implicit in the disaggregative trends we have outlined here and convulsive disruption? Is there something basic to the American political system, and extending to its electoral politics, which rules out a middle ground between drift and mastery?

The fact that these questions were raised by Walter Lippmann more than half a century ago—and have indeed been raised in one form or other in every era of major transitional crisis over the past century—is alone enough to suggest an affirmative answer. The phenomena we have described here provide evidence of a partly quantitative sort which seems to point in the same direction. For electoral disaggregation is the negation of party. Further, it is—or rather, reflects—the negation of structural and behavioral conditions in politics under which linkages between the bottom, the middle and the top can exist and produce the effective carrying out of collective power. Critical realignments are evidence not of the presence of such linkages or conditions in the normal state of American electoral politics, but precisely of their absence. Correspondingly, they are not manifestations of democratic accountability, but infrequent and hazardous substitutes for it.

Taken together, both of these phenomena generate support for the inference that American politics in its normal state is the negation of the public order itself, as that term is understood in politically developed nations. We do not have government in our domestic affairs so much as "nonrule." We do not have political parties in the contemporary sense of that term as understood elsewhere in the Western world; we have antiparties instead. Power centrifuges rather than power concentrators, they have been immensely important not as vehicles of social transformation but for its prevention through political means.

The entire setting of the critical realignments phenomenon bears witness to a deep-seated dialectic within the American political system. From the beginning, the American socioeconomic system has developed and transformed itself with an energy and thrust that has no parallel in modern history. The political system, from parties to policy structures, has seen no such development. Indeed, it has shown astonishingly little substantive transformation over time in its methods of operation. In essence, the political system of this "fragment society" remains based today on the same Lockeian formulation that, as Louis Hartz points out, has dominated its entire history. It is predicated upon the maintenance of a high wall of separation between politics and government on one side and the socioeconomic system on the other. It depends for its effective working on the failure of anything approximating internal sovereignty in the European sense to emerge here.

The Lockeian cultural monolith, however, is based upon a social assumption that has come repeatedly into collision with reality. The assumption, of course, is not only that the autonomy of socioeconomic life from political direction is the prescribed fundamental law for the United States, but that this autonomous development will proceed with enough smoothness, uniformity and generally distributed benefits that it will be entirely compatible with the usual functioning of our antique political structures. Yet the high (though far from impermeable) wall of separation between politics and society is periodically threatened with inundations. As the socioeconomic system develops in the context of unchanging institutions of electoral politics and policy formation, dysfunctions become more and more visible. Whole classes, regions or other major sectors of the population are injured or faced with an imminent threat of injury. Finally the triggering event occurs, critical realignments follow, the universe of policy and of electoral coalitions is broadly redefined, and the tensions generated by the crisis receive some resolution. Thus it can be argued that critical realignment as a periodically recurring phenomenon is as centrally related to the workings of such a system as is the archaic and increasingly rudimentary structure of the major parties themselves.

PARTY VS. SURVIVAL

One is finally left with the sense that the twentieth-century decomposition of partisan links in our electoral system also corresponds closely with the contemporary survival needs of what Samuel P. Huntington has called the American "Tudor polity." Electoral disaggregation and the concentration of certain forms of power in the hands of economic, technological and administrative elites are functional for the short-term survival of non-rule in the United States. They may even somehow be related to the gradual emergence of internal sovereignty in this country —though to be sure under not very promising auspices for participatory democracy of any kind. Were such a development to occur, it would not necessarily entail the disappearance or complete suppression of subgroup tensions or violence in American social life, or of group bargaining and pluralism in the policy process. It might even be associated with increases in both. But it would, after all, reflect the ultimate sociopolitical consequences of the persistence of Lockeian individualism into an era of Big Organization: oligarchy at the top, inertia and spasms of self-defense in the middle, and fragmentation at the base. One may well doubt whether political parties or critical realignments need have much place in such a political universe.

INTRODUCTORY NOTE

Like Walter Dean Burnham, James Mac-Gregor Burns is a political scientist whose mode of analysis is largely historically based, and like Burnham, he is highly critical from a left-of-center perspective of the functioning of the modern American system. But his analysis differs from Burnham's in that it is more structural and institutional, and he does not employ the theory of critical realignment with its attention to elections and the evolution of partisan majorities. Rather, he sees the national Democratic and Republican parties as superimposed upon a Madisonian institutional structure of checks and balances in such a way as to create in effect a four-party system that would roughly be ranked, left-to-right or liberal to conservative across the political spectrum, as follows: (1) Presidential Democrats, (2) Presidential Republicans, (3) Congressional Democrats, and (4) Congressional Republicans. He argues that the congressional perspective is inherently more conservative than the presidential, which he strongly prefers, and he generally deplores the tendency toward deadlock that is inherent in the superimposition of a four-party system over a Madisonian structure of institutionally divided government.

The Deadlock of Democracy

JAMES MacGREGOR BURNS

Ignorance is the first requisite of the historian, ignorance which simplifies and clarifies, which selects and omits," wrote Lytton Strachey in his preface to *Eminent Victorians*. However ironic Strachey meant this remark to be, it is a useful warning for anyone trying to find meaning in history. A long look at the growth of American politics shows a recurring pattern of four parties, especially in recent years. But this pattern may reflect the selecting and distorting process of the one who looks. A study of the raw materials of politics, as in the last chapter, shows some of the forces that might underlie a multiparty system, but Strachey's quip is as relevant to the political scientist looking for current patterns as to the historian looking for long continuing ones.

The crux of the matter is whether the phenomena make up a superficial pattern or show structure and durability. We can ask with the sociologist, do the four parties make up a *system*? The word is used here in its technical sense—the system as a structure of interrelations over time. The structure embraces a set of interdependent behaviors, roles, institutions and motivations; it has good internal communication and leadership; it is adjusted to basic political and social arrangements; it has existed for a long time and will continue indefinitely, barring fundamental alterations. To use a different formulation, institutions, ideas, interests, and individuals are in a condition of stable interaction and adjustment. The four parties are embedded in the political matrix; they are self-maintaining; their behavior and even their effectiveness, in policy terms, is broadly predictable.

From the book *Deadlock of Democracy* by James MacGregor Burns. © 1963 by James MacGregor Burns. Published by Prentice-Hall, Inc., Englewood Cliffs, N.J.

To describe the four parties as a system is not to indulge in meaningless jargon. On the contrary, it is to pose the essence of the problem. If each of the four parties were simply a wing or a faction or a grouping in the two parties, each would possess qualities of impermanence, instability, fluidity, and fragility that would make them entirely different creatures from what they are. But as structures they must be viewed as stable, strong, and persistent. They will not collapse with the death of specific leaders, or a shift in party fortunes, or a tinkering with political machinery. This means, among other things, that the governing of the country is always in the hands of two or more parties, and hence we have coalition government, with the advantages and failings thereof.

This structure is not dead or static. We might picture it as a giant grid, with currents of political energy running back and forth from numberless centers to millions of sub-centers and back to the centers, and also running from sub-center to sub-center. Some areas throb with high tension; others receive no voltage at all and lie cold and dead; most throb feebly as they catch flickering bits of energy. Much of the grid remains stable; but in some places the linkages break off and form new connections, and sometimes a heavy jolt of energy leaves many connections broken and re-fused.

As we turn to the centers of national and state politics we see the high-voltage areas, where politics, as Mr. Dooley said, "ain't bean bag," but a "professional sport, like playin' baseball f'r a livin' or wheelin' a truck." Here the units glow with steady power, at times dully, at times striking off sparks. Here political activity is patterned and institutionalized in city halls and school boards, state capitols and executive mansions, White House and Capitol Hill.

Seeing this grid as a system not only enables us to see patterns and irregularities, and hence perhaps to predict political trends; it also saves us from oversimplification. The American political system today is under sharp scrutiny. The seniority system, the underrepresentation of urban voters dramatized by the Supreme Court decision in *Baker* v. *Carr*, the failure of Congress to enact the bulk of Kennedy's—or even Nixon's— program, has provoked calls for quick reform or simple surgery. But we must see these institutions as outgrowths of a system of power. They are rooted in sets of interrelationships that have great strength and durability. They cannot be cut off like a wart; they are built into the structure of American politics.

STATE PARTIES: THE SHRIVELED ROOTS

The paramount fact about American political parties is their organizational weakness at all levels, from local to national. It has taken Americans a long time to comprehend this fact. There is a conventional wisdom in politics as well as economics. Generations of Americans have been brought up on college textbooks that contrasted the weak national organization with the powerful party "machines" in the states and cities—even while these machines were disintegrating. Really strong party organizations run by party bosses (in contrast to the personal organizations of officeholders such as mayors or governors) hardly exist today. One of the few, the Democratic organization in Albany, New York, is so well preserved that it should be put into the Smithsonian before we forget what a political machine looks like.

At no level, except in a handful of industrial states, do state parties have the attributes of organization. They lack extensive dues-paying memberships; hence they number many captains and sergeants but few foot soldiers. They do a poor job of raising money for themselves as organizations, or even for their candidates. They lack strong and imaginative leadership of their own. They cannot control their most vital function—the nomination of their candidates. Except in a few states, such as Ohio, Connecticut, and Michigan, our parties are essentially collections of small cliques and they are often shunted aside by the politicians who understand political power. Most of the state parties are at best mere jousting grounds for embattled politicians; at worst they simply do not exist, as in the case of Republicans in the rural South or Democrats in the rural Midwest.

Is this too bleak a picture of party organization? If so it seems, we might try a few simple tests. How many of our neighbors are "card-carrying" Democrats or Republicans, paying regular dues to their party as they do to their church group or professional organization? How many of them take part in the affairs of their local parties, as they do in their lodge or union or the PTA? How many of them work for their party at election time, not merely for individual candidates?

This is not to say that party feeling or identification is unimportant; on the contrary, as the last chapter suggested, it is crucial. Our major parties do help keep alive great sets of fuzzy but powerful traditions, goals, and doctrines. Nor is this to assert that winning major party nomination is worthless; it is worth a great deal, but because of party sentiment, not party organization. It is to say that typically the American party is heavily faction-ridden, disorganized at the base, narrow in range of political action, limited in initiative and vision.

Why? Why is the American party, which was a prime agent in the broadening of American democracy, a rather decrepit institution in this Age of Organization? The answer lies in the enormous burden the party must bear and in some internal defects.

The enormous burden is, first of all, our system of federalism. State parties have a double role. They are independent and sovereign entities in their own right, charged with nominating and electing governors and other statewide officials. Each of them is also one of 50 foundations of the national party, charged with electing presidents and senators and congressional delegations. But this is not all. The state party is a holding company for a profusion of county, city, and town parties that must nominate and elect slates of candidates in those jurisdictions, and that must combine in a variety of ways to elect officials representing different parts of the electoral patchwork: state senators, district attorneys, and the like. The party is not only overburdened by the federal system, but also by the "long ballot" with its myriad offices and overlapping jurisdictions. The sheer operational job of the party is overwhelming.

The difficulty goes even deeper. To maintain organizational unity and fighting trim a party should be strong enough to have the intoxicating hope of victory, but not so strong that it grows fat and sluggish and prone to internal discord and disruption. The eternal dilemma of the state or local party is that if it is weak, politicians can ignore it as a route to office, while if it is too big, it disintegrates into factions. Parties need the stimulus of competition. But real two-party competition is precisely what is lacking in many states and localities. The parties, under our federal system, are overrun by national electoral forces that they cannot control. A Republican state party may have served the people well, but a Roosevelt sweep nationally can leave it impotent for years. A Democratic state party might have brought fresh approaches to state problems, only to collapse in the face of a national shift to Eisenhower. Two-party systems in the states are simply not free to find their natural balance of competition. And this may be even more true of parties in the localities. For reasons that may have little to do with the record of Democratic administrations in New York City, Republicans there have little chance of winning the mayoralty on their own. They are fighting something too big—the Al Smith-Roosevelt-Truman tradition of the national Democratic party. Democrats face the same problem in New Hampshire or Kansas.

Even where state or local parties are evenly balanced, the burden of federalism and the long ballot can disorganize the party. For competition carries its own danger: the likelihood that some of the party's statewide candidates will win, and others will fail. In about half of the elections in which a governor won office by a close margin of votes, V. O. Key, Jr. found that candidates of the opposition party gained one or all of the minor state offices. If one of the tasks of party is to concert the actions of its officeholders behind a party program, the state party is thwarted before it can start. It may find itself in the ludicrous position of trying to unite a lieutenant governor, a state commissioner of education, and an auditor against the other party's governor, treasurer, and attorney-general. The result is not party competition but guerrilla warfare.

Hence the eternal dilemma of many state (and local) parties: swept into a majority or minority position by forces they cannot control, they are either unable to win at all, or they win too much, or they win some state offices but not others. The more-or-less rhythmic alternation of control of government by two competitive and united parties—the classic operation of the party pendulum—is hardly to be found in the states. And the party balance is even more frozen in most localities.

Both cause and result of this situation is the party primary. Adopted mainly as a response to the breakdown of competition resulting originally from the Civil War and more immediately from the realignment of '96, the primary has immensely com-

plicated the effort of party leaders to recruit candidates, mobilize the party behind them, and organize a united party government when in office. The primaries are still pulverizing parties
by opening the nominating process to leaders of ethnic and
other groups, to "name" politicians, and to gifted self-promoters;
by swamping the major party primary with too many candidates while starving the minority party with too few; by disrupting collective leadership in the party; and by catering to the
vagrant, shifting, and individualistic forces in American political
life. In this polity of free enterprise, hardheaded politicians gain
nominations by playing up their party faith and gain elections
by playing it down.

If state party leaders are generally impotent, who does run
the political system? The answer is implicit in the foregoing:
officeholders and candidates for office. These are the persons
who recruit candidates for offices (including themselves), set
up active organizational headquarters, raise most political
money, put out the bulk of the more costly propaganda, mobilize
most volunteers, conduct door-to-door canvassing, and even
handle much of the job of getting people to register to vote and
transporting them to the polls on election day. Sometimes state
and local parties seem to be doing all this, but more often some
candidate or officeholder is using the party for his own purposes, or perhaps using it in collaboration with other candidates
or cliques. Significantly, most strong "party" leaders are holders
of strong offices—for example, Mayor Daley of Chicago, Governor Nelson Rockefeller of New York, Senator Abe Ribicoff of
Connecticut, former Governor Mennen Williams of Michigan,
Governor Mark Hatfield of Oregon. The line between officeholder
leadership and collective party leadership is not always clear,
and the situation varies sharply from state to state, but the
typical party is a holding company for contending politicians
rather than an independent source of control over political activity.

In most states, in short, the Madisonian model of politically
fortified checks and balances is far more typical than the Jeffersonian model of competitive parties and majority rule. The
extent and effect of this lack of competition between parties
has been documented by Joseph Schlesinger in an outstanding
piece of research. By combining two basic tests of party competition in the states—the extent of division of control of state

offices between the parties and the rate of alternation of control between the parties (that is, whether the parties shifted control back and forth every few years, as against a long period of control by one party followed by a long period of control by the other party), Schlesinger was able to measure meaningfully the real extent of competition for the major offices in each state. (He did not include the Southern states because, of course, Democrats win practically all state elections there.) In most of the states, he found, most of the offices were non-competitive in this sense. The governorship was the most competitive of the statewide offices—far more so than attorney general or treasurer —but still not highly competitive. United States Senator was not quite so competitive as governor. Least competitive was United States Representative—a fact of the utmost importance.

These findings underline a central fact about American state and local politics: by and large, it is every man for himself, and the devil take the hindmost. In our patchwork of electoral districts each candidate runs on his own, mobilizing his own majority, appealing to his own electorate, bringing together his own unique combination of group interests, independent voters, personal followings, party cliques, and friends and neighbors. Sometimes politicians in one party ally with one another, superficially at least, when they can appeal to a common electorate on the basis of common symbols and promises. Even so, behind the scenes the candidates reach out into special areas of support, even if they have to desert their fellow candidates in the process. They depend more on their own personal followings than on the collective efforts of the party organiza-. tion. The inevitable result is that a party's successful candidates, still depending on their autonomous personal organizations, often deal with one another in office as independent satraps—as indeed they often are.

THE CONGRESSIONAL PARTY SYSTEM

I have noted the heavy impact of national politics on state and local politics—how a presidential sweep of the nation, for example, can upset the competitive balance of parties in the states and leave a swath of one-party states and districts, with the resultant disintegrating and fragmentizing of state and local parties. Now we must look at the reverse process—how the structure of state and local politics, comprising personal organizations surrounding fairly autonomous politicians, reacts back on national party politics. The peculiar interplay in America of national political forces and state-to-local forces makes for a structure of politicians' motives, roles, expectations, and goals that comprise two political systems, the congressional and the presidential.

The base of the congressional system is the one-party district, as established and protected by the state legislatures. Though we hear much about congressmen's "safe seats," it is still hard to grasp the extent of non-competition in congressional elections. Almost half of the House seats never change party hands. Another quarter, roughly, switch only on rare occasions. Aside from great sweeps such as those of 1920 and 1936, about 150 Republican seats and about the same number of Democratic seats never switch to the other party. Reasonably competitive districts number about 125 out of a total of 435. Many Senate seats are also one-party, especially in the South, but not to the same extent as in the House.

These safe seats are only partly accidental in origin. They are also a planned result of the alignment of party forces in the states. The drawing of election districts (congressional as well as state) is in the hands of state legislatures. Most state legislatures are controlled year after year and decade after decade by the same party (at least in one house), and legislators naturally carve up the districts to benefit their own party. Actually, the hottest fights take place mainly within the dominant party as congressmen, to protect their districts, bring influence to bear on state legislators, state legislators maneuver for their own electoral advantage (especially if they have congressional ambitions), and intra-party factions engage in their horse-trading. Sometimes state legislators act positively to protect the congressional party. In 1962 the Mississippi legislature drove a pro-Kennedy Congressman out of office by combining his district with a highly rural and conservative one.

Note the difference between this kind of manipulation and the shenanigans of gerrymandering. A state legislature can make every congressional district approximately equal in population—and hence absolve itself of the charge of gerrymandering—and at the same time carve up the state with such expertness that some districts remain, or become, hopelessly non-

competitive. Indeed, there is a quiet but recurrent battle between state party leaders trying to strengthen the state party as a
whole, and the congressmen and their legislative allies trying
to fortify themselves in their part of the state. The state leaders
want to make as many districts as possible fairly secure for
their party, but not overwhelmingly safe, for they seek to spread
their party's strength widely in order to win as many congressional and legislative elections as possible. The congressman, on
the other hand, is a bit greedy; remembering the occasional
horrible examples of "entrenched" congressmen being unseated,
he usually wants to build up his majorities as high as possible.
And given the diffusion of power in the state party, the congressman can often get his way.

Most one-party districts are made up of villages, small
towns, and small cities. They have a heavily rural bias. Compared to the larger metropolitan areas, these districts tend to be
more homogeneous in social make-up and political attitude.
They usually lack the political competition and vitality that
characterize more urban or mixed areas. The major party, the
local business interests, press and pulpit, the community leaders
combine loosely to represent the dominant interests in the area.
Possible centers of dissent, most notably the opposition party,
trade unions or ethnic groups, cannot carry the burden of competition. The opposition, such as it is, fades away. The result
in these areas is not so much a loud and clear conservatism
(which might be logical in such a social and economic context)
as confusion, conformity, and negativism. But the congressman
does not see it this way. To him the grass roots are the source
of common sense; he would agree with Rousseau that there was
more wisdom in small bands of Swiss peasants gathered under
oak trees to conduct their affairs than in all the governments of
Europe.

We must not exaggerate these urban-rural differences,
given the blurring of social forces in America. Rather we must
see how the political mechanisms are linked to dominant social
forces in typical areas. The link is the politician—in this case
the congressman. He does not relate himself to his district im-
personally. He deals with its political life on his own terms,
kindling some forces and tranquillizing or ignoring others. Thus
he contributes to the political tone of the district as well as
expressing it. The manner in which he does this turns on his

perception of how his political behavior, given the political materials he must work with, can advance his political career.

Typically such a congressman has two major career choices. He can seek to stay in his congressional post and hence rise through the hierarchy in Congress. Or he can use his office as a stepping stone to bigger offices, such as governor or senator. Usually this is not a free choice, for it is influenced by the nature of his district as well as by his own motives and expectations. A man in a safe district often finds himself, as in upstate New York or downstate Illinois, representing a constituency quite different from the state as a whole. Rural districts in particular are likely to be more conservative than the state generally, or at least more opposed to prevailing political and governmental trends in the state. Republican congressmen from the upstate districts of New York, for example, are often at odds with their party's governor and senators. Hence it may be hard for such congressmen to "go statewide"; most of them hesitate to risk a safe seat for the arduous and risky job of appealing to the independents and moderates who might hold the balance of power in a statewide contest.

So the congressman from a safe seat usually follows the easy alternative: he stays put. He placates the dominant social forces in the district; "protects" his district against hostile outside forces; does a great many individual favors; lobbies for benefits for the district; maintains a friends-and-neighbors political organization that scares would-be opponents out of the primary or trounces them if they come in; and comfortably overwhelms the opposition party's candidate—if there is one—on election day. His main commitment politically is to the status quo. He wishes nothing to disrupt his easy relationships with the public officials and private interests that rule the area. He views with alarm the great issues that sweep the nation and threaten to disrupt the familiar and comfortable politics of his district. He does not want to broaden the franchise or encourage more voting, because this might disturb existing arrangements.

Naturally the one-party congressman fares best in the "off-year" (non-presidential) elections. In presidential years the vote in congressional races is over one-third again as large as the comparable turnout in the off-years. Since presidential candidates arouse hosts of independent or apathetic voters who then stay at home in the congressional elections two years later, the one-party congressman faces his greatest risk when the opposition party offers a strong presidential candidate, like Roosevelt or Eisenhower. But such presidential candidates are exceptional, so that in presidential as well as off-year elections the typical one-party congressman is quite safe. And he remains invincibly local. By remaining in the orbit of his congressional area, he stays politically in the orbit of his party's local candidates and officeholders. Thus he operates in a world of political localism, for the electoral and other political forces in the area are largely activated by other local candidates. Hence the congressman, though a national officeholder, is almost as locally oriented as the district attorney or county commissioner, and almost as much beyond the reach of influence by the President or the national party. And this is one more reason he achieves his key aim: unbroken longevity in office.

Longevity in office—this is the crucial nexus between the man in the safe rural district and the congressional party in Washington. The mechanism is well known—the rule of seniority, which promotes congressmen up the committee ladder toward the chairmanship in accordance with his unbroken tenure on the committee. Our man in the safe seat has a wonderful incentive to stay put. He can, with any kind of luck, expect steady promotion to the top councils of the congressional party, regardless of merit. No other major Western democracy rewards its politicians with so much power for so little relevant accomplishment.

But it is dangerous to focus too much on the seniority rule in the committees alone, for this committee rule is merely one instrument, though a central one, in the allocation of power in Congress. Again we must think in terms of a system of power. And that system is today, and has been since 1938, essentially the same as it was in the 1850's, the 1890's, in 1910, and at other turning points in American history.

The leaders of the congressional party are, of course, men who have climbed the seniority ladders and hence the men who come from the safe, usually rural, districts. They are the chairmen, or ranking majority or minority members of the more important committees: the committees that tax and spend, that seek to control other central economic policies, such as prices and investment, that have major influence on the political status and personal privileges of other members of Congress (i.e., special appropriations for members' districts, or special bills affecting individual constituents), and that influence the traffic of legislative business—most notably the House Rules Committee. The statistics are conclusive. In a recent Congress the 217 most urban districts produced 26 per cent of the House chairmen in general, while the 218 least urban accounted for 74 per cent. But the imbalance of rural-urban power becomes even more significant if one notes the relative importance of the committees rather than simply their total number.

This imbalance of urban-rural control of committees is not accidental. The congressional party leaders are the same persons who make assignments to committees. In the House these choices are made by Democratic and Republican committees-on-committees, which are largely composed of rural representatives. Conservative influence in these selection committees is self-perpetuating; by taking on only those members who have already attained some seniority, the committees-on-committees automatically exclude freshman members from the more urban and mixed "swing" districts. Both committees, a careful study concludes, "are so constituted as to be virtually immune to immediate pressures brought about by electoral changes." Using this selection machinery, the congressional parties control access to positions on the key substantive committees and on the Rules Committee. Moreover, House members seeking committee assignments channel their requests through the "dean" or senior member of their state party delegation—one more concession to seniority.

The seniority system is pervasive. It shapes not only key committee memberships and leadership but the whole life and tone of the Congress. Freshman members find themselves treated like freshmen. As they learn the ropes—if they can survive their early re-election campaigns—they learn that the things they need for political survival, such as constituent favors and home-town projects, and the little considerations they want as employees on the Hill, such as office space or congressional patronage, depend on their cooperating with the congressional party leadership. "If you want to get along you've got to go along"—this hoary adage is one of the working principles of congressional life.

How the congressional party operates on a specific and

vital front of public policy can be seen in the House Appropriations Committee. This committee, like the party as a whole, has its own set of roles and norms, rewards and penalties. Its ruling elements consider themselves guardians of the taxpayer's money; they are more prone to cut Administration requests than to shape positive policies of their own, though of course they allow themselves and their congressional allies local appropriations. They operate less as Democrats or Republicans than as elements of a coalition dealing with one another through bargaining, reciprocity, and a united front on the House floor. And appointments to the committee are mainly controlled, of course, by the chairman and senior members. Membership on the committee is not just a job, its members like to say, but a way of life.

The seniors are expert at compounding their influence. Consider Representative Francis E. Walter of Pennsylvania. Not only is he chairman of the Judiciary Committee Immigration Subcommittee, but also of the Un-American Activities Committee and of the House Patronage Committee. Hence he can withhold Capitol Hill patronage jobs from erring members, block private immigration bills (a special problem for urban congressmen trying to get around general immigration restrictions), all the while serving as an astute parliamentarian and as chief guardian of Americanism on Capitol Hill. Other, less noted congressional party leaders operate in the subcommittees of the Appropriations and other committees to compound their influence on the Hill.

I have been emphasizing the House seniority system here, but the Senate shows the same forces at work, though sometimes less visibly. Most Senators, like most Representatives, are lawyers, and about half the Senators in a recent session had begun their careers as state legislators or prosecuting attorneys. In the upper chamber like the lower, men from the safe rural states are more likely to get the choice committee assignments and more likely to acquire greater influence on the committees. Senators "table-hop" from committee to committee over the years to gain better berths, and a senior Senator requesting a vacant committee seat almost always get it, unless, like Estes Kefauver, he has defied Senate norms. Senators from more competitive states are, of course, less likely to build influence in the upper body.

The Senate, like the House, has a set of standing committees that not only provide for division of legislative labor but, as Ralph Huitt says, are part of the allocation of political power. As in the lower chamber, committee chairman control subcommittee appointments. Effectiveness on the Hill depends greatly on conforming with one's elders. The Senate's seniority system "results in the under-representation of liberals among the chairmen of both parties . . . ," Donald R. Matthews concludes. "The seniority system's bias against urban liberals of both parties tends to be self-perpetuating." And the right to filibuster—which is the power of a very few Senators to bargain effectively with all the rest—represents the Madisonian tradition in its most extreme form.

Helping to unite the congressional party is a common ideology. This ideology is, of course generally conservative (defining conservatism as opposition to the increased use of government to redistribute income in favor of lower-income groups) and isolationist (defined as opposition to greater political, diplomatic, and economic concessions and commitments to other nations). But this ideology is intrinsically negative; that is, it is hostile to major governmental trends in the 20th Century, although it offers grudging acceptance of welfare programs and other measures that have won wide support among voters. But on one matter the congressional party ideologists are most articulate and positive—defense of the congressional party system. States' rights, local elections, restricted franchise, minority rights, rural over-representation, checks and balances, congressional power, the danger of majority or "mass" rule, judicial review (at least in the old days), powerful committees, the seniority system, the filibuster—in short, the Madisonian system in all its ramifications—arouse their stout support. And the ideologists in Congress are buttressed outside it by able political thinkers, like James Burnham, by perceptive journalists like William S. White and David Lawrence, and by a host of newspapers, magazines, and commentators.

Congressional party leaders in both houses can exert a wide, though sometimes tenuous, discipline outside their chambers too. Congressmen report cases of Southern members being threatened with primary opposition backed with outside money unless they toed the line. In each house the Republican and Democratic congressional campaign committees, which for decades have operated largely apart from the national party committees, allot money to congressional candidates; and while the sum is not large, there are cases where the committees have given money to conservative candidates from safer districts at the expense of more needy aspirants from more competitive constituencies. The main party discipline of the congressional party, however, is internal. Significantly, the congressional party rarely takes prized committee assignments from members of Congress who bolt the presidential nominee.

Still, the main bulwark of the congressional party system is not this kind of conscious manipulation but, as I have indicated above, a whole system of local power patterns, electoral arrangements, voting behavior, career lines, and institutional arrangements and norms in Congress that together form an operating political system. For we must understand what the congressional party system is not, as well as what it is. It is not a tight, cohesive group of men, conspiring together in a secret chamber and pushing the buttons on a nationwide machine. It is a loose cluster of men, sharing a common concept of the public interest, convinced that they are protecting the nation against radicalism, benefiting from and in turn protecting a set of rules and institutions that bolster their power, and the product of local political patterns. These men deal with one another by bargaining and accommodation rather than by direction and command. They are often divided over specific policies. They have the problem of cooperating across formal party lines between Democrats and Republicans, and across the physical and psychological gap separating Senate and House. And they must share some power with the formally elected leaders in each house, as we will see later. But what unites them is the common defense of a system that consolidates their influence on Capitol Hill. And that system, while not monolithic, is composed of social forces and political mechanisms that are mutually supporting and hence cumulative in their impact. Power in one part of the system can be parlayed into power in another. "The committees with their chairmen," a freshman congressman said recently, "are like a ring of forts."

THE PRESIDENTIAL PARTY SYSTEM

The head of the presidential party is the President. He sets its policies, confirms its ideology, appoints its leaders, and carries its hopes in the quadrennial crisis of the presidential election.

Just as other parties are organized around other officeholders, so a party is organized around the Chief Executive. Beginning with Jefferson and Jackson the man in the White House has acted in varying degrees as "party leader." But he is not head of the whole Democratic or Republican party. There are great sections of the Democratic party beyond the control of President Kennedy today, just as many Republicans never really accepted Mr. Eisenhower as their party leader. But of that section of the whole party that we call the presidential party, the President is undisputed leader.

The President runs his party through a small political staff in the White House and through the chairman of the party's national committee. That chairman, like his own aides, is chosen by him and remains in office only as long as the President wishes. Other leaders of the President's party also remain at his sufferance: Cabinet members, top agency chiefs, and hundreds of administrative aides and operatives in the higher echelons of the Administration. These officials often appear to be non-political but in the final test they will support the presidential party. In the 1930's Harry Hopkins had a clear understanding of the close relation of relief activities to Roosevelt's re-election campaigns. In 1960, according to the testimony of the government official concerned, the Interior Department cancelled the sale of surplus tungsten in an effort to help Vice-President Nixon's election campaign. Some officials, such as the Secretary of Defense and heads of independent commissions, are less in the presidential party orbit, while others like the Attorney General or the Postmaster General hold offices that are much more partisan by tradition. And a few Administration officials may not be in the presidential party at all.

From Washington the presidential party fans out widely. Hundreds of Administration political appointees in the states and cities—federal attorneys, collectors of customs, federal marshals, and the like (except those who mainly owe appointment to Senators at odds with the President)—are expected to protect the Administration's local interests, at least where called on. Both in Washington and in the field the President's men also maintain close relations with many of the state party leaders, though some state committees are the possession of a potent Governor or Senator or big-city mayor, or are hopelessly divided between the President and the state leaders. The organizational reach of the presidential party typically does not extend below the state level, except perhaps in the choosing of national convention delegates.

The national convention shows the presidential party in its full splendor and power. The convention always endorses its leader in the White House, if he wishes it to—a fact of 20th Century history that Harry Truman remembered in the spring of 1948 and his adversaries in the party seemed to forget. The President's men write the platform, determine the content of the major speeches, decide which contested delegations will be seated, control the order of the business on the floor, and roll up the President's endorsement on the first ballot, followed by nomination by acclamation. Rebels are easily put down. The President also controls the nomination of his running-mate. If it is worth his while to make changes in the Vice-Presidency, as Roosevelt did in 1940, he can do so. Usually he does not make the effort, because the Vice-Presidency is not that important. All in all, the presidential party controls the convention as fully as the congressional party controls Congress.

The heart of national politics, Arthur Holcombe wrote, is the presidential campaign. So it is of the presidential party. Its candidate is the focus of the party's effort and the center of national attention. He dominates the national media and sharpens the national debate. He arouses and motivates millions of voters. The campaign is his supreme opportunity to arouse and shape mass opinion, to cut through the babel of voices, to show the voter the direct link between a national problem and doing something about it (i.e., voting for him).

This, indeed, has been the historic achievement of the presidential party—the immense widening of the electorate. "The rise of political parties and the extension of the suffrage produced the plebiscitary Presidency," Schattschneider says. ". . . The Presidency has in turn become the principal instrument for the nationalization of politics"—the destruction of old local power monopolies and sectional power patterns. From Harrison and Jackson in the last century to Eisenhower and Stevenson in 1952 and Kennedy and Nixon in 1960, it has been the presidential party contests that have spectacularly broadened the voting rolls. The reason is clear. The great incentive of the presidential candidates is to widen and "flatten out" their vote, to win states by dependable but not wasteful popular majorities, while the congressional party "bunches" its vote in safe districts.

The stunning impact of the presidential campaign is partly organizational. Roving through the nation, the President's men shake up sleepy committees, set up campaign organizations, raise money, recruit local party leadership. But the regular party organizations, no matter how efficient, are not able to mobilize the majorities that the presidential party seeks. So presidential party candidates establish auxiliary organizations to reach the millions of independents that the regulars disregard. This is an old practice; Horatio Seymour in 1868 set up the "order of the Union Democrats" to bolster the listless Democrats with a vigorous new organization that could cut across party lines. More recently, the Willkie Clubs, Citizens for Eisenhower, Volunteers for Stevenson, Citizens for Kennedy and similar groups have conducted big campaigns separate from, and sometimes at conflict with, the regular organizations. Often they ignore or even "cut" the state and local candidates of the regular parties. Bad feelings always develop between volunteers and regulars. Sometimes the regulars slight the presidential candidate in return. Candidates for governor have been known to hold rallies without a single sign or poster for the presidential candidate of their own party—but the reverse also happens. Sometimes this uneasy marriage ends in disaster. In 1940 Willkie organized a huge force of volunteers through the Willkie clubs; during the war the regulars deserted him, in part because of his war-time support of Roosevelt, and they denied him renomination in 1944. Despite all the bickering, however, this bifurcation of presidential campaigns will continue as long as our parties retain their present character, for the presidential candidate must have machinery for winning independent and even opposition party votes.

Just as the congressional parties benefit from gerrymandered congressional districts, so the presidential party benefits from its own form of gerrymandering. This is the electoral college, which, by allotting all the electoral votes of a state to the candidate winning most popular votes in that state, puts a premium on the big urban states with their handsome electoral-vote plums. Since the big states tend to be highly competitive states, the winner-take-all arrangement plays up the importance of the organized groups, such as Negroes, Catholics, union labor, Jews, ethnic groups that supposedly control the balance of electoral power in the state. This control may be exaggerated, and usually is, but to the presidential parties, locked in fierce combat, this huge, supposedly deliverable vote, looks increasingly irresistible as election day nears. Kennedy's eleventh-hour emphasis on this vote in 1960, and Nixon's apparent unconcern for it when he flew to Alaska at the climactic moment, is bound to enhance the mythology of the electoral-college balance of power. The distortion resulting from the winner-take-all device further separates the bases of the presidential and congressional parties. But even without it, there would be some electoral bifurcation, for the presidential parties, as the more urban, liberally oriented party system, naturally direct their main appeals to the urban and suburban vote.

The career lines in the presidential party are significantly different from those in the congressional. The traditional path to the Presidency has been through a big-state governorship, the party organization around which is likely to be fairly parallel with the presidential party organization in that state (Stevenson in Illinois in 1952, for example). Few governors, on the other hand, rise to high places in the congressional party. Few Senators have become President in the past century, but we now know that the old rule that "Senators don't become President, with Harding as the exception that proves the rule," had a flaw in it (besides the notion that exceptions somehow prove rules). It has not Senators in general but Senators who were committed members of the congressional party that were ineligible for presidential party leadership (Harding *was* an exception to the rule). As if realizing this, John Kennedy moved steadily out of the orbit of the congressional party into that of the presidential during his years in the Senate. It was Lyndon Johnson's failure to do this, and Robert Taft's similar failure earlier, that fatally handicapped them in their quest for the nomination.

The career lines in the presidential and congressional systems seem to diverge at a deeper level too. While evidence on this is limited, it may well be that the presidential party draws on men who have risen through the bureaucracies of big business, universities, unions, large law firms, and state and federal executive departments. Many of these men are "political outsiders," as Mills has defined them; they have spent most of their working life outside strictly political organization. Congressional party leadership is mainly composed of one-time independent entrepreneurs, small-town lawyers, local law enforcement officials, and state legislators. We can guess that the differing vocational, ideological, and institutional worlds of the two groups—one more bureaucratic, hierarchical, and managerial, the other more individualistic and prone to negotiate and bargain—would have a significant impact on the nature of the parties.

All the foregoing discussion presupposes one crucial fact about the presidential party—that its leader is President. What about the presidential party that does not possess the White House? Things then, of course, are very different. There is no office around which the party can be organized, no office to lead it, discipline it, reward it. Defeated at the polls, the presidential party becomes apathetic and disorganized. No one speaks for it with a clear voice. The national chairman, as the executor of the defeated candidate's political estate, is powerless and must yield to the congressional party. The presidential party does not disappear, of course. Its head cut off, the body still lives, waiting for a new head and a new vitality. For the time being, however, it is impotent.

Such, at least, has been the traditional state of the out-of-office presidential party, but there has been an interesting change. After their defeat in 1956, notable presidential Democrats under the leadership of national chairman Paul Butler decided to establish a council to shape party policy and to focus attack on the Eisenhower Administration. Its members came from the presidential party: Harry Truman, Adlai Stevenson, Herbert Lehman, Averell Harriman, among others, with Eleanor Roosevelt as consultant. The committee had little direct influence on policy and was ignored by the congressional Democratic party. But it helped keep alive presidential party doctrine among Democrats and posed well-publicized alternatives to the Eisenhower politics. Much more than the congressional Democrats, the council served as Eisenhower's Loyal Opposition.

That Senator Hubert Humphrey and other liberal Democratic legislators were members of the Advisory Council points up a puzzling but important fact: a large minority of congressmen belong to their presidential party rather than to the congressional. Many of these congressmen are freshmen who represent marginal districts, and perhaps were elected in a presidential party sweep with the head of their presidential party. Kept in essentially a freshman status by the congressional parties, these members of Congress turn to the presidential parties for a political home. Otherwise, the congressional makeup of the two presidential parties varies considerably. Democratic members are mainly those who represent urban dwellers and who are not at home in the rural atmosphere of the congressional parties—for example, Democrats Emanuel Celler of New York, John E. Fogarty of Rhode Island, Chet Holifield of California, Edith Green of Oregon. Republican congressmen in their presidential party are much less numerous and represent more competitive constituencies; Jacob Javits of New York and Clifford P. Case of New Jersey are the outstanding examples. One reason some congressmen move into the orbit of the presidential party is that they see the need for the President's help in gaining re-election. The more marginal and competitive the congressman's district, the closer he will ordinarily be to the presidential party.

The borders between the congressional and presidential parties in Congress are not clear-cut. Many a congressman hedges his bets by shifting back and forth between the two camps, or by keeping a foot in each. And nothing is fuzzier than the role of the elected leadership of Congress—the Speaker of the House, the majority and minority leaders, and the various party conferences and policy committes. Indeed, an interesting question is whether the formal leadership belongs to the presidential or congressional parties. The answer is: it depends.

It depends mainly on whether or not the presidential party is in power. When it is, the leadership ordinarily lines up behind the President. It retains some bargaining power, as Taft did with Eisenhower in 1953. It can always revolt if put under excessive pressure, as Alben Barkley did against Roosevelt in 1944. But generally it goes along, and the meeting of the congressional "Big Four" or "Big Six" with the President has become one of the most durable institutions in Washington. A President's prestige is so great that his fellow partisans in Congress will rarely choose leadership hostile to him. Sometimes he is powerful enough to determine the choice himself. But usually the decision is made largely independent of the White House, as in the selection of Charles Halleck as Republican House leader in 1959 and the election of John W. McCormack as Speaker in 1962. This semi-independence can be of some importance, though; as Neustadt says, "the more an officeholder's power stems from sources outside the President, the stronger will be his potential power *on* the President."

When the presidential party does not occupy the White House, the elected congressional leaders usually move closer to the seniority leadership of the congressional party. This was evident in both Taft's and Johnson's majority leadership in the Senate, and is seen most notably today in Halleck's leadership in the House. The difficulty for the elected leaders, in contrast to the other sets of leaders, is that they lack firm institutional bases of support of their own. The policy committees, caucuses, and other party devices are insubstantial compared with the standing committees. If the majority leader and his whips lack a President to back them up, they are generally, and over the long run, drawn into the vortex of the senior leaders. Consider, for example, Rayburn's and Johnson's refusal to join the Democratic Advisory Council. They treated it as part of a somewhat different party—as indeed it was. Or consider Republican leader Halleck's attitude toward the Republican party platform of 1960. "We will take it out and read it from time to time," he said. "But the congressional people generally have very little to do with writing party platforms."

In this three-way tug of war much also depends on the skill of the elected leader. At times Taft through his experience and doggedness was able to act virtually as a third force in the Senate, as was Lyndon Johnson through his superb parliamentary skill and his grasp of the nuances of Senate life. But when the chips are down the elected leaders usually do not hold the levers of power. Sam Rayburn, despite all his prestige and support in the House, was never really able to vanquish Howard W. Smith, chairman of the Rules Committee. And, as we have seen, Henry Cabot Lodge finally had to yield to the Senate Irreconcilables in his fight against Wilson's League. One problem is that the Senate leader is not sure of his own constituency, as in the case of Senate Democratic majority leader Scott Lucas, who was defeated for re-election to the Senate in 1952. Another inhibiting factor is the fear of failure to be reelected majority leader—the unhappy blow that Republican House leader Joseph W. Martin suffered in 1959. Unlike the seniority leaders, the elected leaders always face possible repudiation at the hands of one or both of their constituencies.

Another type of congressman who has a somewhat equivo-

cal position is the member from a metropolitan, one-party
district. He is ordinarily a Democrat responsive to urban interests and hence takes a liberal position on economic issues.
At the same time he is the beneficiary of a seniority system that
gives him special influence on Capitol Hill—though not so much
influence as it gives rural representatives, who usually gain
the most powerful chairmanships. Many such representatives
of one-party urban districts end up in the awkward position of
supporting the congressional power system at the same time
that they support liberal policies, such as civil rights, that are
blocked by that system. But the city men usually win by such
big margins that their conflicting role positions on the Hill are
not an electoral embarrassment, except possibly in a Democratic
primary.

What of the freshmen congressmen and other congressional members of the presidential party? Sometimes they can
turn to the elected leadership for help, but more often they are
on their own. The freshman congressman quoted earlier as
seeing the committee leadership like a ring of forts went on to
evaluate his own side: "A coalition of Northerners, without interior lines of strength, is a tenuous thing. . . . We have no
unifying philosophy. . . . We have no White House to cajole,
threaten and promise. . . . The analogy with warfare that I
have used is an accurate one. . . . The northern coalition, as
the attackers, are spread out, with poor communications between one another and hence poor coordination. We have no
base of power, with which to menace the chairmen on the one
hand, or to discipline our own members on the other."

The President, as head of the presidential party, has no
more vital task than to lead his presidential forces in Congress,
to unify them, to give them interior lines of strength. For no
section of the presidential party is more dependent on the
President, nor more crucial to him.

FOUR-PARTY POLITICS

We can conclude that the pattern of national politics is essentially a four-party pattern. The Democratic and Republican
parties are each divided into congressional and presidential
structures, with all the elements that comprise the American
type of party.

The division of Democrats and Republicans into two parties each is of course the immediate cause of the national four-party pattern. The four parties would not last long, however, if they lacked strong attitudinal bases in the electorate. They might not continue, for example, if people divided only over economic issues, for such a situation, combined with the tendency of politicians toward combinations, would normally produce two groupings, presumably of those who got smaller slices of the economic loaf against those who got bigger. At least two factors operate against such a simple two-way division in America.

One is the obvious fact that people divide over issues other than economic ones and—a crucial point—that the economic divisions are not congruent with the others. By "other issues" I mean those that have been variously called "moral" or "style" issues but that I will call "way-of-life" issues—that is, issues that pose choices about a nation's whole culture and way of life and that cannot be calculated in terms of immediate and tangible economic return for specific groups of people. Taxes, wages, social security, farm prices, tariffs, public housing are examples of economic issues; while civil liberties, women's rights, disarmament, immigration, corruption in government, defense strategy, racial tolerance and integration, government, and religion are examples of way-of-life issues. The presumed motivational appeal of the former, Berelson, Lazarsfeld, and McPhee suggest, is self-interest of a relatively direct and tangible kind, while that of the latter is self-expression and self-gratification of a more subjective, symbolic, and projective kind. Issues do not fall neatly into the two categories. An expansion of civil rights, such as job opportunity, or of immigration of certain types of workers, or of certain types of defense activities, could mean economic benefits or deprivations for various groups as well as psychic benefits or deprivations for a wider public. But the difference between the two seems sharp enough to affect the shape of our party structure.

Data on the non-congruence of economic and way-of-life issues are limited but highly suggestive. Polls indicate that there has been in recent years little if any relationship between persons' relative positions on domestic and foreign issues. "An interventionist position in foreign affairs was as likely to be taken by a domestic conservative as by a domestic liberal" in

1956, report Campbell and associates, "and the relative isolationist was as likely to favor social welfare activities in Washington as he was to oppose them." By cross-tabulating distributions of responses in 1952 to an "international involvement"
question and a "social welfare activity" question, Key finds four
combinations of opinion: isolationist-liberal, internationalist-
liberal, isolationist-conservative, internationalist-conservative
(with the last the smallest of the four in numbers).

Evidence on the non-congruence of economic and domestic
way-of-life issues is even more limited but still suggestive. Much
of it stems from historians' observations. The political parties
have usually had their "conscience" and "cotton" wings. Under
Theodore Roosevelt the Republican party numbered hosts of
high-income business and professional men who looked on their
party mainly as a weapon to attack the moral and social evils
of the day. The Democratic party in Bryan's and Wilson's days
and also more recently has numbered not only hosts of economic reformers but also workers and farmers who took a
hostile or stunted view of civil liberties, women's rights, civil
rights, civic betterment, and other way-of-life problems.

A second root cause of the four-party pattern is the dis-
articulation of the national and state party systems, stemming
from the workings of federalism in a sectional society combined with some of our special political arrangements. The
impact of national politics on state and local politics in our
sectional nation has been noted in these pages—the creation
of one-party states and districts. Balance and competition at
the national level, especially in presidential contests, helped
produce local noncompetition and imbalance, most notably in
the South and rural North. These one-party areas tended to be
ignored by presidential candidates, who concentrated on the
swing areas, and hence the one-party areas became less important to the presidential parties, but they received extra
representation in Congress because of the seniority system, and
hence became the buttress of the congressional parties.

This double cleavage, institutional and attitudinal, between the presidential parties and the congressional parties is
largely responsible for the conflicting positions that a President,
whether Democratic or Republican, and a Congress, whether
Democratic or Republican controlled, take on the crucial affairs
of state.

Willmore Kendall has pointed to the curious fact that the Executive "is able, with good show of reason, to put itself forward on any particular issue as the spokesman for . . . lofty and enlightened principle. . . . The Executive tends, that is to say, to have the nation's ministers and publicists with it on 'peace,' the nation's professors and moralizers with it on de-segregation, the nation's economists with it on fiscal policy and redistribution, the nation's political scientists with it on political reform and civil rights, etc. . . . The Executive is for world government, for the outlawry of war, for unselfish-ness in our relations with the outside world, for the brotherhood of man, for majority-rule, for progress, for generosity toward the weak and lowly, for freedom of thought and speech, for equality, for the spreading of the benefits of modern civilization to 'underdeveloped' lands, for science and the 'scientific outlook,' for civil rights. . . ." Congress, according to Professor Kendall, stresses other values: small group discussion in the community, deference to highly prestiged and presumably wiser citizens, and an anti-quixotic concern for the "realities, problems, the potential benefits and potential costs (and for whom?)" of presidential proposals.

Why this gap between President and Congress over way-of-life issues? Why, in Professor Kendall's own terms, do the two presidential parties win a much larger share of the "moral-izers" and reformers and utopians than do the two congres-sional parties? Possibly—and here I can only speculate, for we do not have adequate data—because the most persisting major conflicts in American politics have been over economic issues; hence the national parties have offered the most meaningful alternatives in the realm of economic policy; so that if divisions of the voters over economic and way-of-life issues are not con-gruent, as we have reason to think they are not, millions of voters more concerned with way-of-life issues than economic ones have had to operate in a party limbo. They are simply not aroused by the state and local contests, including congres-sional contests, that turn on the old bread-and-butter issues; they have not been geared into the local two-party alignment over the years because they have had no meaningful alternatives presented to them on the issues that mean most to them: cor-ruption, human rights, social reform, and the rest. Hence the voices of the mugwumps have often been ignored in the ob-

scure politics of the local, often non-competitive struggle. But
the presidential contest does reach and arouse such independents because their collective voice nationally is loud, and because in the sharply competitive presidential race the two candidates must move beyond the traditional economic issues and
find way-of-life issues that may reach the uncommitted.

The consequence of the four-party system is that American
political leaders, in order to govern, must manage multi-party
coalitions just as heads of coalition parliamentary regimes in
Europe have traditionally done—as the French did, for example,
before De Gaulle. But the task of governing in a sense is harder
in the United States, for the leaders' job is not simply to pick
up enough parliamentary votes to form a cabinet, or even just to
pass a bill. They must bring together the right combination of
presidential party and congressional party strength to accomplish a great variety of tasks day after day and year after year.
And the leaders' job is further complicated by the fact that
continuous, effective government policy-making is impossible
without a strong working alliance between at least some combination of presidential and congressional parties. For the
presidential side and the congressional side each wields power
not only in its own "constitutional" orbit but in the opposite
side's orbit as well.

The extent to which the congressional and presidential
parties share the same powers and hence can block each other
is extraordinary. The President has a broad range of legislative
power besides his veto: he can issue executive orders that have
the force of law; he can draw up with other nations executive
agreements that are as controlling under international law as
treaties ratified by the Senate; he can make war "by the push
of a button" and let Congress ratify it later, if at all. But Congress inserts itself into the executive process too. The Senate
can refuse to confirm appointments—even one lone Senator can
induce the whole upper body to withhold approval through the
device of "senatorial courtesy." The standing committees closely
affect administrative arrangements through their control of
policy, and the appropriations committees and subcommittees
have a profound impact through their control of funds. The
more "independent" an agency or commission may be of the
President, the more dependent it may be on a committee or
faction of Congress. The relation, of course, changes over time.

After the Civil War Congress tried to control the Administration through such means as the Tenure of Office Act; the act is long since gone but not some of the motivation behind it. Today the Army Chief of Engineers has legislative authority to plan public works and report to Congress without clearing with the President.

In less obvious fields too, the two-party coalitions, the congressional and the presidential, maintain countervailing institutional apparatus. The President can publicize an issue and influence public opinion by appointing a "blue-ribbon" presidential commission controlled by the President's men, and he and his lieutenants can set into action other varieties of Administration inquiries, probes, and explorations. Congress at the same time has its standing committees, including the Un-American Activities Committee, which can investigate at the drop of a hat, and it can set up special committees to conduct grand investigations.

The President can call Congress back into special session after it adjourns, but the houses can recess instead of adjourn and thus retain more control of their own operations. If the President can act on many matters through executive orders not subject to congressional veto, Congress can legislate, at least to a modest extent, through Concurrent Resolutions, which are not subject to presidential veto. Congress can limit White House legislative power by setting statutory expiration dates in the original act, as Ernest Griffith has noted, "as a device to circumvent a possible presidential veto of some future measure designed to change a particular policy to which it has given reluctant or experimental agreement." On the other hand, Congress has had to delegate to the President an immense amount of policy-making power. The bureaucracy of the executive department has grown enormously—but so has that of Congress. The General Accounting Office, which has a theoretically executive duty, supplies information on administrative lapses to congressional watchdogs.

An executive impetus and a legislative tendency confront each other at every junction. The executive impetus is to combine legislative and administrative power, to coordinate functions, to exert control from the top. Whether it is Elihu Root, Theodore Roosevelt's Secretary of War, trying (unsuccessfully) to nationalize the state guard, or Hoover and Truman trying to

centralize administration, or Kennedy trying to reorganize the
executive branch, the instinct of the executive is to integrate
government for the sake of better control. The legislative instinct is pluralistic. Congress and the state legislatures, under
the control of the legislative parties, seek to fragmentize the
executive by means of individual or committee influence over
administrative units, or control of specific budgetary items, or
through hobbling the executive's power to reorganize. State
legislatures have in some instances kept whole sections of the
executive branch out from the governor's control, and have
resisted efforts to shorten the long ballot, which gives state
officials electoral strength independent of the governor.

This bewildering array of countervailing and overlapping
powers compels American political leaders to piece together a
new patchwork of party fragments, factional chieftains, congressional votes, constitutional usage, and bureaucratic officials
in order to put through each major new program. Presidential
party leaders do this through endless persuading, pressuring,
manipulating, and bargaining. Congressional party leaders use
the same methods to balk or modify Administration proposals,
and their task is all the easier because of the many points at
which action can be slowed or stopped in the narrow, twisting,
and crowded legislative channels. Since each set of parties,
congressional or presidential, is a coalition itself, action depends on the alignment of coalition with coalition.

Not that the presidential and congressional party coalitions
are of the same type. The former, to use Dahl's apt expression,
is an "executive-centered coalition." The President has means
of direction and discipline unmatched by the congressional
parties or by the presidential party out of power. He has a
public position, a command of the media, a control over personnel, and a direct electoral link with the people that enable
him to maintain and exploit a somewhat hierarchical system
in the presidential party. The congressional party is led by a
coalition of leaders, allied through their common attitudes and
mutual dependence, and with an internal party system marked
more by bargaining than by hierarchy. The essential operational process differs: the congressional reliance on committees,
with their tendency to protect an existing consensus over the
status quo, contrasts with the executive emphasis on single-
leader activism. The out-of-power presidential party, to use

Dahl's terminology, is a network of "independent sovereignties with spheres of influence." But even this network, inchoate though it is, has the attributes of party—ideology, program, leadership, machinery, and existing or potential electoral support.

Any one of the four parties can—and does—coalesce with any one of the others. We take for granted the coalition of the Democratic presidential and congressional parties, and of the two Republican parties—though often we should not. The durable alliance of the congressional parties has long been publicized by liberals as the "unholy alliance of Old Guard Republicans and Dixie Democrats" in Congress. Less obvious is another alliance, holy or unholy, between presidential Democrats and presidential Republicans. These parties occasionally combine in Congress, as Republicans from urban and suburban districts support the proposals of Democratic Presidents. But the main focus of the presidential party alliance is in the foreign policy and fiscal agencies. Roosevelt's enlistment of Stimson and Knox in his Cabinet in 1940, Truman's appointment of a host of Republicans to foreign-policy and foreign-aid agencies, Eisenhower's choice of Texas Democrat Robert Anderson as Secretary of the Treasury, and Kennedy's retention of Douglas Dillon and other Republicans from the Eisenhower Administration and his selection of an internationalist Republican, McGeorge Bundy, as an assistant, reflect a wide community of interest between the two parties. The alliance is consecrated in the name of "bipartisanship in foreign policy," or the hoary slogan "Party politics stops at the water's edge." What mainly stops at the water's edge is not party politics in general but congressional party politics in particular. The real "unholy alliance" to a good congressional Republican is the historic coalition between the internationalists in both parties. And the internationalist newspapers that approve so highly of foreign-policy bipartisanship today were never so enthusiastic about it in the 1920's and the early 1930's, when it represented a coalition of isolationists.

No political system is neutral—certainly not the congressional and presidential. Power is inseparable from structure. It is not by chance that liberal and internationalist Presidents in this century have been "strong" Presidents, and that men like Taft and Harding are relegated to the ranks of the weak. The stronger the exertion of presidential power, the more liberal and internationalist it will be because of the make-up and dynamics of the presidential party. The stronger the exertion of congressional power, the more conservative and isolationist will be our national policy because of the structure of the congressional forces. The man who is all for liberalism and internationalism "as long as the President's power is not increased" (as for example in the trade agreements act) is a man who has not grasped the relation of ends and means, of power and structure. The man who favors cutting down the powers of Congress because it is "slow and inefficient" is cutting down conservative influence, whether he wants to or not. The structure of coalition politics is inevitably the structure of "who gets what, when and how" in American national politics. As the Madisonian system in being, it is also the structure of slowdown and stalemate in American government.

PART II

The Founders

Writing in the early 1960s, James MacGregor Burns reflected the perspective of a liberal Democrat who, like many of his fellow reformers, had bridled at the relative inaction of the Eisenhower years and had responded with enthusiasm to the successful presidential campaign of John F. Kennedy. Yet President Kennedy had been unable to translate much of his program into effective law, and Burns reflects this frustration in *The Deadlock of Democracy*. Walter Dean Burnham wrote in the late 1960s, and his was a somewhat more radical perspective. He witnessed the enactment under President Lyndon Johnson of the most far-ranging program of liberal reform since the New Deal, then watched the nation erupt in a contagion of violence, and witnessed, in the 1968 election, the apparent degeneration of the two-party system into a confused three-cornered contest from which no clear mandate seemed to emerge. However, Burns and Burnham clearly shared a conviction that flowed from their historical analyses: the founders had both inherited and evolved a widely shared Lockeian-Jeffersonian ideology of classical liberalism and had translated it into a Madisonian system of checks and balances in government that seemed decreasingly responsive to the felt needs of modern political life.

Both Burns and Burnham were primarily concerned, although in somewhat differing ways, with what they regarded as the failures of the American party system. Yet one cannot sensibly turn to the crucially formative era of the Founding Fathers and at once apply party systems analysis to it, because what has been called the first, or the experimental party system, 1789–1824, did not even begin to evolve in any fundamental way until the ratification of the Constitution. This reluctant evolution of a party system within a structural and attitudinal context that was hostile to the very idea of political party is replete with irony, and it is addressed in several of the selections that follow, most notably in the analysis by Richard Hofstadter. But a primary concern must be the prior evolution of a unique American political ideology that was forged by the colonial experience and was both accelerated and sustained by the Revolution. This is not to deny the major commonalities and intellectual indebtedness that linked the thought of Franklin, Paine, Jefferson, and Madison to that of Locke, Bacon, Hume, Pope, Voltaire, Montesquieu, and Rousseau—for all were sons of the eighteenth-century Enlightenment that rejected feudalism, dogmatism, religious intolerance, and restrictions of trade and economic enterprise in appealing to freedom, rationalism, and humanitarianism.

But if the similarities between the violent American and French revolutions were many and genuine, fundamental differences were also profound. The extraordinarily perceptive Alexis de Tocqueville was keenly sensitive to this when he observed in *Democracy in America* that "democratic revolutions make [men] run away from each other and perpetuate, in the midst of equality, hatreds originating in inequality. The Americans have this great advantage, that they attained democracy without the sufferings of a democratic revolution and that they were born equal instead of becoming so."[1] Lacking Europe's feudal past, the Americans embraced classical liberalism's Enlightenment devotion to freedom and rationalism by enshrining in their basic documents a commitment to liberty and equality as society's ultimate and presumably symbiotic goals. But their bitter experience with governmental power, particularly as culminating first under the heavy-handed rule of King George III, then under the feckless wallowing of the Confederation, led them to erect a fascinating structure of government that at once recognized the necessity of power and yet ingeniously sought to shackle it.

[1]Alexis de Tocqueville, *Democracy in America,* New York: Harper & Row, 1966, p. 509.

In the first selection Burnham's concluding paragraph contains a ripe prediction: that "electoral disaggregation and the concentration of certain forms of power in the hands of economic, technological and administrative elites . . . would, after all, reflect the sociopolitical consequences of the *persistence of Lockeian individualism into an era of Big Organization* [emphasis added]: oligarchy at the top, inertia and spasms of self-defense in the middle, and fragmentation at the base." Lockeian individualism, classical Enlightenment liberalism, Jeffersonian republicanism—these familiar phrases are largely interchangeable and represent a constellation of political philosophy that lies at the heart of the American Revolution and is embodied in the Declaration of Independence and the Constitution. But for all its nobility of purpose, its core contains a contradiction that has plagued American political life for two centuries (and mankind's political life for far longer): the equation of liberty and equality. Notice, in Thomas Jefferson's lofty preamble to the Declaration of Independence, how the twin and ostensibly symbiotic goals of liberty and equality are linked in a single crucial sentence. (The balance of the Declaration is a bill of particulars accusing Great Britain and King George III of tyranny, and as such has faded with time in relation to the philosophical principles so powerfully enunciated in the preamble.) Yet liberty and equality often pull in opposite directions because the liberty to exercise unequal talents and energies tends to maximize the unequal distribution of property, especially in an industrial society. But the equation of liberty and equality seemed instinctive to eighteenth-century Americans, where land and opportunity appeared limitless.

Preamble to the Declaration of Independence

THOMAS JEFFERSON

When in the Course of human events, it becomes necessary for one people to disolve the political bands which have connected them with another, and to assume among the powers of the earth, the separate and equal station to which the Laws of Nature and of Nature's God entitle them, a decent respect to the opinions of mankind requires that they should declare the causes that should impel them to the separation. We hold these truths to be self-evident, that all men are created equal, that they are endowed by their Creator with certain unalienable rights, that among these are Life, Liberty, and the pursuit of Happiness. That to secure these rights, Governments are instituted among Men, deriving their just powers from the consent of the governed, That whenever any Form of Government becomes destructive to these ends it is the Right of the People to alter or to abolish it, and to institute new Government, laying its foundation on such principles and organizing its powers in such form, as to them shall seem most likely to effect their Safety and Happiness. Prudence, indeed, will dictate that Governments long established should not be changed for light and transient causes; and accordingly all experience hath shown, that mankind are more disposed to suffer, while evils are sufferable, than to right themselves by abolishing the forms to which they are accustomed. But when a long train of abuses and usurpations, pursuing invariably the same Object evinces a design to reduce them under absolute Despotism, it is their right, it is their duty, to throw off such Government, and to provide new Guards for their future security. Such has been the patient sufferance of these Colonies; and such is now the necessity which constrains them to alter their former Systems of Government. The history of the present King of Great Britain is a history of repeated injuries and usurpations, all having in direct object the establishment of an absolute Tyranny over these States. To prove this, let Facts be submitted to a candid world. . . .

INTRODUCTORY NOTE

John Locke and Thomas Jefferson were giants in their time, sagacious sons of the remarkable Enlightenment epoch in which their tendency to equate liberty and equality made sense, for both were grounded in the then reasonable conviction that the central threat to liberty, and therefore to equality of opportunity, resided in the power of governments. "Life, Liberty, and the pursuit of Happiness" were honorable euphemisms for the common citizen's desire for the kind of fundamental democratic rights about personal liberty and property that Jefferson so eloquently enunciated in his first inaugural address. It was by no means inconsistent then, when Jefferson envisioned a free society of stubbornly independent yeomen in a huge agarian republic, to assume that the only source of potential tyranny was from government, and therefore to isolate governmental power as the prime threat and to give essentially no thought to sources of massive power that then did not exist but that in the future would blossom: big private business in the latter nineteenth century, big labor in the twentieth, plus big foundations and the myriad muscular institutions that in a postindustrial society would generate enormous political pressure. It is unfair to indict Jefferson and the founders for their lack of twentieth-century foresight, but it is apt to point out that the founders' fear of governmental power posed extraordinary dilemmas for subsequent generations of reformers who, although sharing the Jeffersonian dream of a more equalitarian society, perceived that Hamiltonian means were required to achieve it. This has been the abiding dilemma of progressive reformers in America: they inherited a Jeffersonian social goal that was inconsistent with Jeffersonian means. It was Alexander Hamilton who sought a powerful central government, yet Hamilton wanted power to entrench the very commercial and industrial elite that the Jeffersonians deplored. Hence the crowning paradox: when America became an urban-industrial power, liberal reformers sought governmental reforms to ameliorate its abuses, but conservatives could always repair to the Jeffersonian tradition of fear of government, of checking and balancing government into near paralysis, of narrowly circumscribing its jurisdiction, in an effective ploy that indicted reformers for abandoning their generic roots. Reformers called for government regulation of industrial abuses, but conservatives reminded them that the classical liberal pantheon of civic evils held government to be the prime abuser, and that laissez-faire was the true liberal posture. In that sense Barry Goldwater became the quintessential Jeffersonian, and the liberals were deprived of their ideological progenitors. Jefferson's succinct delineation of the principles of republican government in his first inaugural address, which immediately follows, is eloquent and timeless. His call for "a wise and frugal government, which shall restrain men from injuring one another, [but] shall leave them otherwise free to regulate their own pursuits of industry and improvement," was at once true to the eighteenth-century Lockeian faith and a mighty shackle on the hands of future generations of reformers.

First Inaugural Address

THOMAS JEFFERSON

Friends and fellow citizens:

Called upon to undertake the duties of the first executive office of our country, I avail myself of the presence of that portion of my fellow citizens which is here assembled to express my grateful thanks for the favor with which they have been pleased to look toward me, to declare a sincere consciousness that the task is above my talents, and that I approach it with those anxious and awful presentiments which the greatness of the charge and the weakness of my powers so justly inspire. A rising nation, spread over a wide and fruitful land, traversing all the seas with the rich productions of their industry, engaged in commerce with nations who feel power and forget right, advancing rapidly to destinies beyond the reach of mortal eye —when I contemplate these transcendent objects, and see the honor, the happiness, and the hopes of this beloved country committed to the issue and the auspices of this day, I shrink from the contemplation, and humble myself before the magnitude of the undertaking. Utterly indeed should I despair did not the presence of many whom I here see remind me that in the other high authorities provided by our Constitution I shall find resources of wisdom, of virtue, and of zeal on which to rely under all difficulties. To you then, gentlemen, who are charged with the sovereign functions of legislation, and to those associated with you, I look with encouragement for that guidance and support which may enable us to steer with safety the vessel in which we are all embarked amidst the conflicting elements of a troubled world.

During the contest of opinion through which we have passed the animation of discussions and of exertions has sometimes worn an aspect which might impose on strangers unusued to think freely and to speak and to write what they think. But this being now decided by the voice of the nation, announced according to the rules of the constitution, all will of course arrange themselves under the will of the law, and unite in common efforts for the common good. All too will bear in mind this sacred principle, that though the will of the majority is in all cases to prevail, that will, to be rightful, must be reasonable; that the minority possess their equal rights, which equal laws must protect, and to violate would be oppression. Let us then, fellow citizens, unite with one heart and one mind, let us restore to social intercourse that harmony and affection without which liberty and even life itself are but dreary things. And let us reflect that, having banished from our land that religious intolerance under which mankind so long bled and suffered, we have yet gained little if we countenance a political intolerance as despotic, as wicked, and capable of as bitter and bloody persecutions. During the throes and convulsions of the ancient world, during the agonizing spasms of infuriated man, seeking through blood and slaughter his long lost liberty, it was not wonderful that the agitation of the billows should reach even this distant and peaceful shore; that this should be more felt and feared by some and less by others, and should divide opinions as to measures of safety; but every difference of opinion is not a difference of principle. We have called by different names brethren of the same principle. We are all republicans: we are all federalists. If there be any among us who wish to dissolve this Union or to change its republican form, let them stand undisturbed, as monuments of the safety with which error of opinion may be tolerated where reason is left free to combat it. I know, indeed, that some honest men fear that a republican government cannot be strong, that this government is not strong enough. But would the honest patriot, in the full tide of successful experiment, abandon a government which has so far kept us free and firm on the theoretic and visionary fear that this government, the world's best hope, may, by possibility, want energy to preserve itself? I trust not. I believe this, on the contrary, the strongest government on earth. I believe it the only one where every man, at the call of the law, would fly to the standard of the law, and would meet invasions of the public order as his own personal concern. Sometimes it is said that man cannot be trusted with the government of himself. Can he, then, be trusted with the government of others? Or have we found angels in the form of kings to govern him? Let history answer this question.

Let us then pursue with courage and confidence our own federal and republican principles, our attachment to union and representative government. Kindly separated by nature, and a wide ocean, from the exterminating havoc of one quarter of the globe; too high-minded to endure the degradations of the others; possessing a chosen country, with room enough for our descendents to the thousandth and thousandth generation; entertaining a due sense of our equal right to the use of our own facilities, to the acquisitions of our own industry, to honor and confidence from our fellow citizens, resulting not from birth, but from our actions and their sense of them; enlightened by a benign religion, professed, indeed, and practiced in various forms, yet all of them inculcating honesty, truth, temperance, gratitude, and the love of man; acknowledging and adoring an overruling providence, which by all its dispensations proves that it delights in the happiness of man here and his greater happiness hereafter—with all these blessings, what more is necessary to make us a happy and a prosperous people? Still one thing more, fellow citizens—a wise and frugal government, which shall restrain men from injuring one another, shall leave them otherwise free to regulate their own pursuits of industry and improvement, and shall not take from the mouth of labor the bread it has earned. This is the sum of good government, and this is necessary to close the circle of our felicities.

About to enter, fellow citizens, on the exercise of duties which comprehend everything dear and valuable to you, it is proper you should understand what I deem the essential principles of this government, and consequently those which ought to shape its administration. I will compress them in the narrowest compass they will bear, stating the general principle, but not all its limitations. Equal and exact justice to all men, of whatever state or persuasion, religious or political; peace, commerce, and honest friendship with all nations, entangling alliances with none; the support of the state governments in all their rights, as the most competent administrations for our domestic concerns and the surest bulwarks against anti-republican tendencies; the preservation of the general government in its whole constitutional vigor, as the sheet anchor of our peace at home and safety abroad; a jealous care of the right of election by the people, a mild and safe corrective of abuses which are lopped by the sword of revolution where peaceable remedies are unprovided; absolute acquiescence in the decisions of the majority, the vital principle of republics from which is no appeal but to force, the vital principle and immediate parent of despotism; a well disciplined militia, our best reliance in peace and for the first moments of war, till regulars may relieve them; the supremacy of the civil over the military authority; economy in the public expence, that labor may be lightly burthened; the honest payment of our debts and sacred preservation of the public faith; encouragement of agriculture, and of commerce as its handmaid; the diffusion of information and arraignment of all abuses at the bar of the public reason; freedom of religion; freedom of the press, and freedom of person under the protection of the habeas corpus, and trial by juries impartially selected. These principles form the bright constellation which has gone before us and guided our steps through an age of revolution and reformation. The wisdom of our sages and blood of our heroes have been devoted to their attainment. They should be the creed of our political faith, the text of civic instruction, the touchstone by which to try the services of those we trust; and should we wander from them in moments of error or of alarm, let us hasten to retrace our steps and to regain the road which alone leads to peace, liberty, and safety.

I repair, then, fellow-citizens, to the post you have assigned me. With experience enough in subordinate stations to know the difficulties of this the greatest of all, I have learnt to expect that it will rarely fall to the lot of imperfect man to retire from this station with the reputation and the favor which bring him into it. Without pretensions to that high confidence you reposed in our first and greatest revolutionary character, whose preeminent services had entitled him to the first place in his country's love and destined for him the fairest page in the volume of faithful history, I ask so much confidence only as may give firmness and effect to the legal administration of your affairs. I shall often go wrong through defect of judgment. When right, I shall often be thought wrong by those whose positions will not command a view of the whole ground. I ask your indulgence for my own errors, which will never be intentional, and your support against the errors of others, who may condemn what they would not if seen in all its parts. The approbation implied by your suffrage is a great consolation to me for the past, and my future solicitude will be to retain the good opinion of those who have bestowed it in advance, to conciliate that of others by doing them all the good in my power, and to be instrumental to the happiness and freedom of all.

Relying, then, on the patronage of your good will, I advance with obedience to the work, ready to retire from it whenever you become sensible how much better choices it is in your power to make. And may that infinite power which rules the destinies of the universe lead our councils to what is best, and give them a favorable issue for your peace and prosperity.

March 4, 1801.

The fundamentally negative view of government that was broadly shared by the generation of the founders is aptly reflected in the following excerpt from Thomas Paine's *Common Sense* (1776), which contains the famous and telling observation that "government, like dress, is the badge of lost innocence." *Common Sense* was a powerful tract of propaganda, and like the Declaration of Independence, the major portion of it was devoted to a list of specific grievances against the king and the colonial system. But Paine began *Common Sense,* as did Jefferson the preamble to the Declaration, with a more generalized and theoretical discussion of the nature of government. The English-born Paine's intellectual indebtedness to the ideals of the Enlightenment is clearly reflected in his metaphor of the state of nature and the social compact. Paine's profound faith in the immutable law and order of nature, the omnipotence of reason, the necessity for tolerance and for freedom to debate all questions, and the equal rights and dignity of the individual may seem naive to a more cynical generation; but his enunciation of this faith struck powerfully responsive chords throughout the colonies on the eve of the Revolution.

Common Sense

THOMAS PAINE

Some writers have so confounded society with government, as to leave little or no distinction between them; whereas they are not only different, but have different origins. Society is produced by our wants, and government by our wickedness; the former promotes our happiness *positively* by uniting our affections, the latter *negatively* by restraining our vices. The one encourages intercourse, the other creates distinctions. The first is a patron, the last a punisher.

Society in every state is a blessing, but government even in its best state is but a necessary evil; in its worst state an intolerable one; for when we suffer, or are exposed to the same miseries *by a government*, which we might expect in a country *without government*, our calamity is heightened by reflecting that we furnish the means by which we suffer. Government, like dress, is the badge of lost innocence; the palaces of kings are built on the ruins of the bowers of paradise. For were the impulses of conscience clear, uniform, and irresistibly obeyed, man would need no other lawgiver; but that not being the case, he finds it necessary to surrender up a part of his property to furnish means for the protection of the rest; and this he is induced to do by the same prudence which in every other case advises him out of two evils to choose the least. *Wherefore,* security being the true design and end of government, it unanswerably follows, that whatever *form* thereof appears most likely to ensure it to us, with the least expence and greatest benefit, is preferable to all others.

In order to gain a clear and just idea of the design and end of government, let us suppose a small number of persons settled in some sequestered part of the earth, unconnected with the rest, they will then represent the first peopling of any country, or of the world. In this state of natural liberty, society will be their first thought. A thousand motives will excite them thereto, the strength of one man is so unequal to his wants, and his mind so unfitted for perpetual solitude, that he is soon obliged to seek assistance and relief of another, who in his turn requires the same. Four or five united would be able to raise a tolerable dwelling in the midst of a wilderness, but *one* man might labour out the common period of life without accomplishing any thing; when he had felled his timber he could not remove it, nor erect it after it was removed; hunger in the mean time would urge him from his work, and every different want call him a different way. Disease, nay even misfortune would be death, for though neither might be mortal, yet either would disable him from living, and reduce him to a state in which he might rather be said to perish than to die.

Thus necessity, like a gravitating power, would soon form our newly arrived emigrants into society, the reciprocal blessings of which, would supersede, and render the obligations of law and government unnecessary while they remained perfectly just to each other; but as nothing but heaven is impregnable to vice, it will unavoidably happen, that in proportion as they surmount the first difficulties of emigration, which bound them together in a common cause, they will begin to relax in their duty and attachment to each other; and this remissness will point out the necessity of establishing some form of government to supply the defect of moral virtue.

Some convenient tree will afford them a State-House, under the branches of which, the whole colony may assemble to deliberate on public matters. It is more than probable that their first laws will have the title only of REGULATIONS, and be enforced by no other penalty than public disesteem. In this first parliament every man, by natural right, will have a seat.

But as the colony increases, the public concerns will increase likewise, and the distance at which the members may be separated, will render it too inconvenient for all of them to meet on every occasion as at first, when their number was small, their habitations near, and the public concerns few and trifling. This will point out the convenience of their consenting to leave the legislative part to be managed by a select number chosen from the whole body, who are supposed to have the same concerns at stake which those have who appointed them, and who will act in the same manner as the whole body would act, were they present. If the colony continue increasing, it will become necessary to augment the number of the representatives, and that the interest of every part of the colony may be attended to, it will be found best to divide the whole into convenient parts, each part sending its proper number; and that the *elected* might never form to themselves an interest separate from the *electors*, prudence will point out the propriety of having elections often; because as the *elected* might by that means return and mix again with the general body of the *electors* in a few months, their fidelity to the public will be secured by the prudent reflexion of not making a rod for themselves. And as this frequent interchange will establish a common interest with every part of the community, they will mutually and naturally support each other, and on this (not on the unmeaning name of king) depends the *strength of government, and the happiness of the governed.*

Here then is the origin and rise of government; namely, a mode rendered necessary by the inability of moral virtue to govern the world; here too is the design and end of government, viz. freedom and security. And however our eyes may be dazzled with show, or our ears deceived by sound; however prejudice may warp our wills, or interest darken our understanding, the simple voice of nature and of reason will say, it is right.

INTRODUCTORY NOTE

It is important to emphasize the degree to which Jefferson and Paine regarded government, at best, as a necessary evil whose powers must be severely limited to minimizing the harm that citizens might inflict upon one another. Historically the commonplace equation of Lockeian and Jeffersonian Enlightenment liberalism, and of the American and French revolutionary traditions—the one for "Life, Liberty, and the pursuit of Happiness," the other for "Liberté, Eqalité, Fraternité"—has led to the adoption of a common conflict model for explaining political events in both the Old World and the New. According to this model the inequalities that persist in society generate class conflict, causing forces on the political right to seek (through control of government) to preserve the status quo, and forces on the political left to seek (through control of government) to reform its inequitable distribution of rewards and punishments. Over time these recurrent conflicts generate flood tides of liberal reform and ebb tides of conservative retrenchment, which in America have produced the stairstep history of reform efforts that were celebrated by such notable Progressive historians as Frederick Jackson Turner, Charles and Mary Beard, Carl L. Becker, Arthur Meier Schlesinger, and Vernon L. Parrington. The Great Crash of 1929 and the subsequent political triumph of the New Deal greatly reinforced this progressive school of interpretation, which was rooted in assumptions of ideological, sectional, and class conflict; was essentially optimistic; contained a pronounced liberal bias; and came to dominate the basic textbooks.

Following World War II, however, and particularly in the wake of the cold war, the conflict model came under sharp attack in America—especially in regard to its implicit equation of the European and American experiences with economic class as the crucial political variable—for there were fundamental dissimilarities that it could not explain. Why, for instance, did the impact of the industrial revolution in Europe lead the working masses to turn toward socialism, while in the United States the socialist left had remained pathetically weak, even in times of severe economic depression? Conversely, how could the conflict model account for the fact that, under the brutal strains of the Great Depression of the 1930s, bourgeois flights toward fascism occurred in Germany, Italy, Spain, and, to a greater extent than has generally been realized, France, but in the United States the appeal of fascism remained marginal? Some historical force seemed to have radically truncated the political spectrum in America, politically clustering the masses rather tightly around the moderate center. The rhetorical wars of Federalists and Republicans, Whigs and Democrats, Democrats and Republicans had apparently disguised a consensual core of political values.

The new "consensus" school of historians that emerged in the 1950s was led by such conservative intellectuals as Daniel Boorstin, Clinton Rossiter, and David M. Potter. They regarded the American Revolution as essentially a conservative catharsis that, through severance of European ties, preserved a remarkably homogeneous and unique social order that had emerged through generations of what Edmund Burke called "salutary neglect" from Great Britain and the Old World. As such it differed radically from the bloody class warfare of the French Revolution. The consensus historians have argued that despite the two-party system that evolved in America, Americans historically have agreed with one another on fundamental values to a much greater extent than they have disagreed.

A ranking member of the consensus school is Louis Hartz. His seminal analysis of the political thought of American's revolutionary generation, reprinted in part here, was published in 1952.[1] But prior to its reading, several preliminary observations are in order. First, Hartz (who like Rossiter is both a historian and political scientist) was writing for the sophisticated readers of *The American Political Science Review,* and his essay is sensitive to the often bewildering paradoxes and astonishing ironies that enrich his analysis, making it both intellectually rewarding and— especially for the student not steeped in the history of political theory—fairly difficult reading. Because his frequent allusions to such European theoreticians as Reynal, Condorcet, Turgot, Harrington, Bonald, and Maistre are apt to be confusing or distracting, students should have some initial grasp of his argument,

---

[1]For a full explication of Hartz's thesis, see his *The Liberal Tradition in America,* New York: Harcourt Brace Javanovich, 1955.

which is keyed not so much to what *was achieved* as to what was *not achieved* because, uniquely in America, *it did not have to be achieved.* Central to this thesis is America's lack of the feudal past that Europe had inherited, which involved a complex snarl of such myriad associations as class, church, guild, and place—to such a degree that any fundamental reordering of society, which the Enlightenment liberals so fervently desired, would require a liberal government heavily endowed with the raw power necessary to sustain the reformation of the tenacious *ancien regime.* To survive in Europe, liberalism would have to endure a cataclysmic social revolution. But America, having inherited her democratic society without the severe constraints of feudalism, could have her liberalism without having to endure the lasting disruptions of a democratic revolution.

A major implication of this analysis, which bears on the Burnham interpretation with which we began, is that unlike European liberalism, American liberalism was virtually the *only* political tradition. However, in the absence of feudal institutions, American liberalism felt no need to nurture power, so its natural tendency to fear and disperse governmental power reigned supreme. Ironically, future generations of reformers would pay a heavy price for this unique eighteenth-century luxury that blessed the efforts of our founders.

The Liberal Tradition
in America

LOUIS HARTZ

"The great advantage of the American," Tocqueville once wrote, "is that he has arrived at a state of democracy without having to endure a democratic revolution. . . ." Fundamental as this insight is, we have not remembered Tocqueville for it, and the reason is rather difficult to explain. Perhaps it is because, fearing revolution in the present, we like to think of it in the past, and we are reluctant to concede that its romance has been missing from our lives. Perhaps it is because the plain evidence of the American revolution of 1776, especially the evidence of its social impact that our newer historians have collected, has made the comment of Tocqueville seem thoroughly enigmatic. But in the last analysis, of course, the question of its validity is a question of perspective. Tocqueville was writing with the great revolutions of Europe in mind, and from that point of view the outstanding thing about the American effort of 1776 was bound to be, not the freedom to which it led, but the established feudal structure it did not have to destroy. He was writing too, as no French liberal of the nineteenth century could fail to write, with the shattered hopes of the Enlightenment in mind. The American revolution had been one of the greatest of them all, a precedent constantly appealed to in 1793. In the age of Tocqueville there was ground enough for reconsidering the American image that the Jacobins had cherished.

Even in the glorious days of the eighteenth century, when America suddenly became the revolutionary symbol of Western liberalism, it had not been easy to hide the free society with which it started. As a matter of fact, the liberals of Europe had themselves romanticized its social freedom, which put them in

From Louis Hartz, "American Political Thought and the American Revolution," *The American Political Science Review*, 46 (June 1952), pp. 321–342, *passim*. Published by the American Political Science Association, Washington, D.C.

a rather odd position; for if Reynal was right in 1772, how could Condorcet be right in 1776? If America was from the beginning a kind of idyllic state of nature, how could it suddenly become a brilliant example of social emancipation? Two consolations were being extracted from a situation which could at best yield only one. But the mood of the Americans themselves, as they watched the excitement of Condorcet seize the Old World, is also very revealing. They did not respond in kind. They did not try to shatter the social structure of Europe in order to usher in a Tenth and Final Epoch in the history of man. Delighted as they were with the support that they received, they remained, with the exception of a few men like Paine and Barlow, curiously untouched by the crusading intensity we find in the French and the Russians at a later time. Warren G. Harding, arguing against the League of Nations, was able to point back at them and say, "Mark you, they were not reforming the world." And James Fenimore Cooper, a keener mind than Harding, generalized their behavior into a comment about America that America is only now beginning to understand: "We are not a nation much addicted to the desire of proselytizing."

There were, no doubt, several reasons for this. But clearly one of the most significant is the sense that the Americans had themselves of the liberal history out of which they came. In the midst of the Stamp Act struggle, young John Adams congratulated his colonial ancestors for turning their backs on Europe's class-ridden corporate society, for rejecting the "canon and feudal law." The pervasiveness of Adam's sentiment in American thought has often been discussed, but what is easily overlooked is the subtle way in which it corroded the spirit of the world crusader. For this was a pride of inheritance, not a pride of achievement; and instead of being a message of hope for Europe, it came close to being a damning indictment of it. It saturated the American sense of mission, not with a Christian universalism, but with a curiously Hebraic kind of separatism. The two themes fought one another in the cosmopolitan mind of Jefferson, dividing him between a love of Europe and fear of its "contamination"; but in the case of men like Adams and Gouverneur Morris, the second theme easily triumphed over the first. By the time the crusty Adams had gotten through talking to politicians abroad, he had buried the Enlightenment con-

cept of an oppressed humanity so completely beneath the national concept of a New World that he was ready to predict a
great and ultimate struggle between America's youth and
Europe's decadence. As for Morris, our official ambassador to
France in 1789, he simply inverted the task of the Comintern
agent. Instead of urging the French on to duplicate the American experience, he badgered them by pointing out that they
could never succeed in doing so. "They want an American
constitution," he wrote contemptuously, "without realizing they
have no Americans to uphold it."

Thus the fact that the Americans did not have to endure a
"democratic revolution" deeply conditioned their outlook on
people elsewhere who did; and by helping to thwart the crusading spirit in them, it gave to the wild enthusiasms of Europe
an appearance not only of analytic error but of unrequited
love. Symbols of a world revolution, the Americans were not in
truth world revolutionaries. There is no use complaining about
the confusions implicit in this position, as Woodrow Wilson
used to complain when he said that we had "no business" permitting the French to get the wrong impression about the
American revolution. On both sides the reactions that arose
were well-nigh inevitable. But one cannot help wondering about
something else: the satisfying use to which our folklore has
been able to put the incongruity of America's revolutionary
role. For if the "contamination" that Jefferson feared, and that
found its classic expression in Washington's Farewell Address,
has been a part of the American myth, so has the "round the
world" significance of the shots that were fired at Concord.
We have been able to dream of ourselves as emancipators of
the world at the very moment that we have withdrawn from
it. We have been able to see ourselves as saviours at the very
moment that we have been isolationists. Here, surely, is one of
the great American luxuries that the twentieth century has
destroyed.

When the Americans celebrated the uniqueness of their own
society, they were on the track of a personal insight of the profoundest importance. For the nonfeudal world in which they
lived shaped every aspect of their social thought: it gave them
a frame of mind that cannot be found anywhere else in the
eighteenth century, or in the wider history of modern revolutions. . . .

Sir William Ashley, discussing the origins of the "American spirit," once remarked that "as feudalism was not transplanted to the New World, there was no need for the strong arm of a central power to destroy it." This is a simple statement, but, like many of Ashley's simple statements, it contains a neglected truth. For Americans usually assume that their attack on political power in 1776 was determined entirely by the issues of the revolution, when as a matter of fact it was precisely because of the things they were not revolting against that they were able to carry it through. The action of England inspired the American colonists with a hatred of centralized authority; but had that action been a transplanted American feudalism, rich in the chaos of ages, then they would surely have had to dream of centralizing authority themselves.

They would, in other words, have shared the familiar agony of European liberalism—hating power and loving it too. The liberals of Europe in the eighteenth century wanted, of course, to limit power; but confronted with the heritage of an ancient corporate society, they were forever devising sharp and sovereign instruments that might be used to put it down. Thus while the Americans were attacking Dr. Johnson's theory of sovereignty, one of the most popular liberal doctrines in Europe, cherished alike by Bentham and Voltaire, was the doctrine of the enlightened despot, a kind of political deism in which a single force would rationalize the social world. While the Americans were praising the "illustrious Montesquieu" for his idea of checks and balances, that worthy was under heavy attack in France itself because he compromised the unity of power on which so many liberals relied. Even the English Whigs, men who were by no means believers in monarchical absolutism, found it impossible to go along with their eager young friends across the Atlantic. When the Americans, closing their eyes to 1688, began to lay the axe to the concept of parliamentary sovereignty, most of the Whigs fled their company at once.

A philosopher, it is true, might look askance at the theory of power the Americans developed. It was not a model of lucid exposition. The trouble lay with their treatment of sovereignty. Instead of boldly rejecting the concept, as Franklin was once on the verge of doing when he said that it made him "quite sick," they accepted the concept and tried to qualify it out of existence. The result was a chaotic series of forays and retreats in which a sovereign Parliament was limited, first by the distinction between external and internal taxation, then by the distinction between revenue and regulation, and finally by the remarkable contention that colonial legislatures were as sovereign as Parliament was. But there is a limit to how much we can criticize the Americans for shifting their ground. They were obviously feeling their way; and they could hardly be expected to know at the time of the Stamp Act what their position would be at the time of the first Continental Congress. Moreover, if they clung to the concept of sovereignty, they battered it beyond belief, and no one would confuse their version of it with the one advanced by Turgot or even by Blackstone in Europe. The meekness of the American sovereign testifies to the beating he had received. Instead of putting up a fierce and embarrassing battle against the limits of natural law and the separation of powers, as he usually did in the theories of Europe, he accepted those limits with a vast docility. . . .

The question, again, was largely a question of the free society in which the Americans lived. Nor ought we to assume that its impact on their view of political power disappeared when war and domestic upheaval finally came. Of course, there was scattered talk of the need for a "dictator," as Jefferson angrily reported in 1782, and until new assemblies appeared in most places, Committees of Public Safety had authoritarian power. But none of this went deep enough to shape the philosophic mood of the nation. A hero is missing from the revolutionary literature of America. He is the Legislator, the classical giant who almost invariably turns up at revolutionary moments to be given authority to lay the foundations of the free society. He is not missing because the Americans were unfamiliar with images of ancient history, or because they had not read the Harringtons or the Machiavellis and Rousseaus of the modern period. Harrington, as a matter of fact, was one of their favorite writers. The Legislator is missing because, in truth, the Americans had no need for his services. Much as they liked Harrington's republicanism, they did not require a Cromwell, as Harrington thought he did, to erect the foundations for it. Those foundations had already been laid by history.

The issue of history itself is deeply involved here. On this score, inevitably, the fact that the revolutionaries of 1776 had inherited the freest society in the world shaped their thinking in a most intricate way. It gave them, in the first place, an appearance of outright conservatism. We know, of course, that most liberals of the eighteenth century, from Bentham to Quesnay, were bitter opponents of history, posing a sharp antithesis between nature and tradition. And it is an equally familiar fact that their adversaries, including Burke and Blackstone, sought to break down this antithesis by identifying natural-law with the slow evolution of the past. The militant Americans, confronted with these two positions, actually took the second. Until Jefferson raised the banner of independence, and even in many cases after that time, they based their claims on a philosophic synthesis of Anglo-American legal history and the reason of natural law. Blackstone, the very Blackstone whom Bentham so bitterly attacked in the very year 1776, was a rock on which they relied.

The explanation is not hard to find. The past had been good to the Americans, and they knew it. Instead of inspiring them to the fury of Bentham and Voltaire, it often produced a mystical sense of Providential guidance akin to that of Maistre —as when Rev. Samuel West, surveying the growth of America's population, anticipated victory in the revolution because "we have been prospered in a most wonderful manner." The troubles they had with England did not alter this outlook. Even these, as they pointed out again and again, were of recent origin, coming after more than a century of that "'salutary neglect" which Burke defended so vigorously. And in a specific sense, of course, the record of English history in the seventeenth century and the record of colonial charters from the time of the Virginia settlement provided excellent ammunition for the battle they were waging in defense of colonial rights. A series of circumstances had conspired to saturate even the revolutionary position of the Americans with the quality of traditionalism—to give them, indeed, the appearance of outraged reactionaries. "This I call an innovation," thundered John Dickinson, in his attack on the Stamp Act, "a most dangerous innovation."

Now here was a frame of mind that would surely have troubled many of the illuminated liberals in Europe, were it not for an ironic fact. America piled on top of this paradox another one of an opposite kind, and thus as it were, by misleading them twice, gave them a deceptive sense of understanding.

Actually, the form of America's traditionalism was one thing, its content quite another. Colonial history had not been the slow and glacial record of development that Bonald and Maistre loved to talk about. On the contrary, since the first sailing of the *Mayflower*, it had been a story of new beginnings, daring enterprises, and explicitly stated principles—it breathed, in other words, the spirit of Bentham himself. The result was that the traditionalism of the Americans, like a pure freak of logic, often bore amazing marks of anti-historical rationalism. The clearest case of this undoubtedly is to be found in the revolutionary constitutions of 1776, which evoked, as Franklin reported, the "rapture" of European liberals everywhere. In America, of course, the concept of a written constitution, including many of the mechanical devices it embodied, was the end-product of a chain of historical experience that went back to the Mayflower Compact and the Plantation Covenants of the New England towns: it was the essence of political traditionalism. But in Europe just the reverse was true. The concept was the darling of the rationalists—a symbol of the emancipated mind at work.

Thus Condorcet was untroubled. Instead of bemoaning the fact that the Americans were Blackstonian historicists, he proudly welcomed them into the fraternity of the illuminated. American constitutionalism, he said, "had not grown, but was planned"; it "took no force from the weight of centuries but was put together mechanically in a few years." When John Adams read this comment, he spouted two words on the margin of the page: "Fool! Fool!" But surely the judgment was harsh. After all, when Burke clothes himself in the garments of Siéyès, who can blame the loyal rationalist who fraternally grasps his hand? The reactionaries of Europe, moreover, were often no keener in their judgment. They made the same mistake in reverse. Maistre gloomily predicted that the American Constitution would not last because it was created out of the whole cloth of reason.

But how then are we to describe these baffling Americans? Were they rationalists or were they traditionalists? The truth is, they were neither, which is perhaps another way of saying that they were both. For the war between Burke and Bentham on the score of tradition, which made a great deal of sense in a society where men had lived in the shadow of feudal institutions, made comparatively little sense in a society where for years they had been creating new states, planning new settlements, and, as Jefferson said, literally building new lives. In such a society a strange dialectic was fated to appear, which would somehow unite the antagonistic components of the European mind; the past became a continuous future, and the God of the traditionalists sanctioned the very arrogance of the men who defied Him.

This shattering of the time categories of Europe, this Hegelian-like revolution in historic perspective, goes far to explain one of the enduring secrets of the American character: a capacity to combine rock-ribbed traditionalism with high inventiveness, ancestor worship with ardent optimism. Most critics have seized upon one or the other of these aspects of the American mind, finding it impossible to conceive how both can go together. That is why the insight of Gunnar Myrdal is a very distinguished one when he writes: "America is . . . conservative. . . . But the principles conserved are liberal and some, indeed, are radical." Radicalism and conservatism have been twisted entirely out of shape by the liberal flow of American history. . . .

When we study national variations in political theory, we are led to semantic considerations of a delicate kind, and it is to these, finally, that we must turn if we wish to get at the basic assumption of American thought. We have to consider the peculiar meaning that American life gave to the words of Locke.

There are two sides to the Lockean argument: a defense of the state that is implicit, and a limitation of the state that is explicit. The first is to be found in Locke's basic social norm, the concept of free individuals in a state of nature. This idea untangled men from the myriad associations of class, church, guild, and place, in terms of which feudal society defined their lives; and by doing so, it automatically gave to the state a much higher rank in relation to them than ever before. The state became the only association that might legitimately coerce them at all. That is why the liberals of France in the eighteenth century were able to substitute the concept of absolutism for Locke's conclusions of limited government and to believe that that they were still his disciples in the deepest sense. When Locke came to America, however, a change appeared. Because the basic feudal oppressions of Europe had not taken root, the fundamental social norm of Locke ceased in large part to look like a norm and began, of all things, to look like a sober description of fact. The effect was significant enough. When the Americans moved from that concept to the contractual idea of organizing the state, they were not conscious of having already done anything to fortify the state, but were conscious only that they were about to limit it. One side of Locke became virtually the whole of him. Turgot ceased to be a modification of Locke, and became, as he was for John Adams, the destruction of his very essence.

It was a remarkable thing—this inversion of perspectives that made the social norms of Europe the factual premises of America. History was on a lark, out to tease men, not by shattering their dreams, but by fulfilling them with a sort of satiric accuracy. In America one not only found a society sufficiently fluid to give a touch of meaning to the individualist norms of Locke, but one also found letter-perfect replicas of the very images he used. There was a frontier that was a veritable state of nature. There were agreements, such as the Mayflower Compact, that were veritable social contracts. There were new communities springing up in *vacuis locis*, clear evidence that men were using their Lockean right of emigration, which Jefferson soberly appealed to as "universal" in his defense of colonial land claims in 1774. A purist could argue, of course, that even these phenomena were not enough to make a reality out of the pre-social men that liberalism dreamt of in theory. But surely they came as close to doing so as anything history has ever seen. Locke and Rousseau themselves could not help lapsing into the empirical mood when they looked across the Atlantic. "Thus, in the beginning," Locke once wrote, "all the world was America. . . ."

In such a setting, how could the tremendous, revolutionary social impact that liberalism had in Europe be preserved? The impact was not, of course, missing entirely; for the attack on the vestiges of corporate society in America that began in 1776, the disestablishment of the Anglican church, the abolition of quitrents and primogeniture, the breaking up of the Tory estates, tinged American liberalism with its own peculiar fire. Nor must we therefore assume that the Americans had wider political objectives than the Europeans, since even their new governmental forms were, as Becker once said, little more than the "colonial institutions with the Parliament and king left out." But after these cautions have been taken, the central point is clear. In America the first half of Locke's argument was bound to become less a call to arms than a set of preliminary remarks essential to establishing a final conclusion: that the power of the state must be limited. Observe how it is treated by the Americans in their great debate with England, even by original thinkers like Otis and Wilson. They do not lavish upon it the fascinated inquiry that we find in Rousseau or Priestley. They advance it mechanically, hurry through it, anxious to get on to what is really bothering them: the limits of the British Parliament, the power of taxation. In Europe the idea of social liberty is loaded with dynamite; but it America it becomes, to a remarkable degree, the working base from which argument begins.

Here, then, is the master assumption of American political thought, the assumption from which all of the American attitudes discussed in this essay flow: the reality of atomistic social freedom. It is instinctive to the American mind, as in a sense the concept of the polis was instinctive to Platonic Athens or the concept of the church to the mind of the middle ages. Catastrophes have not been able to destroy it, proletariats have refused to give it up, and even our Progressive tradition, in its agonized clinging to a Jeffersonian world, has helped to keep it alive. There has been only one major group of American thinkers who have dared to challenge it frontally: the Fitzhughs and Holmeses of the pre-Civil War South who, identifying slavery with feudalism, tried to follow the path of the European reaction and of Comte. But American life rode roughshod over them—for the "prejudice" of Burke in America was liberal and the positive reality of Locke in America transformed them into the very metaphysicians they assailed. They were soon forgotten, massive victims of the absolute temper of the American mind, shoved off the scene by Horatio Alger, who gave to the Lockean premise a brilliance that lasted until the crash of 1929. And even the crash, though it led to a revision of the premise, did not really shatter it.

It might be appropriate to summarize with a single word, or even with a single sentence, the political outlook that this premise has produced. But where is the word and where is the sentence one might use? American political thought, as we have

seen, is a veritable maze of polar contradictions, winding in and
out of each other hopelessly: pragmatism and absolutism, his-
toricism and rationalism, optimism and pessimism, materialism
and idealism, individualism and conformism. But, after all, the
human mind works by polar contradictions; and when we have
evolved an interpretation of it which leads cleanly in a single
direction, we may be sure that we have missed a lot. The task
of the cultural analyst is not to discover simplicity, or even to
discover unity, for simplicity and unity do not exist, but to
drive a wedge of rationality through the pathetic indecisions
of social thought. In the American case that wedge is not hard
to find. It is not hidden in an obscure place. We find it in what
the West as a whole has always recognized to be the distinctive
element in American civilization: its social freedom, its social
equality. And yet it is true, for all of our Jeffersonian nationalism, that the interpretation of American political thought
has not been built around this idea. On the contrary, instead
of interpreting the American revolution in terms of American
freedom, we have interpreted it in terms of American oppression, and instead of studying the nineteenth century in terms
of American equality, we have studied it in terms of a series of
cosmic Beardian and Parrington struggles against class exploitation. We have missed what the rest of the world has seen and
what we ourselves have seen whenever we have contrasted the
New World with the Old. But this is a large issue which brings
us not only to the Progressive historians but to the peculiar
subjectivism of the American mind that they reflect, and it is
beyond the scope of our discussion now.

The liberals of Europe in 1776 were obviously worshiping
a very peculiar hero. If the average American had been suddenly thrust in their midst, he would have been embarrassed by
the millennial enthusiasms that many of them had, would have
found their talk of classes vastly overdone, and would have re-
acted to the Enlightenment synthesis of absolutism and liberty
as if it were little short of dishonest doubletalk. Bred in a
freer world, he had a different set of perspectives, was animated
by a different set of passions, and looked forward to different
goals. He was, as Crèvecoeur put it, a "new man" in Western
politics.

But, someone may ask, where did the liberal heritage of

the Americans come from in the first place? Didn't they have to create it? And if they did, were they not at one time or another in much the same position as the Europeans?

These questions drive us back to the ultimate nature of the American experience, and, in so doing, confront us with a queer twist in the problem of revolution. No one can deny that conscious purpose went into the making of the colonial world, and that the men of the seventeenth century who fled to America from Europe were keenly aware of the oppressions of European life. But they were revolutionaries with a difference, and the fact of their fleeing is no minor fact: for it is one thing to stay at home and fight the "canon and feudal law," and it is another to leave it far behind. It is one thing to try to establish liberalism in the Old World, and it is another to establish it in the New. Revolution, to borrow the words of T. S. Eliot, means to murder and create, but the American experience has been projected strangely in the realm of creation alone. The destruction of forests and Indian tribes—heroic, bloody, legendary as it was— cannot be compared with the destruction of a social order to which one belongs oneself. The first experience is wholly external and, being external, can actually be completed; the second experience is an inner struggle as well as an outer struggle, like the slaying of a Freudian father, and goes on in a sense forever. Moreover, even the matter of creation is not in the American case a simple one. The New World, as Lord Baltimore's ill-fated experiment with feudalism in the seventeenth century illustrates, did not merely offer the Americans a virgin ground for the building of a liberal system: it conspired itself to help that system along. The abundance of land in America, as well as the need for a lure to settlers, entered so subtly into the shaping of America's liberal tradition, touched it so completely at every point, that Sumner was actually ready to say, "We have not made America, America has made us."

It is this business of destruction and creation which goes to the heart of the problem. For the point of departure of great revolutionary thought everywhere else in the world has been the effort to build a new society on the ruins of an old society, and this is an experience America has never had. Tocqueville saw the issue clearly, and it is time now to complete the sentence of his with which we began this essay: "The great advantage of the American is that he has arrived at a state of democracy without having to endure a democratic revolution; *and that he is born free without having to become so.*"

Born free without having to become so: this idea, especially in light of the strange relationship which the revolutionary Americans had with their admirers abroad, raises an obvious question. Can a people that is born free ever understand peoples elsewhere that have to become so? Can it ever lead them? Or to turn the issue around, can peoples struggling for a goal understand those who have inherited it? This is not a problem of antitheses such, for example, as we find in Locke and Filmer. It is a problem of different perspectives on the same ideal. But we must not for that reason assume that it is any less difficult of solution; it may in the end be more difficult, since antitheses define each other and hence can understand each other, but different perspectives on a single value may, ironically enough, lack this common ground of definition. Condorcet might make sense out of Burke's traditionalism, for it was the reverse of his own activism, but what could he say about Otis, who combined both concepts in a synthesis that neither had seen? America's experience of being born free has put it in a strange relationship to the rest of the world.

INTRODUCTORY NOTE

With independence from Great Britain secured by the Revolutionary War, the Continental Congress, by 1781, had obtained the ratification by all 13 states of its "Articles of Confederation and Perpetual Union," under which the new nation was governed for eight years. Hypersensitive to the threat of centralized governmental power, the revolutionary generation of Americans had insisted upon keeping tight local control over their affairs, and as a consequence the new Confederation was so loose that the Congress was essentially powerless to enforce measures exercised under even its limited jurisdiction—which included only foreign and Indian affairs, coinage, the postal system, borrowing money, and settling disputes between states. Lacking a federal executive or judiciary, the impotent Confederation floundered, setting the stage for the Constitutional Convention of 1787–1789.

Leading the campaign for ratification of the new Constitution was Alexander Hamilton, who together with James Madison and John Jay (who soon dropped out because of illness) engineered the construction of the most famous political commentary in American History. *The Federalist Papers* were issued in two volumes in 1788 and contained 85 essays that were widely reprinted in newspapers and were heavily instrumental in securing ratification.[1] The authors of *The Federalist Papers* faced the fundamental problem of overcoming widespread fears that a more national or centralized government might violate the principles of the Revolution and of limited republican government in general. Scholars have observed that their efforts produced a collection with a split personality. Hamilton tended unabashedly to call for a powerful national government to order the economic chaos of the Confederation and to sternly put down such frightening popular uprisings as Shays' Rebellion. Madison, a more subtle thinker, preferred less to concentrate power than to balance and blend it.

[1]See Roy P. Fairfield, ed., *The Federalist Papers*, Garden City, N.Y.: Doubleday, 1961.

Madison's essays have become the classics that justify reference to him was Philosopher of the Constitution. In the essay that follows, *The Federalist No. 39,* Madison (under the pen name of Publius) argues that the Constitution, if ratified, would create a government in which the federal and national character of its powers would be blended in a fashion that would be consistent with the cardinal principle of republican government: one "which derives all its powers directly or indirectly from the great body of the people, and is administered by persons holding their offices during pleasure, for a limited period, or during good behavior."

The Federalist No. 39

"PUBLIUS" (JAMES MADISON)

To the People of the State of New York:

The last paper having concluded the observations which were meant to introduce a candid survey of the plan of government reported by the convention, we now proceed to the execution of that part of our undertaking.

The first question that offers itself is, whether the general form and aspect of the government be strictly republican. It is evident that no other form would be reconcilable with the genius of the people of America; with the fundamental principles of the Revolution; or with that honorable determination which animates every votary of freedom, to rest all our political experiments on the capacity of mankind for self-government. If the plan of the convention, therefore, be found to depart from the republican character, its advocates must abandon it as no longer defensible.

What, then, are the distinctive characters of the republican form? Were an answer to this question to be sought, not by recurring to principles, but in the application of the term by political writers, to the constitutions of different States, no satisfactory one would ever be found. Holland, in which no particle of the supreme authority is derived from the people, has passed almost universally under the denomination of a republic. The same title has been bestowed on Venice where absolute power over the great body of the people is exercised in the most absolute manner by a small body of hereditary nobles. Poland, which is a mixture of aristocracy and of monarchy in their worst forms, has been dignified with the same appellation. The government of England, which has one republican branch only, combined with an hereditary aristocracy and monarchy, has, with equal impropriety, been frequently placed on the list of republics. These examples, which are nearly as dissimilar to each other as to a genuine republic, show the extreme inaccuracy with which the term has been used in political disquisitions.

If we resort for a criterion to the different principles on which different forms of government are established, we may define a republic to be, or at least may bestow that name on, a government which derives all its powers directly or indirectly from the great body of the people, and is administered by persons holding their offices during pleasure, for a limited period, or during good behavior. It is *essential* to such a government that it be derived from the great body of the society, not from an inconsiderable proportion, or a favored class of it; otherwise a handful of tyrannical nobles, exercising their oppressions by a delegation of their powers, might aspire to the rank of republicans and claim for their government the honorable title of republic. It is *sufficient* for such a government that the persons administering it be appointed, eitheir directly or indirectly, by the people; and that they hold their appointments by either of the tenures just specified; otherwise every government in the United States, as well as every other popular government that has been or can be well organized or well executed, would be degraded from the republican character. According to the constitution of every State in the Union, some or other of the officers of government are appointed indirectly only by the people. According to most of them, the chief magistrate himself is so appointed. And according to one, this mode of appointment is extended to one of the coordinate branches of the legislature. According to all the constitutions, also, the tenure of the highest offices is extended to a definite period, and in many instances, both within the legislative and executive departments, to a period of years. According to the provisions of most of the constitutions, again, as well as according to the most respectable and received opinions on the subject, the members of the judiciary department are to retain their offices by the firm tenure of good behavior.

On comparing the Constitution planned by the convention with the standard here fixed, we perceive at once that it is, in the most rigid sense, conformable to it. The House of Representatives, like that of one branch at least of all the State legislatures, is elected immediately by the great body of the people. The Senate, like the present Congress, and the Senate of Maryland, derives its appointment indirectly from the people. The President is indirectly derived from the choice of the people, according to the example in most of the States. Even the judges with all other officers of the Union, will, as in the several States, be the choice, though a remote choice, of the people themselves. The duration of the appointments is equally conformable to the republican standard and to the model of State constitutions. The house of Representatives is periodically elective, as in all the States; and for the period of two years, as in the State of South Carolina. The Senate is elective for the period of six years; which is but one year more than the period of the Senate of Maryland, and but two more than that of the Senates of New York and Virginia. The President is to continue in office for the period of four years; . . . in New York and Delaware the chief magistrate is elected for three years, and in South Carolina for two years. In the other States the election is annual. In several of the States, however, no constitutional provision is made for the impeachment of the chief magistrate. And in Delaware and Virginia he is not impeachable till out of office. The President of the United States is impeachable at any time during his continuance in office. The tenure by which the judges are to hold their places is, as it unquestionably ought to be, that of good behavior. The tenure of the ministerial offices generally, will be a subject of legal regulation, conformably to the reason of the case and the example of the State constitutions.

Could any further proof be required of the republican complexion of this system, the most decisive one might be found in its absolute prohibition of titles of nobility, both under the federal and the State governments; and in its express guaranty of the republican form to each of the latter.

"But it was not sufficient," say the adversaries of the proposed Constitution, "for the convention to adhere to the republican form. They ought, with equal care, to have preserved the *federal* form, which regards the Union as a *Confederacy* of sovereign states; instead of which, they have framed a *national* government, which regards the Union as a *consolidation* of the States." And it is asked by what authority this bold and radical innovation was undertaken? The handle which has been made of this objection requires that it should be examined with some precision.

Without inquiring into the accuracy of the distinction on

which the objection is founded, it will be necessary to a just estimate of its force, first, to ascertain the real character of the government in question; secondly, to inquire how far the convention were authorized to propose such a government; and thirdly, how far the duty they owed to their country could supply any defect of regular authority.

First.—In order to ascertain the real character of the government, it may be considered in relation to the foundation on which it is to be established; to the sources from which its ordinary powers are to be drawn; to the operation of those powers; to the extent of them; and to the authority by which future changes in the government are to be introduced.

On examining the first relation, it appears, on one hand, that the Constitution is to be founded on the assent and ratification of the people of America, given by deputies elected for the special purpose; but, on the other, that this assent and ratification is to be given by the people, not as individuals composing one entire nation, but as composing the distinct and independent States to which they respectively belong. It is to be the assent and ratification of the several States, derived from the supreme authority in each State,—the authority of the people themselves. The act, therefore, establishing the Constitution, will not be a *national,* but a *federal* act.

That it will be a federal and not a national act, as these terms are understood by the objectors, the act of the people as forming so many independent States, not as forming one aggregate nation is obvious from this single consideration: that it is to result neither from the decision of a *majority* of the people of the Union, nor from that of a *majority* of the States. It must result from the *unanimous* assent of the several States that are parties to it, differing no otherwise from their ordinary assent than in its being expressed, not by the legislative authority, but by that of the people themselves. Were the people regarded in this transition as forming one nation, the will of the majority of the whole people of the United States would bind the minority in the same manner as the majority in each State must bind the minority; and the will of the majority must be determined either by a comparison of the individual votes, or by considering the will of the majority of the States as evidence of the will of a majority of the people of the United States. Neither of these rules has been adopted.

Each State, in ratifying the Constitution, is considered as a sovereign body, independent of all others, and only to be bound by its own voluntary act. In this relation, then, the new Constitution will, if established, be a *federal*, and not a *national* constitution.

The next relation is to the sources from which the ordinary powers of government are to be derived. The House of Representatives will derive its powers from the people of America; and the people will be represented in the same proportion, and on the same principle, as they are in the legislature of a particular State. So far the government is *national*, not *federal*. The Senate, on the other hand, will derive its powers from the States, as political and coequal societies; and these will be represented on the principle of equality in the Senate, as they now are in the existing Congress. So far the government is *federal*, not *national*. The executive power will be derived from a very compound source. The immediate election of the President is to be made by the States in their political characters. The votes allotted to them are in a compound ratio, which considers them partly as distinct and coequal societies, partly as unequal members of the same society. The eventual election, again, is to be made by that branch of the legislature which consists of the national representatives; but in this particular act they are to be thrown into the form of individual delegations, from so many distinct and coequal bodies politic. From this aspect of the government it appears to be of a mixed character, presenting at least as many *federal* as *national* features.

The difference between a federal and national government, as it relates to the *operation of the government*, is supposed to consist in this, that in the former the powers operate on the political bodies composing the Confederacy in their political capacities; in the latter, on the individual citizens composing the nation in their individual capacities. On trying the Constitution by this criterion, it falls under the *national*, not the *federal* character; though perhaps not so completely as has been understood. In several cases, and particularly in the trial of controversies to which States may be parties, they must be viewed and proceeded against in their collective and political capacities only. So far the national countenance of the government on this side seems to be disfigured by a few federal features. But this blemish is perhaps unavoidable in any plan; and the operation of the government on the people, in their individual capacities, in its ordinary and most essential proceedings, may, on the whole designate it in this relation, a *national* government.

But if the government be national with regard to the *operation* of its powers, it changes its aspect again when we contemplate it in relation to the extent of its powers. The idea of a national government involves in it, not only an authority over the individual citizens, but an indefinite supremacy over all persons and things, so far as they are objects of lawful government. Among a people consolidated into one nation, this supremacy is completely vested in the national legislature. Among communities united for particular purposes, it is vested partly in the general and partly in the municipal legislatures. In the former case, all local authorities are subordinate to the supreme; and may be controlled, directed, or abolished by it at pleasure. In the latter, the local or municipal authorities form distinct and independent portions of the supremacy, no more subject within their respective spheres to the general authority, than the general authority is subject to them within its own sphere. In this relation, then, the proposed government cannot be deemed a *national* one; since its jurisdiction extends to certain enumerated objects only, and leaves to the several States a residuary and inviolable sovereignty over all other objects. It is true that in controversies relating to the boundary between the two jurisdictions, the tribunal which is ultimately to decide, is to be established under the general government. But this does not change the principle of the case. The decision is to be impartially made, according to the rules of the Constitution; and all the usual and most effectual precautions are taken to secure this impartiality. Some such tribunal is clearly essential to prevent an appeal to the sword and a dissolution of the compact; and that it ought to be established under the general rather than under the local governments, or, to speak more properly, that it could be safely established under the first alone, is a position not likely to be combated.

If we try the Constitution by its last relation to the authority by which amendments are to be made, we find it neither wholly *national* nor wholly *federal*. Were it wholly national, the supreme and ultimate authority would reside in the *ma-*

jority of the people of the Union; and this authority would be competent at all times, like that of a majority of every national society, to alter or abolish its established government. Were it wholly federal, on the other hand, the concurrence of each State in the Union would be essential to every alteration that would be binding on all. The mode provided by the plan of the convention is not founded on either of these principles. In requiring more than a majority, and particularly in computing the proportion by *States*, not by *citizens*, it departs from the *national* and advances towards the *federal* character; in rendering the concurrence of less than the whole number of States sufficient, it loses again the *federal* and partakes of the *national* character.

The proposed Constitution, therefore, is, in strictness, neither a national nor a federal Constitution, but a composition of both. In its foundation it is federal, not national; in the sources from which the ordinary powers of the government are drawn, it is partly federal and partly national; in the operation of these powers, it is national, not federal; in the extent of them, again, it is federal, not national; and, finally, in the authoritative mode of introducing amendments, it is neither wholly federal nor wholly national.

INTRODUCTORY NOTE

In *The Federalist No. 51,* Madison reflects the essentially pessimistic view of many of his tumultuous generation: that human nature was unchangeable and that mankind was a sorry lot, governed by self-interest and given to anarchy or tyranny. Hence, vice could not be controlled by virtue, but by setting vice against vice in a kind of bearable equilibrium that resembled the Newtonian mechanics of a planetary system. Government would not be a creature of virtue, but one of checks and balances that so dispersed power and set interest against interest, in sufficiently great a sphere, that neither transient majorities nor minorities could capture it. In place of the old Whig concept of an organic society, in which government strove to incorporate the basic social forces of the state structure, the founders envisioned a society of hostile individuals in which liberty was personal and private and the interests of society and the rights of individuals were distinct.[1] Government, then, need only be an honest, if shackled, broker.

[1]See Gordon S. Wood, *The Creation of the American Republic, 1776–1787,* Chapel Hill, N.C.: University of North Carolina Press, 1969.

The Federalist No. 51

"PUBLIUS" (JAMES MADISON)

To the People of the State of New York:

To what expedient, then, shall we finally resort for maintaining in practice the necessary partition of power among the several departments as laid down in the Constitution? The only answer that can be given is, that as all these exterior provisions are found to be inadequate, the defect must be supplied by so contriving the interior structure of the government as that its several constituent parts may, by their mutual relations, be the means of keeping each other in their proper places. Without presuming to undertake a full development of this important idea, I will hazard a few general observations, which may perhaps place it in a clearer light, and enable us to form a more correct judgment of the principles and structure of the government planned by the convention.

In order to lay a due foundation for that separate and distinct exercise of the different powers of government, which to a certain extent is admitted on all hands to be essential to the preservation of liberty, it is evident that each department should have a will of its own; and consequently should be so constituted that the members of each should have as little agency as possible in the appointment of the members of the others. Were this principle rigorously adhered to, it would require that all the appointments for the supreme executive, legislative, and judiciary magistrates should be drawn from the same fountain of authority, the people, through channels having no communication whatever with one another. Perhaps such a plan of constructing the several departments would be less difficult in practice than it may in contemplation appear. Some difficulties, however, and some additional expense would attend the execution of it. Some deviations, therefore, from the principle must be admitted. In the constitution of the judiciary department in particular, it might be inexpedient to insist rigorously on the principle: first, because peculiar qualifications being essential in the members, the primary consideration ought to be to select that mode of choice which best secures these qualifications; secondly, because the permanent tenure by which the appointments are held in that department must soon destroy all sense of dependence on the authority conferring them.

It is equally evident, that the members of each department should be as little dependent as possible on those of the others for the emoluments annexed to their offices. Were the executive magistrate or the judges not independent of the legislature in this particular, their independence in every other would be merely nominal.

But the great security against a gradual concentration of the several powers in the same department, consists in giving to those who administer each department the necessary constitutional means and personal motives to resist encroachments of the others. The provision for defense must in this, as in all other cases, be made to counteract ambition. The interest of the man must be connected with the constitutional rights of the place. It may be a reflection on human nature, that such devices should be necessary to control the abuses of government. But what is government itself, but the greatest of all reflections on human nature? If men were angels, no government would be necessary. If angels were to govern men, neither external nor internal controls on government would be necessary. In framing a government which is to be administered by men over men, the great difficulty lies in this: you must first enable the government to control the governed; and in the next place oblige it to control itself. A dependence on the people is, no doubt, the primary control on the government; but experience has taught mankind the necessity of auxiliary precautions.

This policy of supplying, by opposite and rival interests, the defect of better motives might be traced through the whole system of human affairs, private as well as public. We see it particularly displayed in all the subordinate distributions of power, where the constant aim is to divide and arrange the several offices in such a manner as that each may be a check on the other—that the private interest of every individual may be a sentinel over the public rights. These inventions of prudence cannot be less requisite in the distribution of the supreme powers of the State.

But it is not possible to give to each department an equal

power of self-defence. In republican government the legislative authority necessarily predominates. The remedy for this inconveniency is to divide the legislature into different branches; and to render them, by different modes of election and different principles of action, as little connected with each other as the nature of their common functions and their common dependence on the society will admit. It may even be necessary to guard against dangerous encroachments by still further precautions. As the weight of the legislative authority requires that it should be thus divided, the weakness of the executive may require, on the other hand, that it should be fortified. An absolute negative on the legislature appears, at first view, to be the natural defence with which the executive magistrate should be armed. But perhaps it would be neither altogether safe nor alone sufficient. On ordinary occasions it might not be exerted with the requisite firmness, and an extraordinary occasions it might be perfidiously abused. May not this defect of an absolute negative be supplied by some qualified connection between this weaker department and the weaker branch of the stronger department, by which the latter may be held to support the constitutional rights of the former, without being too much detached from the rights of its own department?

If the principles on which these observations are founded be just . . . and they be applied as a criterion to the several State constitutions and to the federal Constitution, it will be found that if the latter does not perfectly correspond with them, the former are infinitely less able to bear such a test.

There are, moreover, two considerations particularly applicable to the federal system of America, which place that system in a very interesting point of view.

First. In a single republic, all the power surrendered by the people is submitted to the administration of a single government; and the usurpations are guarded against by a division of the government into district and separate departments. In the compound republic of America, the power surrendered by the people is first divided between two distinct governments, and then the portion allotted to each subdivided among distinct and separate departments. Hence a double security arises to the rights of the people. The different governments will control each other, at the same time that each will be controlled by itself.

Second. It is of great importance in a republic not only to guard the society against the oppression of its rulers, but to guard one part of the society against the injustices of the other part. Different interests necessarily exist in different classes of citizens. If a majority be united by a common interest, the rights of the minority will be insecure. There are but two methods of providing against this evil: the one by creating a will in the community independent of the majority—that is, of the society itself; the other by comprehending in the society so many separate descriptions of citizens as will render an unjust combination of a majority of the whole very improbable, if not impracticable. The first method prevails in all governments possessing an hereditary or self-appointed authority. This, at best, is but a precarious security; because a power independent of the society may as well espouse the unjust views of the major, as the rightful interests of the minor party, and may possibly be turned against both parties. The second method will be exemplified in the federal republic of the United States. Whilst all authority in it will be derived from and dependent on the society, the society itself will be broken into so many parts, interests and classes of citizens, that the rights of individuals or of the minority will be in little danger from interested combinations of the majority. In a free government the security for civil rights must be the same as that for religious rights. It consists in the one case in the multiplicity of interests and in the other in the multiplicity of sects. The degree of security in both cases will depend on the number of interests and sects; and this may be presumed to depend on the extent of country and number of people comprehended under the same government. This view of the subject must particularly recommend a proper federal system to all the sincere and considerate friends of republican government, since it shows that in exact proportion as the territory of the Union may be formed into more circumscribed Confederacies or States, oppressive combinations of a majority will be facilitated; the best security under the republican forms for the rights of every class of citizens will be diminished; and consequently the stability and independence of some member of the government, the only other security, must be proportionally increased. Justice is the end of government. It is the end of civil society. It ever has been and ever will be pursued until it be obtained, or until liberty be lost in the pursuit. In a society under the forms of which the stronger faction can readily unite and oppress the weaker, anarchy may as truly be said to reign as in a state of nature, where the weaker individual is not secured against the violence of the stronger; and, as in the latter state even the stronger individuals are prompted, by the uncertainty of their condition, to submit to a government which may protect the weak as well as themselves; so, in the former state will the more powerful factions or parties be gradually induced by a like motive to wish for a government which will protect all parties, the weaker as well as the more powerful. It can be little doubted that if the State of Rhode Island was separated from the Confederacy and left to itself, the insecurity of rights under the popular form of government within such narrow limits would be displayed by such reiterated oppressions of factious majorities that some power altogether independent of the people would soon be called for by the voice of the very factions whose misrule had proved the necessity of it. In the extended republic of the United States and among the great variety of interests, parties, and sects which it embraces, a coalition of a majority of the whole society could seldom take place on any other principles than those of justice and the general good; whilst there being thus less danger to a minor from the will of a major party, there must be less pretext, also, to provide for the security of the former, by introducing into the government a will not dependent on the latter, or, in other words, a will independent of the society itself. It is no less certain than it is important, notwithstanding the contrary opinions which have been entertained, that the larger the society, provided it lie within a practical sphere, the more duly capable it will be of self-government. And happily for the *republican cause*, the practicable sphere may be carried to a very great extent by a judicious modification and mixture of the *federal principle*.

INTRODUCTORY NOTE

In view of the intensity of the debate over ratification of the Constitution, it is astonishing how rapidly the controversy ebbed and the Constitution came to be venerated as a sacrosanct document. Widely copied at home, in the form of new state constitutions, and abroad, the Constitution survived even the climax of its most spectacular failure: the Civil War. Indeed, it would likely have survived even if the South had won, for the constitution of the Confederate States of America was essentially a replica of the original.

But by the turn of the century, the processes of industrialization and urbanization had severely torn the social fabric of the nation; great fortunes were accumulated against a background of growing discontent on the part of the rural and urban poor. Coalitions of reformers occasionally engineered the passage of laws designed to regulate business enterprise, only to see them struck down by a conservative Supreme Court on the grounds that they violated the Constitution. So the progressive reformers struck out at the Constitution itself and at the founders who had constructed it. In 1913 Charles A. Beard published *An Economic Interpretation of the Constitution of the United States,* in which he argued with a ruthless economic determinism "that substantially all of the merchants, money lenders, security holders, manufacturers, shippers, capitalists, and financiers and their professional associates are to be found on one side in support of the Constitution and that substantially all or a major portion of the opposition came from the non-slaveholding farmers and the debtors." Beard concluded that "our fundamental law was not the product of an abstraction known as 'the whole people,' but of a group of economic interests which must have expected beneficial results from its adoption." Viewed in this light, the Constitution could be regarded as a kind of Thermidorian reaction, the product of a counterrevolution that had betrayed the equalitarian values of the Revolution, had lined the pockets of the self-interested founders, and had played into the hands of the robber barons ever since.

This sort of degrading of the Constitution and the founders

is as hyperbolic as the veneration in which they had previously been held, but the Progressive era was much given to muckraking hyperbole. Actually, Professor Beard was careful not to press the moral judgment that was implicit in his analysis, but critics have argued that this was the equivalent of describing a series of murders and tortures and inviting the readers to make any moral judgment they pleased. But the work of Beard and his fellow Progressive historians profoundly influenced the liberal thrust of scholarly interpretation for decades. The essay that follows was written by Pulitzer Prize-winning historian Richard Hofstadter, who has acknowledged his intellectual debt to Beard and the Progressive historians, but who focuses on the political thought of the Founding Fathers rather than on their financial portfolios. Although he acknowledges the consistent republicanism and the statesmanlike moderation of the founders, Hofstadter is critical of their political legacy. A master of the felicitous phrase, he summarizes their belief in a properly designed state that "would check interest with interest, class with class, faction with faction, and one branch of government with another in a harmonious system of mutual frustration."

The Founding Fathers: An Age of Realism

RICHARD HOFSTADTER

I

Long ago Horace White observed that the Constitution of the United States "is based upon the philosophy of Hobbes and the religion of Calvin. It assumes that the natural state of mankind is a state of war, and that the carnal mind is at enmity with God." Of course, the Constitution was founded more upon experience than any such abstract theory; but it was also an event in the intellectual history of Western civilization. The men who drew up the Constitution in Philiadelphia during the summer of 1787 had a vivid Calvinistic sense of human evil and damnation and believed with Hobbes that men are selfish and contentious. They were men of affairs, merchants, lawyers, planter-businessmen, speculators, investors. Having seen human nature on display in the market place, the courtroom, the legislative chamber, and in every secret path and alleyway where wealth and power are courted, they felt they knew it in all its frailty. To them a human being was an atom of self-interest. They did not believe in man, but they did believe in the power of a good political constitution to control him.

This may be an abstract notion to ascribe to practical men, but it follows the language that the Fathers themselves used. General Knox, for example, wrote in disgust to Washington after the Shays Rebellion that Americans were, after all, "men —actual men possessing all the turbulent passions belonging to that animal." Throughout the secret discussions at the Constitutional Convention it was clear that this distrust of man was first and foremost a distrust of the common man and democratic rule. As the Revolution took away the restraining hand of the British government, old colonial grievances of farmers,

From *The American Political Tradition,* by Richard Hofstadter. Copyright 1948 by Alfred A. Knopf, Inc. Reprinted by permission of the publisher.

debtors, and squatters against merchants, investors, and large landholders had flared up anew; the lower orders took advantage of new democratic constitutions in several states, and the possessing classes were frightened. The members of the Constitutional Convention were concerned to create a government that could not only regulate commerce and pay its debts but also prevent currency inflation and stay laws, and check such uprisings as the Shays Rebellion.

Cribbing and confining the popular spirit that had been at large since 1776 were essential to the purposes of the new Constitution. Edmund Randolph, saying to the Convention that the evils from which the country suffered originated in "the turbulence and follies of democracy," and that the great danger lay in "the democratic parts of our constitutions"; Elbridge Gerry, speaking of democracy as "the worst of all political evils"; Roger Sherman, hoping that "the people . . . have as little to do as may be about the government"; William Livingston, saying that "the people have ever been and ever will be unfit to retain the exercise of power in their own hands"; George Washington, the presiding officer, urging the delegates not to produce a document of which they themselves could not approve simply in order to "please the people"; Hamilton, charging that the "turbulent and changing" masses "seldom judge or determine right" and advising a permanent governmental body to "check the imprudence of democracy"; the wealthy young planter Charles Pinckney, proposing that no one be president who was not worth at least one hundred thousand dollars—all these were quite representative of the spirit in which the problems of government were treated.

Democratic ideas are most likely to take root among discontented and oppressed classes, rising middle classes, or perhaps some sections of an old, alienated, and partially disinherited aristocracy, but they do not appeal to a privileged class that is still amplifying its privileges. With a half-dozen exceptions at the most, the men of the Philadelphia Convention were sons of men who had considerable position and wealth, and as a group they had advanced well beyond their fathers. Only one of them, William Few of Georgia, could be said in any sense to represent the yeoman farmer class which constituted the overwhelming majority of the free population. In the late eighteenth century "the better kind of people" found themselves set off from the mass by a hundred visible, tangible, and audible distinctions of dress, speech, manners, and education. There was a continuous lineage of upper-class contempt, from pre-Revolutionary Tories like Peggy Hutchinson, the Governor's daughter, who wrote one day: "The dirty mob was all about me as I drove into town," to a Federalist like Hamilton, who candidly disdained the people. Mass unrest was often received in the spirit of young Gouverneur Morris: "The mob begin to think and reason. Poor reptiles! . . . They bask in the sun, and ere noon they will bite, depend upon it. The gentry begin to fear this." Nowhere in America or Europe—not even among the great liberated thinkers of the Enlightenment—did democratic ideas appear respectable to the cultivated classes. Whether the Fathers looked to the cynically illuminated intellectuals of contemporary Europe or to their own Christian heritage of the idea of original sin, they found quick confirmation of the notion that man is an unregenerate rebel who has to be controlled.

And yet there was another side to the picture. The Fathers were intellectual heirs of seventeenth-century English republicanism with its opposition to arbitrary rule and faith in popular sovereignty. If they feared the advance of democracy, they also had misgivings about turning to the extreme right. Having recently experienced a bitter revolutionary struggle with an external power beyond their control, they were in no mood to follow Hobbes to his conclusion that any kind of government must be accepted in order to avert the anarchy and terror of a state of nature. They were uneasily aware that both military dictatorship and a return to monarchy were being seriously discussed in some quarters—the former chiefly among unpaid and discontented army officers, the latter in rich and fashionable Northern circles. John Jay, familiar with sentiment among New York's mercantile aristocracy, wrote to Washington, June 27, 1786, that he feared that "the better kind of people (by which I mean the people who are orderly and industrious, who are content with their situations, and not uneasy in their circumstances) will be led, by the insecurity of property, the loss of confidence in their rulers, and the want of public faith and rectitude, to consider the charms of liberty as imaginary and delusive." Such men, he thought, might be prepared for "almost any change that may promise them quiet and security."

Washington, who had already repudiated a suggestion that he become a military dictator, agreed, remarking that "we are apt to run from one extreme to the other."

Unwilling to turn their backs upon republicanism, the Fathers also wished to avoid violating the prejudices of the people. "Notwithstanding the oppression and injustice experienced among us from democracy," said George Mason, "the genius of the people is in favor of it, and the genius of the people must be consulted." Mason admitted "that we had been too democratic," but feared that "we should incautiously run into the opposite extreme." James Madison, who has quite rightfully been called the philosopher of the Constitution, told the delegates: "It seems indispensable that the mass of citizens should not be without a voice in making the laws which they are to obey, and in choosing the magistrates who are to administer them." James Wilson, the outstanding jurist of the age, later appointed to the Supreme Court by Washington, said again and again that the ultimate power of government must of necessity reside in the people. This the Fathers commonly accepted, for if government did not proceed from the people, from what other source could it legitimately come? To adopt any other premise not only would be inconsistent with everything they had said against British rule in the past but would open the gates to an extreme concentration of power in the future. Hamilton saw the sharp distinction in the Convention when he said that "the members most tenacious of republicanism were as loud as any in declaiming the vices of democracy." There was no better expression of the dilemma of a man who has no faith in the people but insists that government be based upon them than that of Jeremy Belknap, a New England clergyman, who wrote to a friend: "Let it stand as a principle that government originates from the people; but let the people be taught . . . that they are not able to govern themselves."

II

If the masses were turbulent and unregenerate, and yet if government must be founded upon their suffrage and consent, what could a Constitution-maker do? One thing that the Fathers did not propose to do, because they thought it impossible, was to change the nature of man to conform with a more ideal system.

They were inordinately confident that they knew what man always had been and what he always would be. The eighteenth-century mind had great faith in universals. Its method, as Carl Becker has said, was "to go up and down the field of history looking for man in general, the universal man, stripped of the accidents of time and place." Madison declared that the causes of political differences and of the formation of factions were "sown in the nature of man" and could never be eradicated. "It is universally acknowledged," David Hume had written, "that there is a great uniformity among the actions of men, in all nations and ages, and that human nature remains still the same, in its principles and operations. The same motives always produce the same actions. The same events always follow from the same causes."

Since man was an unchangable creature of self-interest, it would not do to leave anything to his capacity for restraint. It was too much to expect that vice could be checked by virtue; the Fathers relied instead upon checking vice with vice. Madison once objected during the Convention that Gouverneur Morris was "forever inculcating the utter political depravity of men and the necessity of opposing one vice and interest to another vice and interest." And yet Madison himself in the *Federalist Number 51* later set forth an excellent statement of the same thesis:

> Ambition must be made to counteract ambition. . . . It may be a reflection on human nature that such devices should be necessary to control the abuses of government. But what is government itself, but the greatest of all reflections on human nature? If men were angels, no government would be necessary. . . . In framing a government which is to be administered by men over men, the great difficulty lies in this: you must first enable the government to control the governed; and in the next place oblige it to control itself.

Political economists of the laissez-faire school were saying that private vices could be public benefits, that an economically beneficient result would be providentially or "naturally" achieved if self-interest were left free from state interference and allowed to pursue its ends. But the Fathers were not so optimistic about politics. If, in a state that lacked constitutional balance, one class or one interest gained control, they believed, it would surely plunder all other interests. The Fathers, of course, were especially fearful that the poor would plunder the rich, but most of them would probably have admitted that the rich, unrestrained, would also plunder the poor. Even Gouverneur Morris, who stood as close to the extreme aristocratic position as candor and intelligence would allow, told the Convention: "Wealth tends to corrupt the mind and to nourish its love of power, and to stimulate it to oppression. History proves this to be the spirit of the opulent."

What the Fathers wanted was known as "balanced government," an idea at least as old as Aristotle and Polybius. This ancient conception had won new sanction in the eighteenth century, which was dominated intellectually by the scientific work of Newton, and in which mechanical metaphors sprang as naturally to men's minds as did biological metaphors in the Darwinian atmosphere of the late nineteenth century. Men had found a rational order in the universe and they hoped that it could be transferred to politics, or, as John Adams put it, that governments could be "erected on the simple principles of nature." Madison spoke in the most precise Newtonian language when he said that such a "natural" government must be so constructed "that its several constituent parts may, by their mutual relations, be the means of keeping each other in their proper places." A properly designed state, the Fathers believed, would check interest with interest, class with class, faction with faction, and one branch of government with another in a harmonious system of mutual frustration.

In practical form, therefore, the quest of the Fathers reduced primarily to a search for constitutional devices that would force various interests to check and control one another. Among those who favored the federal Constitution three such devices were distinguished.

The first of these was the advantage of a federated government in maintaining order against popular uprisings or majority rule. In a single state a faction might arise and take complete control by force; but if the states were bound in a federation, the central government could step in and prevent it. Hamilton quoted Montesquieu: "Should a popular insurrection happen in one of the confederate states, the others are able to quell it." Further, as Madison argued in the *Federalist Number 10,* a

majority would be the most dangerous of all factions that might
arise, for the majority would be the most capable of gaining
complete ascendancy. If the political society were very extensive, however, and embraced a large number and variety of local
interests, the citizens who shared a common majority interest
"must be rendered by their number and local situation, unable
to concert and carry into effect their schemes of oppression."
The chief propertied interests would then be safer from "a rage
for paper money, for an abolition of debts, for an equal division
of property, or for any other improper or wicked project."

The second advantage of good constitutional government
resided in the mechanism of representation itself. In a small
direct democracy the unstable passions of the people would
dominate lawmaking; but a representative government, as
Madison said, would "refine and enlarge the public views by
passing them through the medium of a chosen body of citizens."
Representatives chosen by the people were wiser and more
deliberate than the people themselves in mass assemblage.
Hamilton frankly anticipated a kind of syndical paternalism in
which the wealthy and dominant members of every trade or
industry would represent the others in politics. Merchants, for
example, were "the natural representatives" of their employees
and of the mechanics and artisans they dealt with. Hamilton
expected that Congress, "with too few exceptions to have any
influence on the spirit of the government, will be composed of
landholders, merchants, and men of the learned professions."

The third advantage of the government the Fathers were
designing was pointed out most elaborately by John Adams
in the first volume of his *Defence of the Constitutions of Government of the United States of America*, which reached Philadelphia while the Convention was in session and was cited
with approval by several delegates. Adams believed that the
aristocracy and the democracy must be made to neutralize
each other. Each element should be given its own house of the
legislature, and over both houses there should be set a capable,
strong, and impartial executive armed with the veto power.
This split assembly would contain within itself an organic check
and would be capable of self-control under the governance of
the executive. The whole system was to be capped by an independent judiciary. The inevitable tendency of the rich and the
poor to plunder each other would be kept in hand.

III

It is ironical that the Constitution, which Americans venerate so deeply, is based upon a political theory that at one crucial point stands in direct antithesis to the main stream of American democratic faith. Modern American folklore assumes that democracy and liberty are all but identical, and when democratic writers take the trouble to make the distinction, they usually assume that democracy is necessary to liberty. But the Founding Fathers thought that the liberty with which they were most concerned was menaced by democracy. In their minds liberty was linked not to democracy but to property.

What did the Fathers mean by liberty? What did Jay mean when he spoke of "the charms of liberty"? Or Madison when he declared that to destroy liberty in order to destroy factions would be a remedy worse than the disease? Certainly the men who met at Philadelphia were not interested in extending liberty to those classes in America, the Negro slaves and the indentured servants, who were most in need of it, for slavery was recognized in the organic structure of the Constitution and indentured servitude was no concern of the Convention. Nor was the regard of the delegates for civil liberties any too tender. It was the opponents of the Constitution who were most active in demanding such vital liberties as freedom of religion, freedom of speech and press, jury trial, due process, and protection from "unreasonable searches and seizures." These guarantees had to be incorporated in the first ten amendments because the Convention neglected to put them in the original document. Turning to economic issues, it was not freedom of trade in the modern sense that the Fathers were striving for. Although they did not believe in impeding trade unnecessarily, they felt that failure to regulate it was one of the central weaknesses of the Articles of Confederation, and they stood closer to the mercantilists than to Adam Smith. Again, liberty to them did not mean free access to the nation's unappropriated wealth. At least fourteen of them were land speculators. They did not believe in the right of the squatter to occupy unused land, but rather in the right of the absentee owner or speculator to pre-empt it.

The liberties that the constitutionalists hoped to gain were chiefly negative. They wanted freedom from fiscal uncertainty and irregularities in the currency, from trade wars

among the states, from economic discrimination by more powerful foreign governments, from attacks on the creditor class or
on property, from popular insurrection. They aimed to create a
government that would act as an honest broker among a variety
of propertied interests, giving them all protection from their
common enemies and preventing any one of them from becoming too powerful. The Convention was a fraternity of types of
absentee ownership. All property should be permitted to have its
proportionate voice in government. Individual property interests
might have to be sacrificed at times, but only for the community of propertied interests. Freedom for property would result
in liberty for men—perhaps not for all men, but at least for all
worthy men. Because men have different faculties and abilities,
the Fathers believed, they acquire different amounts of property.
To protect property is only to protect men in the exercise of
their natural faculties. Among the many liberties, therefore,
freedom to hold and dispose property is paramount. Democracy, unchecked rule by the masses, is sure to bring arbitrary
redistribution of property, destroying the very essence of liberty.

The Fathers' conception of democracy, shaped by their
practical experience with the aggressive dirt farmers in the
American states and the urban mobs of the Revolutionary
period, was supplemented by their reading in history and
political science. Fear of what Madison called "the superior force
of an interested and overbearing majority" was the dominant
emotion aroused by their study of historical examples. The
chief examples of republics were among the city-states of antiq-
uity, medieval Europe, and early modern times. Now, the history
of these republics—a history, as Hamilton said, "of perpetual
vibration between the extremes of tyranny and anarchy"—was
alarming. Further, most of the men who had overthrown the
liberties of republics had "begun their career by paying an
obsequious court to the people; commencing demagogues and
ending tyrants."

All the constitutional devices that the Fathers praised in
their writings were attempts to guarantee the future of the
United States against the "turbulent" political cycles of previous
republics. By "democracy," they meant a system of government
which directly expressed the will of the majority of the people,
usually through such an assemblage of the people as was possible in the small area of the city-state.

A cardinal tenet in the faith of the men who made the Constitution was the belief that democracy can never be more than a transitional stage in government, that it always evolves into either a tyranny (the rule of the rich demagogue who has patronized the mob) or an aristocracy (the original leaders of the democratic elements). "Remember," wrote the dogmatic John Adams in one of his letters to John Taylor of Caroline, "democracy never lasts long. It soon wastes, exhausts, and murders itself. There never was a democracy yet that did not commit suicide." Again:

> If you give more than a share in the sovereignty to the demo-crats, that is, if you give them the command or preponderance in the . . . legislature, they will vote all property out of the hands of you aristocrats, and if they let you escape with your lives, it will be more humanity, consideration, and generosity than any triumphant democracy ever displayed since the creation. And what will follow? The aristocracy among the demo-crats will take your places, and treat their fellows as severely and sternly as you have treated them.

Government, thought the Fathers, is based on property. Men who have no property lack the necessary stake in an orderly society to make stable or reliable citizens. Dread of the propertyless masses of the towns was all but universal. George Washington, Gouverneur Morris, John Dickinson, and James Madison spoke of their anxieties about the urban working class that might arise some time in the future—"men without property and principle," as Dickinson described them—and even the democratic Jefferson shared this prejudice. Madison, stating the problem, came close to anticipating the modern threats to conservative republicanism from both communism and fascism:

> In future times, a great majority of the people will not only be without landed but any other sort of property. These will either combine, under the influence of their common situation —in which case the rights of property and the public liberty will not be secure in their hands—or, what is more probable, they will become the tools of opulence and ambition, in which case there will be equal danger on another side.

What encouraged the Fathers about their own era, how-ever, was the broad dispersion of landed property. The small land-owning farmers had been troublesome in recent years, but there was a general conviction that under a properly made Constitution a *modus vivendi* could be worked out with them. The possession of moderate plots of property presumably gave them a sufficient stake in society to be safe and responsible citizens under the restaints of balanced government. Influence in government would be proportionate to property: merchants and great landholders would be dominant, but small property owners would have an independent and far from negligible voice. It was "politic as well as just," said Madison, "that the interests and rights of every class should be duly represented and understood in the public councils," and John Adams declared that there could be "no free government without a democratical branch in the constitution."

The farming element already satisfied the property requirements for suffrage in most of the states, and the Fathers generally had no quarrel with their enfranchisement. But when they spoke of the necessity of founding government upon the consent of "the people," it was only these small property-holders that they had in mind. For example, the famous Virginia Bill of Rights, written by George Mason, explicity defined those eligible for suffrage as all men "having sufficient evidence of permanent common interest with and attachment to the community"— which meant, in brief, sufficient property.

However, the original intention of the Fathers to admit the yeoman into an important but sharply limited partnership in affairs of state could not be perfectly realized. At the time the Constitution was made, Southern planters and Northern merchants were setting their differences aside in order to meet common dangers—from radicals within and more powerful nations without. After the Constitution was adopted, conflict between the ruling classes broke out anew, especially after powerful planters were offended by the favoritism of Hamilton's policies to Northern commercial interests. The planters turned to the farmers to form an agrarian alliance, and for more than half a century this powerful coalition embraced the bulk of the articulate interests of the country. As time went on, therefore, the main stream of American political conviction deviated more and more from the antidemocratic position of the Constitution makers. Yet, curiously, their general satisfaction with the Constitution together with their growing nationalism made

Americans deeply reverent of the founding generation, with
the result that as it grew stronger, this deviation was increasingly overlooked.

There is common agreement among modern critics that
the debates over the Constitution were carried on at an intellectual level that is rare in politics, and that the Constitution
itself is one of the world's masterpieces of practical statecraft.
On other grounds there has been controversy. At the very
beginning contemporary opponents of the Constitution foresaw
an apocalyptic destruction of local government and popular
institutions, while conservative Europeans of the old regime
thought the young American Republic was a dangerous leftist
experiment. Modern critical scholarship, which reached a high
point in Charles A. Beard's *An Economic Interpretation of the
Constitution of the United States*, started a new turn in the
debate. The antagonism, long latent, between the philosophy
of the Constitution and the philosophy of American democracy
again came into the open. Professor Beard's work appeared in
1913 at the peak of the Progressive era, when the muckraking
fever was still high; some readers tended to conclude from his
findings that the Fathers were selfish reactionaries who do not
deserve their high place in American esteem. Still more recently,
other writers, inverting this logic, have used Beard's facts to
praise the Fathers for their opposition to "democracy" and as
an argument for returning again to the idea of a "republic."

In fact, the Fathers' image of themselves as moderate
republicans standing between political extremes was quite
accurate. They were impelled by class motives more than
pietistic writers like to admit, but they were also controlled,
as Professor Beard himself has recently emphasized, by a statesmanlike sense of moderation and a scrupulously republican
philosophy. Any attempt, however, to tear their ideas out of the
eighteenth-century context is sure to make them seem starkly
reactionary. Consider, for example, the favorite maxim of
John Jay: "The people who own the country ought to govern it."
To the Fathers this was simply a swift axiomatic statement of
the stake-in-society theory of political rights, a moderate conservative position under eighteenth-century conditions of property distribution in America. Under modern property relations
this maxim demands a drastic restriction of the base of political
power. A large portion of the modern middle class—and it is the

strength of this class upon which balanced government depends
—is propertyless; and the urban proletariat, which the Fathers
so greatly feared, is almost one half the population. Further,
the separation of ownership from control that has come with
the corporation deprives Jay's maxim of twentieth-century
meaning even for many propertied people. The six hundred
thousand stockholders of the American Telephone & Telegraph
Company not only do not acquire political power by virtue of
their stock-ownerships, but they do not even acquire economic
power: they cannot control their own company.

  From a humanistic standpoint there is a serious dilemma
in the philosophy of the Fathers, which derives from their
conception of man. They thought man was a creature of rapa-
cious self-interest, and yet they wanted him to be free—free,
in essence, to contend, to engage in an umpired strife, to use
property to get property. They accepted the mercantile image
of life as an eternal battleground, and assumed the Hobbesian
war of each against all; they did not propose to put an end to
this war, but merely to stabilize it and make it less murderous.
They had no hope and they offered none for any ultimate
organic change in the way men conduct themselves. The result
was that while they thought self-interest the most dangerous
and unbrookable quality of man, they necessarily underwrote it
in trying to control it. They succeeded in both respects: under
the competitive capitalism of the nineteenth century America
continued to be an arena for various grasping and contending
interests, and the federal government continued to provide
a stable and acceptable medium within which they could contend; further, it usually showed the wholesome bias on behalf
of property which the Fathers expected. But no man who is as
well abreast of modern science as the Fathers were of eighteenth-century science believes any longer in unchanging
human nature. Modern humanistic thinkers who seek for a
means by which society may transcend external conflict and
rigid adherence to property rights as its integrating principles
can expect no answer in the philosophy of balanced government as it was set down by the Constitution-makers of 1787.

INTRODUCTORY NOTE

Although the creative genius of the founders must be acknowledged with pride, hindsight has proved them to have been dead wrong on four crucial assumptions that underlay their work.[1] First, they thought—or rather feared—that the popular House of Representatives would be dynamic, equalitarian, populistic, and democratically leveling, and therefore a dangerous center of power that needed restraint. Second, they assumed that the president would represent the wellborn and the few, screened from the raw electorate by the elitist electoral college, and that he would use his veto against popular majorities lodged in the House. They were wrong, for the relationship they envisaged has been reversed. It is the presidency that has proved to be the dynamic center that, certainly since Jackson, could claim to be the only representative of a national majority in the whole constitutional system. Increasingly the president has become the policymaker and creator of legislation as self-appointed spokesman for the majority, whereas the power of Congress has been increasingly that of the veto, often exercised on behalf of groups whose privileges are threatened by presidential policy. A corollary to this role reversal, more recently evolved, is the degree to which the Senate has performed less conservatively than the House—a transformation that the founders would not have guessed. Third, there is no evidence in the records of the Convention or *The Federalist Papers* to suggest that the founders anticipated the evolution of judicial review, whereby the judiciary would function from time to time as policymaker and legislator in its own right, even to the point of nullifying acts of Congress signed by the president.

Finally, and most revealingly, the founders did not foresee the great and crucial organizational function that political parties would perform. The Constitution makes no provision for them, indeed no mention of them. For the founders' generation, party

[1]See Robert A. Dahl, *A Preface to Democratic Theory,* Chicago: The University of Chicago Press, 1956; especially chap. 1 and pp. 141–143.

was a dirty word, synonymous with faction—a self-interested clique of willful men whose purpose was destructive of the common weal and subversive of the unity that was so crucial to the survival of a revolutionary new nation. But in *The Federalist Papers*, Madison shrewdly seized upon this general animosity toward party or faction in order to frame an argument that would ingeniously stand a commonplace notion upon its head in defense of the Constitution. That notion was the conventional view that democratic governments could function only when small areas and numbers of citizens were involved. The debates of the founders are liberally sprinkled with historical allusions to the city-state democracies of ancient Greece and to more recent but similar European experiences in which democratic regimes degenerated either into anarchy or tyranny. The implicit corollary was that the odds against a viable democracy were severe enough in a small community, and that democratic government was quite impossible when large areas and numbers of citizens were involved. The antifederalists made much of this, insisting that the local control and loose governmental structure of the Confederation was more conducive to liberty. But Madison reversed this axiom by tightly arguing in *The Federalist No. 10* that the larger the sphere of government in a republic, where public opinion was filtered through representation, the less chance there would be for transient majority factions to capture the apparatus of government and thereby threaten liberty.

The Federalist No. 10

"PUBLIUS" (JAMES MADISON)

To the People of the State of New York:

Among the numerous advantages promised by a well-constructed Union, none deserves to be more accurately developed than its tendency to break and control the violence of faction. The friend of popular governments never finds himself so much alarmed for their character and fate, as when he contemplates their propensity to this dangerous vice. He will not fail, therefore, to set a due value on any plan which, without violating the principles to which he is attached, provides a proper cure for it. The instability, injustice, and confusion introduced into the public councils, have, in truth, been the mortal diseases under which popular governments have everywhere perished; as they continue to be the favorite and fruitful topics from which the adversaries to liberty derive their most specious declamations. The valuable improvements made by the American constitutions on the popular models, both ancient and modern, cannot certainly be too much admired; but it would be an unwarrantable partiality, to contend that they have as effectually obviated the danger on this side, as was wished and expected. Complaints are everywhere heard from our most considerate and virtuous citizens, equally the friends of public and private faith, and of public and personal liberty, that our governments are too unstable; that the public good is disregarded in the conflicts of rival parties; and that measures are too often decided, not according to the rules of justice and the rights of the minor party, but by the superior force of an interested and overbearing majority. However anxiously we may wish that these complaints had no foundation, the evidence of known facts will not permit us to deny that they are in some degree true. It will be found, indeed, on a candid review of our situation, that some of the distresses under which we labor have been erroneously charged on the operation of our governments; but it will be found, at the same time, that other causes will not alone account for many of our heaviest misfortunes; and, particularly, for that prevailing and increasing distrust of public engagements, and alarm for private rights, which are echoed from one end of the continent to the other. These must be chiefly, if not wholly, effects of the unsteadiness and injustice with which a factious spirit has tainted our public administrations.

By a faction, I understand a number of citizens, whether amounting to a majority or minority of the whole, who are united and actuated by some common impulse of passion, or of interest, adverse to the rights of other citizens, or to the permanent and aggregate interests of the community.

There are two methods of curing the mischiefs of faction: the one, by removing its causes; the other, by controlling its effects.

There are again two methods of removing the causes of faction: the one, by destroying the liberty which is essential to its existence; the other, by giving to every citizen the same opinions, the same passions, and the same interests.

It could never be more truly said than of the first remedy, that it is worse than the disease. Liberty is to faction what air is to fire, an ailment without which it instantly expires. But it could not be less folly to abolish liberty, which is essential to political life, because it nourishes faction, than it would be to wish the annihilation of air, which is essential to animal life, because it imparts to fire its destructive agency.

The second expedient is as impracticable as the first would be unwise. As long as the reason of man continues fallible, and he is at liberty to exercise it, different opinions will be formed. As long as the connection subsists between his reason and his self-love, his opinions and his passions will have a reciprocal influence on each other; and the former will be objects to which the latter will attach themselves. The diversity in the faculties of men, from which the rights of property originate, is not less an insuperable obstacle to a uniformity of interests. The protection of these faculties is the first object of government. From the protection of different and unequal faculties of acquiring property, the possession of different degrees and kinds of property immediately results; and from the influence of these on the sentiments and views of the respective proprietors, ensues a division of the society into different interests and parties.

The latent causes of faction are thus sown in the nature of man; and we see them everywhere brought into different degrees of activity, according to the different circumstances of civil society. A zeal for different opinions concerning religion, concerning government, and many other points, as well of speculation as of practice; an attachment to different leaders ambitiously contending for pre-eminence and power; or to persons of other descriptions whose fortunes have been interesting to the human passions, have, in turn, divided mankind into parties, inflamed them with mutual animosity, and rendered them much more disposed to vex and oppress each other than to co-operate for their common good. So strong is this propensity of mankind to fall into mutual animosities, that where no substantial occasion presents itself, the most frivolous and fanciful distinctions have been sufficient to kindle their unfriendly passions and excite their most violent conflicts. But the most common and durable source of factions has been the various and unequal distribution of property. Those who hold and those who are without property have ever formed distinct interests in society. Those who are creditors, and those who are debtors, fall under a like discrimination. A landed interest, a mercantile interest, a moneyed interest, with many lesser interests, grow up of necessity in civilized nations, and divide them into different classes, actuated by different sentiments and views. The regulation of these various and interfering interests forms the principal task of modern legislation, and involves the spirit of party and faction in the necessary and ordinary operations of the government.

No man is allowed to be a judge in his own cause, because his interest would certainly bias his judgment, and, not improbably, corrupt his integrity. With equal, nay with greater reason, a body of men are unfit to be both judges and parties at the same time; yet what are many of the most important acts of legislation, but so many judicial determinations, not indeed concerning the rights of single persons, but concerning the rights of large bodies of citizens? and what are the different classes of legislators but advocates and parties to the causes which they determine? Is a law proposed concerning private debts? It is a question to which the creditors are parties on one side and the debtors on the other. Justice ought to hold the balance between them. Yet the parties are, and must be, themselves the judges; and the most numerous party, or, in other words, the most powerful faction must be expected to prevail. Shall domestic manufactures be encouraged, and in what degree, by restrictions on foreign manufactures? are questions which would be differently decided by the landed and the manufacturing classes, and probably by neither with a sole regard to justice and the public good. The apportionment of taxes on the various descriptions of property is an act which seems to require the most exact impartiality; yet there is, perhaps, no legislative act in which greater opportunity and temptation are given to a predominant party to trample on the rules of justice. Every shilling with which they overburden the inferior number is a shilling saved to their own pockets.

It is in vain to say that enlightened statesmen will be able to adjust these clashing interests and render them all subservient to the public good. Enlightened statesmen will not always be at the helm. Nor, in many cases, can such an adjustment be made at all without taking into view indirect and remote considerations, which will rarely prevail over the immediate interest which one party may find in disregarding the rights of another or the good of the whole.

The inference to which we are brought is, that the *causes* of faction cannot be removed, and that relief is only to be sought in the means of controlling its *effects*.

If a faction consists of less than a majority, relief is supplied by the republican principle, which enables the majority to defeat its sinister views by regular vote. It may clog the administration, it may convulse the society; but it will be unable to execute and mask its violence under the forms of the Constitution. When a majority is included in a faction, the form of popular government, on the other hand, enables it to sacrifice to its ruling passion or interest both the public good and the rights of other citizens. To secure the public good and private rights against the danger of such a faction, and at the same time to preserve the spirit and the form of popular government, is then the great object to which our inquiries are directed. Let me add that it is the great desideratum by which this form of government can be rescued from the opprobrium under which it has so long labored, and be recommended to the esteem and adoption of mankind.

By what means is this object attainable? Evidently by one

of two only. Either the existence of the same passion or interest in a majority at the same time must be prevented, or the majority, having such coexistent passion or interest, must be rendered by their number and local situation unable to concert and carry into effect schemes of oppression. If the impulse and the opportunity be suffered to coincide, we well know that neither moral nor religious motives can be relied on as an adequate control. They are not found to be such on the injustice and violence of individuals, and lose their efficacy in proportion to the number combined together, that is, in proportion as their efficacy becomes needful.

From this view of the subject it may be concluded that a pure democracy, by which I mean a society consisting of a small number of citizens, who assemble and administer the government in person, can admit of no cure for the mischiefs of faction. A common passion or interest will, in almost every case, be felt by a majority of the whole; a communication and concert result from the form of government itself; and there is nothing to check the inducements to sacrifice the weaker party or an obnoxious individual. Hence it is that such democracies have ever been spectacles of turbulence and contention; have ever been found incompatible with personal security or the rights of property; and have in general been as short in their lives as they have been violent in their deaths. Theoretic politicians, who have patronized this species of government, have erroneously supposed that by reducing mankind to a perfect equality in their political rights, they would, at the same time, be perfectly equalized and assimilated in their possessions, their opinions, and their passions.

A republic, by which I mean a government in which the scheme of representation takes place, opens a different prospect, and promises the cure for which we are seeking. Let us examine the points in which it varies from pure democracy, and we shall comprehend both the nature of the cure and the efficacy which it must derive from the Union.

The two great points of difference between a democracy and a republic are: first, the delegation of the government in the latter to a small number of citizens elected by the rest; secondly, the greater number of citizens and greater sphere of country over which the latter may be extended.

The effect of the first difference is, on the one hand, to refine and enlarge the public views, by passing them through the medium of a chosen body of citizens, whose wisdom may best discern the true interest of their country, and whose patriotism and love of justice will be least likely to sacrifice it to temporary or partial considerations. Under such a regulation, it may well happen that the public voice, pronounced by the representatives of the people, will be more consonant to the public good than if pronounced by the people themselves, convened for the purpose. On the other hand, the effect may be inverted. Men of factious tempers, of local prejudices, or of sinister designs, may by intrigue, by corruption, or by other means, first obtain the suffrages, and then betray the interests of the people. The question resulting is, whether small or extensive republics are more favorable to the election of proper guardians of the public weal; and it is clearly decided in favor of the latter by two obvious considerations.

In the first place, it is to be remarked that, however small the republic may be, the representatives must be raised to a certain number in order to guard against the cabals of a few; and that, however large it may be, they must be limited to a certain number in order to guard against the confusion of a multitude. Hence, the number of representatives in the two cases not being in proportion to that of the two constituents, and being proportionately greater in the small republic, it follows that, if the proportion of fit characters be not less in the large than in the small republic, the former will present a greater option and consequently a greater probability of a fit choice.

In the next place, as each representative will be chosen by a greater number of citizens in the large than in the small republic, it will be more difficult for unworthy candidates to practise with success the vicious arts by which elections are too often carried; and the suffrages of the people being more free, will be more likely to centre in men who possess the most attractive merit and the most diffusive and established characters.

It must be confessed that in this, as in most other cases, there is a mean, on both sides of which inconvenience will be found to lie. By enlarging too much the number of electors, you render the representative too little acquainted with all their local circumstances and lesser interests: as by reducing it too much, you render him unduly attached to these, and too little fit to comprehend and pursue great and national objects. The federal Constitution forms a happy combination in this respect; the great and aggregate interests being referred to the national, the local and particular to the State legislatures.

The other point of difference is, the greater number of citizens and extent of territory which may be brought within the compass of republican than of democratic government; and it is this circumstance principally which renders factious combinations less to be dreaded in the former than in the latter. The smaller the society, the fewer probably will be the distinct parties and interests composing it; the fewer the distinct parties and interests, the more frequently will a majority be found of the same party; and the smaller the number of individuals composing a majority, and the smaller the compass within which they are placed, the more easily will they concert and execute their plans of oppression. Extend the sphere, and you take in a greater variety of parties and interests; you make it less probable that a majority of the whole will have a common motive to invade the rights of other citizens; or if such a common motive exists, it will be more difficult for all who feel it to discover their own strength and to act in unison with each other. Besides other impediments, it may be remarked that, where there is a consciousness of unjust or dishonorable purposes, communication is always checked by distrust in proportion to the number whose concurrence is necessary.

Hence, it clearly appears that the same advantage which a republic has over a democracy in controlling the effects of faction is enjoyed by a large over a small republic,—is enjoyed by the Union over the States composing it. Does the advantage consist in the substitution of representatives whose enlightened views and virtuous sentiments render them superior to local prejudices and to schemes of injustice? It will not be denied that the representation of the Union will be most likely to possess these requisite endowments. Does it consist in the greater security afforded by a greater variety of parties, against the event of any one party being able to outnumber and oppress the rest? In an equal degree does the increased variety of parties comprised within the Union, increase this security. Does it, in fine, consist in the greater obstacles opposed to the concert and accomplishment of the secret wishes of an unjust and interested majority? Here, again, the extent of the Union gives it the most palpable advantage.

The influence of factious leaders may kindle a flame within their particular States, but will be unable to spread a general conflagration through the other States. A religious sect may degenerate into a political faction in a part of the Confederacy; but the variety of sects dispersed over the entire face of it must secure the national councils against any danger from that source. A rage for paper money, for an abolition of debts, for an equal division or property, or for any other improper or wicked project, will be less apt to pervade the whole body of the Union than a particular member of it; in the same proportion as such a malady is more likely to taint a particular county or district, than an entire State.

In the extent and proper structure of the Union, therefore, we behold a republican remedy for the diseases most incident to republican government. And according to the degree of pleasure and pride we feel in being republicans, ought to be our zeal in cherishing the spirit and supporting the character of Federalists.

Madison's argument (in *The Federalist No. 10*) prevailed, and the Constitution, as ratified with the Bill of Rights added, remained—and remains to this day—eloquently silent about party. Yet it is ironic how quickly the first modern party system in the history of the world evolved in the United States under a constitution whose fundamental assumptions were essentially antiparty. It is also ironic how the party of the founding regime under Washington and Adams, the Federalist party, in effect committed suicide because its leaders refused to perceive that they *were* a party, and that the opposition Republicans were a legitimate party also, rather than a disloyal faction that needed curbing by alien and sedition laws. The irony is compounded by the gravitation of Madison, philosopher of the Constitution, toward the opposition party of Jeffersonian republicanism.

If Charles Beard's thesis was too narrow and dogmatic, it was nonetheless telling; the founders were anxious to protect the sanctity of property rights from the leveling tendencies of radical democracy. But as the political theoretician Robert Dahl has observed, they misunderstood the dynamics of their own society:

> They failed to predict correctly the social balance of power that was to prevail even in their own lifetime. They did not really understand that in an agrarian society lacking feudal institutions and possessing an open and expanding frontier, radical democracy was almost certain to become the dominant and conventional view, almost certain to prevail in politics, and almost certain to be conservative about property.[1]

That the modern party system should evolve under the umbrella of a constitution that was hostile to it is fascinating. In the essay that follows, Richard Hofstadter probes the ambiguities of Madisonian pluralism, particularly its central assumption that sets liberty against party, which is the reverse of the assumption upon which the modern party system stands.

[1]Dahl, *A Preface to Democratic Theory*, p. 142.

A Constitution
Against Parties

RICHARD HOFSTADTER

I

That political parties did not hold a respectable place in eighteenth-century American political theory was a reflection of the
low estimate put upon their operation in practice. Wherever the
Americans looked, whether to the politics of Georgian England,
their own provincial capitals, or the republics of the historical
past, they thought they saw in parties only a distracting and
divisive force representing the claims of unbridled, selfish,
special interests. I do not intend here to try to penetrate the
thickets of eighteenth-century politics either in England or in
the American provinces. We long ago learned not to identify
the Whigs and Tories of the eighteenth century with the highly
developed British political parties of modern times, and not
to imagine that England had a well-developed two-party system
at the close of the eighteenth century or even during the early
decades of the nineteenth. Modern parties have grown up in
response to (and in turn have helped to stimulate) the development of large electorates, and their institutional structures are
in good measure an outgrowth of the efforts necessary to connect the parliamentary party and the mass party. The modern
party is, in this respect, the disciplined product of regular party
competition in the forum of public opinion. It also deals with
legislative issues, over which the established parties differ. But
this concern with issues and legislation—and hence with competing programs—which we now take for granted as a focus
of party politics did not have at all the same degree of development in the politics of late eighteenth-century England or of
the American colonies. It is the need to legislate frequently that
imposes a constant discipline within a parliamentary body, as

From *The Idea of a Party System*, by Richard Hofstadter. Originally published by the University of California Press (1969); reprinted by permission of The Regents of the University of California.

it is the need to carry issues to an electorate of considerable size that requires permanent organizations within the constituencies.

Although a suddenly enlarged electorate, active political contests, and the presence before Parliament of important issues coincided with a strong tendency toward a two-party system in the early eighteenth century, this state of affairs, which began to wane after the death of Queen Anne, was a matter of the rather distant past by the time of George III's accession. British politics in the era of George III, with the cabinet system not yet developed, with its relatively small electorate, its pocket boroughs, its connections of leading families, its management by purchase and arrangement, its lack of highly focused issues, its multiple, shifting factions, its high proportion of unaligned members of Parliament, bore only a vague germinal relation to the highly developed modern British party system. Historians may argue about details, but even as late as the 1820's, Richard Pares once suggested, one should perhaps speak only of a tendency toward a two-party system. The modern procedure for a change of ministry was first foreshadowed, though in a rudimentary way, only in 1830, when Wellington's cabinet was forced to resign and give way to the Whig ministry headed by Earl Grey. An adverse vote in the House of Commons now became established as the occasion for the end of a ministry, but it was not until 1868 that a prime minister (in this case Disraeli) first took the popular verdict in an election as a clear mandate and resigned without testing his position in Parliament. It was only after the Reform Acts of 1832 and 1867 that Britain moved toward the extended electorate of the sort that had been established in the United States. Efforts to organize machinery to mobilize a large electorate, which had reached a high state of development in the United States by the 1820's were being made in England during the 1860's. In party development, therefore, the United States proved to be the avantgarde nation.

Though today we think of the party system, party organization, and party identifications among the electorate as being much more fully developed in Britain than in the United States, it is easy to see why eighteenth-century Americans found in the state of English politics little that was edifying and less to imitate. However we may now assess the English political system in the last half of the eighteenth century, it seems safe to say that most Americans saw in it even less merit than it had, that they regarded it with a certain self-righteous puritanism, emphasizing its evil and corrupt character, which they contrasted with the robust and virtuous character of their own politics. Although there were still Anglophiles of a sort, one finds few Americans near the close of the century who could, with Hamilton, look upon English political culture, with all its faults, as the most advanced in the West, or who could understand why he thought it was the only government in the world that united "public strength with individual security." One can find perhaps none at all who could see in the historic division between Whigs and Tories any precursor of the highly functional party system of the future.

On the eve of the Revolution, most colonials thought of recent English history simply as a story of moral degeneracy, political corruption, and increasing despotism, marking a sharp and perhaps irreversible decline from the glories of that earlier England whose principles had been the inspiration of American liberties. Indeed one reason for the Revolution was the felt necessity of severing connections with a state that was losing the pristine purity of its constitution and was cutting itself adrift upon the seas of corrupt and tyrannical government. Americans saw this corruption when they visited the mother country; they read about it in the English political pamphleteers; they saw it at work on their own premises in the behavior of the Customs Commissioners during the 1760's. Benjamin Franklin had commented on the increasing "corruption and degeneracy of the people" in England during the 1750's, and shortly before Lexington and Concord was still complaining about "an extream corruption prevalent among all orders of men in this rotten state." All he could see was "Numberless and needless places, enormous salaries, pensions, perquisites, groundless quarrels, foolish expeditions, false accounts or no accounts, contracts and jobbs" which "devour all revenue and produce continual necessity in the midst of natural plenty." James Otis thought that the House of Lords was filled with peers who had not risen above what they learned at Oxford and Cambridge—"nothing at all but whoring, smoking, and drinking"—and that the Commons were "a parcel of button-makers, pinmakers, horse jockeys, gamesters, pensioners, pimps, and whore masters." John Adams believed that the virtue of England was done for: "Corruption, like a cancer . . . eats faster and faster every hour. The revenue creates pensioners, and the pensioners urge for more revenue. The people grow less steady, spirited, and virtuous, the seekers more numerous and corrupt, and every day increases the circles of their dependents and expectants, until virtue, integrity, public spirit, simplicity, and frugality, become the objects of ridicule and scorn, and vanity, foppery, selfishness, meanness, and downrght venality swallowing up the whole society," Jefferson, writing under the stress of wartime animosity in his *Notes on Virginia,* concluded that Great Britain was nearly finished: "The sun of her glory is fast descending on the horizon. Her philosophy has crossed the channel, her freedom the Atlantic, and herself seems passing to that awful dissolution whose issue is not given human foresight to scan."

II

Although the Americans thought of their own political condition as being much healthier than England's—it was in the New World that they expected old English liberties to be preserved—they thought they had no reason to attribute the comparative soundness of their own policies, as they saw it, to any evidences of party government. Though many historians would probably want to make an exception for Pennsylvania, and some perhaps for New York, most would agree with the general judgment that "no colony had what could be appropriately designated as a party structure." Certainly if a rigorous definition of party structure is laid down, demanding not merely parliamentary factions in the assemblies but clearly developed and permanent mass parties, this judgment would hold.

A great deal of political energy went into the repeated battles with the royal governors, and this put a premium on methods of organization that united rather than divided the assemblies. In the conduct of their struggles, and in securing legislation, the colonists had recourse to more or less disciplined caucusing groups, sometimes called "Juntos" which made life difficult for the governors but greatly increased the effectiveness of those who wanted to assert colonial prerogatives. After 1776, with royal governors out of the way, the state legislators, released from the unifying discipline imposed by the struggle for their prerogatives, were more free to break up into factional groupings. Political contests could now take on more clearly the form of struggles between rival groups of citizens within the state. But of course many respectable men saw this period as one of alarming disorder, and they could see little promise of good in the local factionalism that developed. "To many, the very word 'party' carried anti-republican connotations."

Pennsylvania, which had the closest thing to a two-party system, was sometimes pointed to as an example of the evil effects of party strife under constitutional government. Madison, for example, in the Fiftieth *Federalist*, cited the "two fixed and violent parties" of Pennsylvania as a primary reason for the failure of that state's Council of Revision. The state had been "for a long time before, violently heated and distracted by the rage of party," Madison pointed out, and this was a difficulty that the other states must also except to experience. Yet one may wonder about the justice of this judgment on Pennsylvania. The factions in Pennsylvania may have been as bad as they were thought to be—the politics of that province had always been contentious—but the existence of parties did not prevent the Pennsylvanians from going through the fires of the Revolution, the British ensconced on their very doorstep, without slipping into tyranny or giving way to indiscriminate reprisals, or from emerging with a free and quite democratic constitution.

No doubt the factors that combined to produce free government were numerous, and party conflict was only one of them. Provincial factionalism had its seamy side and its social costs; and the pre-party factions may be criticized by contrast with the highly developed parties of a later day. But factional differences taught the Americans to argue, polemicize, legislate, and on occasion to make compromises; the modern political party is an evolutionary product resting on a large fund of political experience, of which this early factional politics was a part.

The truth seems to be, however, that free government could struggle along with or without these rudimentary forms of party. Virginia must here concern us especially; and Virginia— which, along with Connecticut, was the least faction-ridden of the colonies—represents the strongest challenge to the notion that the political party had to be a decisive force in the development of a free state. If we compare the political culture of the

Old Dominion, which was, after all, the political culture that the Virginia dynasts knew best, with most other colonies, we are impressed by its partyless condition and the relaltive uneventfulness of its domestic politics in the eighteenth century up to about 1763. One may argue whether the government of colonial Virginia was brilliant, but it was certainly competent as governments went then and as most of them go now; and Virginia bequeathed to the new nation an impressive, if preponderantly parochial, gallery of talents, unmatched by any of the other states.

It is Virginia that may serve to remind us that, for all the claims that have been made for the "democratic" character of colonial politics, colonial society was a deferential society and its politics were ordered accordingly. In his elegant little study of the methods of political control in Washington's Virginia, there was one conception for which Charles S. Sydnor had no use, beyond a need to explain its absence, and that is the conception of party. In eighteenth-century Virginia men were elected not because of the group they were associated with or what they proposed to do about this or that issue but because of what they were. An election promise might be made here or there—though political promises were rather frowned on and might even be made the object of investigation or cause an elected candidate to be refused his seat—but in the main men put themselves forward on their social position and character and manners, and on their willingness to treat their constituencies in the right and liberal fashion, not least on their willingness to ply them with rum punch. It was rare for a man to run on issues or policies; and no one could run on factional identifications, since these were thin, ephemeral, and spare of meaning.

"Perhaps the most striking characteristic of Virginia politics between 1689 and 1763," writes Jack P. Greene in his study of the Southern colonial assemblies, "was its tranquillity." Even the governors, he concludes, were in the main able, prudent, and moderate. The aristocracy was tightly knit and mutually accommodating. There was no serious rivalry between the Council and the Burgesses. Sectional divisions there were, but before the Revolution they were not of grave consequence. Class differences there were also, and occasional personal rivalries, but they produced no parties, not even permanent factions, and St. George Tucker was able to recall with satisfaction long after the Revolution that he had never seen anything in the Burgesses "that bore the appearance of *party spirit*."

A generation nurtured in this environment had no successful example of party government anywhere in its experience, but it had an example of a partyless government of a free and relatively benign character, and the statements of the Virginia dynasts about party, though conventional among their entire generation in America as well as in their own particular cherished locale, have a uniquely firm root in Virginia soil.

III

Let us turn from the state of practice to the state of theory. The Founding Fathers, thinking along lines drawn by the old struggle against British authority, by the works of dissenters, radical Whigs, and libertarian publicists, and by the violent pre-Revolutionary controversy itself, were concerned with one central issue: liberty versus power. Because men are fallible, wicked, and self-aggrandizing, they thought, power tends always to extend itself and to encroach upon liberty. "From the nature of man," said George Mason at the Federal Convention, "we can be sure that those who have power in their hands . . . will always, when they can, . . . increase it." "Power," said Madison, "is of an encroaching nature." The basic problem of republicanism, as most of them saw it, was to protect liberty by devising foolproof checks upon power. The basic problem of good American republicans like Madison, who nevertheless wanted a stronger Union, was to protect liberty by checking power, without at the same time weakening government to a point at which its stability would be in danger.

Liberty, then, was the basic value. As to what it consisted of, Americans sometimes assumed so much that their passionate claims for liberty seemed to mask a demand for license or anarchy. But they would have answered that liberty prevailed when men were free to exercise their natural rights. As an answer to the abstract question, What is liberty? this was enough for them, and they had no difficulty at all in spelling out what natural rights were or what institutions threatened liberty or sustained it. It was endangered by many things they saw in contemporary England: monarchy and aristocracy, a standing army, corruption, bribery, and patronage, a decadent state of morals. It could best be protected under a government which had within it a strong popular house in the legislature, a broad freehold suffrage, a system of mutual checks and balances among the arms of government, an independent judiciary, explicit guarantees of rights (among these, civil and religious liberties and trial by jury), and frequent (some said annual) elections.

The necessity of checks on power is a theme struck over and over. But it is important that for the Fathers these checks had to be built *into the constitutional structure itself*. They were not content—and still less were the people they had to persuade—to rest their hopes on those checks that might arise in the political process alone, and this is one reason why they put no faith in party competition. Their hopes were pinned on a formal, written system of internal checks and balances, the precise enumeration of limited powers, and the explicit statement of constitutional guarantees, such as the opponents of the Constitution insisted on adding to it. Such informal forces in politics as the temper of the public, the process of opposition, the institutionalization of party structures, which to us seem so vital in democracy, seemed to them too slender a reliance, too inadequate a substitute for explicit constitutional specifications.

Here, it is important to realize, the ideas about constitutional structure that prevailed in America were derived both from Anglo-American experience and from the traditions of classical political thought. What had come down as the authoritative prescription for just and stable government from the times of Polybius and Aristotle was the idea of mixed government—that is, a government that would incorporate representation of the three basic orders in society. The three indispensable arms of government would act for the sovereign, the nobility, and the people. The prevalent eighteenth-century passion for balanced government, which was founded on the conviction that liberty and justice would be most secure if the elements of the state and of society were counterposed in such a way as to check and control each other, was sought for in constitutional systems that separated the powers of government and put the several arms of government in a state of watchful mutual tension. The necessary mutual checks would thus be provided by the elements of the constitution, and not by parties, which were indeed usually thought of, when they were thought of at all, as forces likely to upset the desired constitutional balance by mobilizing too much force and passion in behalf of one limited interest.

When they were thought of at all: in classical political theory, in the great books from Aristotle and Machiavelli to Locke and Montesquieu, which were read by the Founding Fathers when they consulted literature for political wisdom, parties played only an incidental, illustrative historical role, usually as examples of some difficult problem or some historical mischief. Most of the classical political writers had mentioned party here and there, but none of them discussed parties at substantial length or offered a theory of the role of the party in the state. Even such empirically minded thinkers as Aristotle and Machiavelli had little to say on the subject; and so strong was this tradition that even as late as 1861, long after his own country was well launched upon the development of its two-party system, John Stuart Mill could write a entire treatise, *Considerations on Representative Government,* in which he never elaborated upon the role of party. Indeed, it was the great cumulative and collective merit of writers like Bolingbroke, Hume, Burke, and Madison that they showed a new understanding of the importance of party and a strong disposition to move it somewhat closer to the center of concern in political thought.

However, the point remains that in the thinking of the Founding Fathers, the truly useful and reliable antithesis of politics, the counterpoises upon which they were disposed to rely for liberty and stability, were still embodied not in the mutual checks of political parties but in the classic doctrine of the separation of powers, in the mutual checks of the houses of legislature, or in the checks exerted upon each other by the executive and the legislature, and in that exerted by the judiciary over the other two. Checks were to be built into planned constitutional forms instead of being left to the hurly-burly of politics. James Madison, for example, assuring the Federal Convention that the new constitution would have safeguards against the betrayal of trust by officials, explained: "An obvious precaution against this danger would be to divide the trust between different bodies of men, who might watch and check each other." John Jay, speaking for the Constitution in the New York ratifying convention, said: "The two houses will naturally be in a state of rivalship. This will make them always vigilant, quick to discern a bad measure, and ready to oppose it." It was two *houses*, not two parties.

While most of the Fathers did assume that partisan oppositions would form from time to time, they did not expect that valuable permanent structures would arise from them which would have a part to play in the protection and exercise of liberties or in reconciling the stability and effectiveness of government with the exercise of popular freedoms. The solution, then, lay in a nicely balanced constitutional system, a well-designed state which would hold in check a variety of evils, among which the divisive effects of parties ranked high. The Fathers hoped to create not a system of party government under a constitution but rather a constitutional government that would check and control parties.

This conviction, as Cecelia Kenyon has pointed out, was shared by both sides in the debate over the adoption of the Constitution. Although Federalists and Anti-Federalists differed over many things, they do not seem to have differed over the proposition that an effective constitution is one that successfully counteracts the work of parties. The Anti-Federalists often expressed a sweeping opposition to the idea of political organization as such, and, as Miss Kenyon has observed, "the contemporary opponents of the Constitution feared parties or factions in the Madisonian sense just as much as did Madison, and . . . they feared parties in the modern sense even more than Madison did. They feared and distrusted concerted group action for the purpose of 'centering votes' in order to obtain a plurality, because they believed this would distort the automatic or natural expression of the people's will."

IV

We have come now to the point at which we can examine the problem of party as it was expressed in the minds of the Virginia dynasts. It seems fitting to begin with Madison: he was a more systematic, and I believe a more deliberate and profound thinker than Thomas Jefferson; as the philosopher of the Constitution, he gives the clearest and most authoritative statement of the conflict between the rationale of the Constitution and the spirit of party; and, as the man who began, before Jefferson, to play the central role in organizing what came to be considered Jefferson's party, he illustrates even more sharply than Jefferson our central paradox of party government instituted by anti-party thinkers.

The great achievement of Madison was to provide for his contemporaries a statement of the checks-and-balances view of government in which a pluralistic view of society itself was linked to the plural constitutional structure. Like John Adams, he saw with great clarity the importance of supplementing the internal balance of the constitution with the external balance of the various interests and forces that made up society.

Here Madisonian pluralism owes a great deal to the example of religious toleration and religious liberty that had already been established in eighteenth-century America. The traditions of dissenting Protestantism had made an essential contribution to political pluralism. That fear of arbitrary power which is so marked in American political expression had been shaped to a large degree by the experience men of dissenting sects had had with persecution. Freedom of religion became for them a central example of freedoms in general, and it was hardly accidental that the libertarian writers who meant so much to the colonials so often stemmed from the tradition of religious dissent. In the colonies, Americans fought unrelentingly against the proposal to introduce an Anglican episcopate among them, an idea that excited in their minds a remarkable terror that religious liberty, and then all liberty, would be invaded. In their campaign against an American episcopate, the colonials cooperated with dissenters in the mother country with such admirable system and regularity that they established a veritable trans-Atlantic Protestant anti-episcopal union, whose members gave a great deal of thought to the problems of liberty, toleration, and pluralism.

In 1768 an Anglican chaplain was quoted by one of his anti-establishment opponents in New York as having said that American experience showed that "republican principles in religion naturally engender the same in civil government." It was an appropriate remark. The whole Protestant enterprise had made for the decentralization of structure within the churches themselves, and at the same time within the structure of society. There were no longer a State and a Church standing together as unified, firm ordered hierarchies, but two spheres of values that could sometimes compete. The presence of dissenters, and the necessity of appeasing them in the interests of secular stability, meant that the imperatives of the state and those of the church might not coincide, and that the latter might in some respects be sacrificed for the former. The presence of a variety of theologies, a plurality of views within Protestantism itself, also made toleration a necessary precondition for the secular values of peace and social stability. The coexistence of the sects and the growth of toleration led to a premium on argument and persuasion, as against main force. The dissenters, with the law against them and no other instrument of suasion available to them, had had to defend their interests in this way. It became clear in England that there could no longer be such a thing as a single enforceable orthodoxy. Even error had to be tolerated, and if error could be endured where profound matters of faith were concerned, a model had been created for the political game, in which also one might learn to endure error in the interests of social peace.

Of course the advancing secularism of educated men brought strong reinforcement to this tendency. One notices the common sense of relief shared by such different theorists of party as Bolingbroke, Hume, and Burke at the passing of the old religiously inspired, bigotry-animated political divisions of the seventeenth century, and Hume indeed had made a central principle of it in his political writings. The advanced, enlightened, more or less secular man could take a genial view of the competitions of sects, so long as they were all free and not at each others' throats. So Franklin, a Deist, patronized the churches, and Jefferson in time forged a curious political alliance between Enlightenment liberalism and the passion of the minority sects for religious freedom.

The intellectual transition from the pluralism engendered by religious denominations to that of parties was clearly illustrated by William Livingston in New York during the 1750's. A young man still in his late twenties when he started writing in 1752, Livingston was soon to cut quite a figure in the politics of the province as a partisan in the De Lancey-Livingston party battle. The De Lancey's were Anglicans, the Livingstons and their allies Presbyterians and keen enemies of episcopacy. In

1752 Livingston launched his *Independent Reflector*, a journal which aped the style of the *Tatler* and the *Spectator* but which took much of its argument from *Cato's Letters*. Though a strong partisan, Livingston had been put off by dogmatic doctrinal religion at Yale. His Presbyterianism was qualified by a certain broad tolerance of other dissenting groups and yet fortified by an intense, almost anti-clerical animus against the Anglican Church. His own doctrines on faction were hewn out of the current orthodoxy. ("Unspeakably calamitous have been the consequences of party-division. It has occasioned deluges of blood, and subverted kingdoms.") But still, as an ardent partisan, Livingston, like Bolingbroke with his country party to end all parties, had to have an exception: "To infer . . . that the liberties of the people are safe and unendanger'd, because there are no political contests, is illogical and fallacious." We all have a right to look into the conduct of our superiors, and if we find in them "a combination of roguery" it is our common right to "form a party against their united strength: and such a party, I hope we may never want the spirit to form."

Livingston, who never lacked such spirit, was roused to one of his keenest efforts in 1753 during the controversy over the founding of King's College (later Columbia). He was afraid that the college, should it receive a charter from the Crown, would become an exclusively Anglican institution, "an academy founded in bigotry and reared by party-spirit." He proposed instead that the college should be created by the legislature, and established on such a non-sectarian basis that all the groups in the province could use it together, and that all the youths sent there could be educated free of indoctrination in any particular set of religious or partisan tenets. "*For as we are split into so great a variety of opinions and professions; had each individual his share in the government of the academy, the jealousy of all parties combating each other, would inevitably produce a perfect freedom for each particular party.*" Next to a patriot king and wise laws, Livingston argued, "an equal toleration of conscience is justly deem'd the basis of the public liberty of this country. And will not this foundation be undermined? Will it not be threatened with a total subversion, should one party obtain the sole management of the education of our youth?"

Note that the term "party" is applied by Livingston more or less indifferently to a religious or a political group, a circumstance that arises not only out of their interconnection in the provincial politics of New York but also, and more importantly, out of his understanding of the principles of mutuality involved both in religious liberty and civic peace. For him libertarian principles in religion did indeed have a bearing on the problems of civil government.

A similar awareness of the relation between multiple sects and liberty is evident in a remarkable address before a convention of the Congregational clergy of Rhode Island delivered by the Reverend Ezra Stiles in 1760 and published the following year. Stiles was really addressing the Congregational world of New England, which, though badly divided for twenty years by the effects of the Great Awakening, was still united in its anxiety about episcopal incursions. In *A Discourse on the Christian Union* Stiles pleaded for an ecumenical tolerance. "Every sect," he said, "have a right to vindicate their particular forms." Theological differences, which he hoped to minimize among good Christians, might survive, but: "Their conviction . . . is not to be laboured by the coercion of civil or ecclesiastical punishment, but by the gentle force of persuasion and truth— not by appeals to the tenets of parties and great men; not by an appeal to the position of Arminius or Calvin; but by an appeal to the inspired writings." In arguing that even church councils or consociations had no authority over individual churches, Stiles added strikingly: "Coercive uniformity is neither necessary in politics nor religion." This conclusion was premised upon a remarkable statement of harmony in plurality: "Providence has planted the British America with a variety of sects, which will unavoidably become a mutual balance upon one another. Their temporary collisions, like the action of acids and alcalies, after a short ebullition will subside in harmony and union, not by the destruction of either, but in the friendly cohabitation of all. . . . Resplendent and all-pervading TRUTH will terminate the whole in universal harmony. All surreptitious efforts and attempts on public liberty will unavoidably excite the public vigilance of the sects, till the terms of general union be defined and honorably adjusted. The notion of erecting the polity of either sect into universal dominion to the destruction of the rest, is but an airy vision . . . all the present sects will subsist and increase into distinct respectable bodies, continuing their distinctions for a long time yet to come in full life and vigor. Indeed mutual oppression will more and more subside from their mutual balance of one another. Union may subsist on these distinctions, coalescence only on the sameness of public sentiment, which can again be effected in the Christian world only by the gentle but almighty power of truth. . . . The sects cannot destroy one another: all attempts this way will be fruitless—they may effect a temporary disturbance, but cannot produce a dissolution—each one subserves the mutual security of all. . . . Nothing however will content us but actual experiment—this experiment will be made in one century, and then perhaps we shall be satisfied."

It remained for James Madison to make still more explicit than Livingston or Stiles the analogy between the religious and the civic spheres. From this earliest days Madison had had a deep and passionate commitment to religious liberty. The Madison family was never warmly disposed toward the Anglican establishment in Virginia, and Madison's father appears to have been unsympathetic to the persecution of Baptists that raged during James's youth in neighboring Culpeper County. Madison himself, who was tutored by a Princeton-educated Presbyterian, made the significant choice to go to Princeton rather than to Anglican William and Mary. His undergraduate years at Princeton coincided with the regime of President John Witherspoon, who was later to be a signer of the Declaration of Independence. Although his religion was more severe than Madison's, Witherspoon may have heightened his antipathy to establishments. At Princeton Madison also appears to have read Voltaire surreptitiously, and of all the Voltairean aphorisms that he might have chosen to fasten upon, he became particularly fond of Voltaire's saying that in England one sect would have produced slavery and two a civil war, but that a multiplicity of sects caused the people to live at peace. He was also apparently familiar with William Livingston's *Independent Reflector*, which was often read at Princeton. When he went back to Virginia, it was as a firm advocate of religious liberty and an alert foe of an Anglican episcopate. The editors of his papers have concluded that religious issues were more important than economic ones in stimulating his earliest interest in politics. When he began to correspond with a college friend from Pennsylvania, William Bradford, it was religious issues that chiefly aroused him, and he began to make unfavorable comparisons between

Virginia's persecutions and the broad tolerance displayed in Pennsylvania.

At twenty-three, he denounced "that diabolical Hell conceived principle of persecution" and the Anglican clergy for abetting it, and professed that this troubled him more than any other public issue. Concerning a new outbreak of persecution in Culpeper County he wrote to Bradford in January 1774: "There are at this [time] in the adjacent county not less than five or six well-meaning men in close [jail] for publishing their religious sentiments which in the main are very orthodox. I have neither patience to hear, talk, or think of anything relative to this matter, for I have squabbled and scolded, abused and ridiculed about it to so little purpose, that I am without common patience." By contrast he admired "that liberal catholic and equitable way of thinking as to the rights of Conscience, which is one of the characteristics of a free people" that he believed to be prevalent in Pennsylvania. Later it was Madison who would take the leadership in the struggle to go beyond the limited principle of toleration to espouse complete religious liberty and achieve disestablishment in the first constitution of Virginia.

As Madison was well aware in the less discouraged moments of his maturity, an answer to the "hell-conceived principle" was already apparent in America. The growth of a multiplicity of denominations and sects had made religious freedom a practical necessity, and had provided the political forces to make it possible. Madison's insight into the strength and viability of a pluralistic society seems at least to have been heightened by, if it did not derive from, the model already before him of various religious groups coexisting in comparative peace and harmony. He told the Virginia ratifying convention of 1788 that the remarkable freedom of religion now achieved "arises from that multiplicity of sects, which pervades America, and which is the best and only security for religious liberty in any society. . . . The United States abound in such a variety of sects, that it is a strong security against religious persecution, and it is sufficient to authorize a conclusion that no one sect will ever be able to outnumber or depress the rest."

A monopolistic religious establishment, Madison saw, is in a position to persecute, just as a single interest in society or a single arm of government, when unchecked, is in a position to be tyrannical. A plurality of sects militates against religious oppression just as a plurality of varying social interests militates against political oppression. Madison put this analogy very explicitly in Number 51 of *The Federalist*, where he spoke of the desirability of guarding against the oppression of minorities by a single consolidated majority. This, he thought, could be done in the proposed federal republic of the United States "by comprehending in the society so many separate descriptions of citizens as will render an unjust combination of a majority of the whole very improbable, if not impracticable." While all authority in the proposed republic, he went on, "will be derived from and dependent on the society, the society itself will be broken into so many parts, interests, and classes of citizens, that the rights of individuals, or of the minority, will be in little danger from interested combinations of the majority. *In a free government the security for civil rights must be the same as that for religious rights. It consists in the one case in the multiplicity of interests, and in the other in the multiplicity of sects.* The degree of security in both cases will depend on the number of interests and sects; and this may be presumed to depend on the extent of country and number of people comprehended under the same government."

V

The best statement of Madison's pluralism, of course, is in the familiar Number 10 of *The Federalist*, a work which shows a powerful obligation to the theory of party laid down in David Hume's essays. Madison's basic concern in that essay was to show that a large federal union would be better than a small republic at sustaining free representative government; but his point of departure was the problem of controlling parties and the "violence" and threat to liberty that are connected with them. Always, in *The Federalist* the fundamental thing government has to control is the "assertive selfishness of human nature." But the basic manifestation of this selfishness in political life is the party, or faction. Possibly the greatest of the many advantages that would come with a well-constructed Union, Madison argued, was "its tendency to break and control the violence of faction." (Madison, it should be noted, used the terms party and faction as synonymous.) The classical

problem of the republics known to previous history, their instability, injustice, and confusion, had already been much rem-
edied by the constitutions of the American states, he admitted.
But now complaints were being heard everywhere by public-
spirited men that "the public good is disregarded in the conflicts of rival parties"—and particularly that measures were
being decided "by the superior force of an increased and overbearing majority." Such injustices were largely if not wholly the
consequence of "a factious spirit" in government. "By a faction,"
Madison goes on, "I understand a number of citizens, whether
amounting to a majority or a minority of the whole, who are
united and actuated by some common impulse of passion, or of
interest, adverse to the rights of other citizens, or to the
permanent and aggregate interests of the community."

How best to remedy this state of affairs? You can destroy
liberty, which makes faction possible, but that remedy is clearly
far worse than the disease. You can try to give all citizens the
same opinions, passions, and interests, but that is impracticable.
Men have different faculties and different abilities in acquiring
property; and protecting these faculties is the first object of
government. But out of these differences arise different kinds
and degrees of property, hence differing political interests and
parties. "The latent causes of factions are thus sown in the
nature of man." Passions will make men form factions and
"vex and oppress each other." But different propertied interests
—landed, moneyed, mercantile, manufacturing, debtors, and
creditors—are the most common and durable sources of factions. "The regulation of these various and interfering interests
forms the principal task of modern legislation, and involves
the spirit of party and faction in the necessary and ordinary
operations of government."

This last sentence, because of the ambiguity of the word
"involves," has led some readers to think that Madison had
found, after all, a strong positive function for parties. But it is
one thing to say that legislation or government cannot be carried on without having parties make their appearance—i.e., that
they are *involved*—and another that they are *valuable* in the
process; and I think the whole context of Madison's work, with
its pejorative definition of party and its many invidious refer-
ences to party, makes it clear that it was the former meaning he
was trying to convey.

Since the causes of faction cannot be safely or wisely re-moved, Madison was saying, we have to look for relief in the means of controlling its effects. The most dangerous faction is the most powerful, the majority faction, and it is above all the tyranny of the majority that we must be concerned with. A minority faction, he admitted, could be temporarily ob-structive, and could even convulse society. But in the normal course of events in a republic, it will be outvoted, and it will be "unable to execute and mask its violence under the forms of the Constitution." However, a majority faction can sacrifice the public good and the rights of other citizens to its ruling passion, and it is this above all that must be prevented. "To secure the public good and private rights against the danger of such [majority] faction, and at the same time to preserve the spirit and form of popular government, is then the great ob-ject to which our inquiries are directed."

How can this be done? It is useless to rely on enlightened statesmen: they may not always be there; and it is the very essence of good constitution-making to provide safeguards against ordinary human frailties. The answer lies in a repre-sentative republic, which will avoid the turbulance of direct democracy, and in an extensive republic rather than a small one.

In making this last point, Madison was trying to establish a view which thus far had had the status of a heresy. It was standard eighteenth-century doctrine—made canonical by Mon-tesquieu though questioned by Hume—that republican govern-ments, whatever their merits, are not strong enough for the government of an extended territory. Madison was concerned to assert the opposite: that an extended territory such as that of the United States bodes well for the survival and stability of representative republican government precisely because, be-ing large, it embraces a healthy and mutually balancing variety of economic and social interests. It is just this plurality and variety that he believes will prevent the emergence of a co-hesive and oppressive majority. "Extend the sphere, and you take in a greater variety of parties and interests; you will make it less probable that a majority of the whole will have a com-mon motive to invade the rights of other citizens; or if such a common motive exists, it will be more difficult for all who feel it to discover their own strength, and to act in unison with each other."

In a large federal republic, Madison argued, a majority faction was less likely to be achieved than in a small one. The greater variety of parties is the greatest security "against the event of any one party being able to outnumber and oppress the rest." Thus the parties themselves are mobilized against the great danger of party. A multilateral equipoise, a suspended harmony of conflicting elements, very Newtonian in conception, is established. In Pope's words:

> Not chaos-like, together crushed and bruised
> But, as the world harmoniously confused
> Where order in variety we see,
> And where, though all things differ, all agree.

With the Madisonian formulation, thinking on the role of party had thus reached a stage of profound but sterile ambiguity. To unravel the ambiguity would require an entire additional generation of political experience.

VI

Certain aspects of the Madisonian model require comment here, since they point to difficulties unresolved either in the theory or the construction of the Constitution. Madison is not, for example, wholly clear by just what mechanisms the formation of an oppressive majority is to be prevented. It is not certain whether he is saying that in a properly balanced society under a properly balanced constitution it will be impossible for a majority to form at all, or whether he simply believes that the majority, if formed, will be too weak or too impermanent, or both, to execute its "schemes of oppression." But more important than this is the question whether Madison has left room enough in his ingenious model for the formation of a majority sufficiently effective to govern at all. If the "energetic" government he and Hamilton sought was to become a reality, it would surely carry out a number of policies of sweeping consequence for the people, policies which in most cases would be the object of doubt and dispute. How could any such policies be formed and executed, if not through the periodic formation of majority coalitions? Again, how could they be better legitimated under a republican system than by reference to the majority will? Madison himself would soon enough begin to see the cogency of these questions.

Another problem that has stimulated much comment is that Madison seems to show so little fear of minority tyranny or even of minority obstruction, both of which he dismisses in a phrase. He does not address himself to the possibility that, since majorities are to be weak and precarious, a large, aggressive minority, though incapable of taking the reins of government, might veto whatever policy it likes, and thus in effect tyrannize over the majority. There is, in short, no protection of the majority against grave deprivations imposed by the minority. (And as we shall see in due course, Madison was forced to confront this possibility near the end of his life, when he was compelled by his opposition to nullification to rephrase his view of the majority.) Neither, it must be added, does Madison address himself to the possibility that a minority interest in the population, by virtue of superior wealth, organization, and influence, can actually come into the firm possession of power against a pluralistic and divided majority. Yet with a few years after the Constitution was in operation this was precisely what the leaders of the emergent Republican party were saying about the Federalists.

Then, again, Madison's argument hardly anticipates the next step in the political game. What was he to say about the dangers of a majority coalition when his own party, the Republicans, had finally organized one? Were the Republicans a faction or party in the sense in which Madison had used that word? Were they too, then, a danger to liberty? Were they a danger to liberty when, having two of the arms of government and finding the opposition entrenched in the third, the judiciary, they tried to subordinate the third arm also? Was this a fatal invasion of the sacred principle of the separation of powers?

There is another set of problems arising from the tension between Madison's two great objectives, to create a more "energetic" national government and to protect liberty. Professor Alpheus T. Mason has remarked that *The Federalist* was a "split personality." Certainly there was a breach between Hamilton's clear and uncluttered concern for greater governmental energy and his tendency to consider that in a country like America liberty would be sure to take care of itself, and Madison's passionate desire, without sacrificing energy, to check the majority, to be sure that liberty was secured in a more certain way than had ever been done in the history of republics.

The balance of social interests, the separation and balance of powers, were meant to secure liberty, but it was still uncertain, after the instrument had been framed and ratified, whether the balance would not be too precarious to come to rest anywhere; and whether the arms of government, separated in the parchment, could come together in reality to cooperate in the formation and execution of policy. As we shall see, a mechanism had to be found, for example, by which men could put together what God, in the shape of the Constitution, had sundered—to make it possible for the President and Congress to work in harness. Both the Federalists and the Republicans had to find a solution to this—the Federalists by making Hamilton a kind of prime minister to bridge the gap, and the Republicans by having President Jefferson exert through his agents and his direct influence a great power in Congress. The framers, discussing the method of election of the President, had expressed a good deal of concern that this should not happen—that the Executive should not be in league with, or the leader of, a party. But both sides, in order to make policy, found the agency of party a practical necessity. And in the end it seems doubtful whether this Constitution, devised against party, could have been made to work if such a functional agency as the party had not sprung into the gap to remedy its chief remaining deficiencies.

At an early point, then, parties were to become a part of the machinery of government in a manner that went well beyond Madison's resigned acceptance of them as evils that would always be there. In a country which was always to be in need of the cohesive force of institutions, the national parties, for all their faults, were to become at an early hour primary and necessary parts of the machinery of government, essential vehicles to convey men's loyalties to the State under a central government that often seemed rather distant and abstract. So much so that we may say that it was the parties that rescued this Constitution-against-parties and made of it a working instrument of government. When Lord Bryce came to evaluate American government in *The American Commonwealth,* he noted: "The whole machinery, both of national and State governments, is worked by the political parties. . . . The spirit and force of party has in America been as essential to the action of the machinery of government as steam is to a locomotive engine; or, to vary the simile, party association and organization are to the organs of government almost what the motor nerves are to the muscles, sinews, and bones of the human body. They transmit the motive power, they determine the direction by which the organs act. . . . The actual working of party government is not only full of interest and instruction, but is so unlike what a student of the Federal Constitution could have expected or foreseen, that it is the thing of all others which anyone writing about America ought to try to portray."

A final word must be said about the character of Madison's pluralism. His was a pluralism *among* the parties, whereas the course of our national history has produced a pluralism *within* the parties. It was natural for Madison in 1787–88 to think of the country as having not merely a wide variety of interests but also a rather wide variety of party groupings and sub-groupings within the states. Historians will almost certainly disagree about the details, but Forrest McDonald's delineation of the various political factions existing during the Confederation may be suggestive. He found, leaving out a miscellany of very small factions, one state (Pennsylvania) with two parties, five states with two major factions, five with three or four major factions, and one (Delaware) with multiple cliques. We need not be surprised that Madison's thought had to be adapted to this existing political disorganization—thirteen states, each in its way a kind of separate political interest, and all together containing within them something like thirty discernible political groupings. What Madison did not see in advance was that the Constitution, by focusing more attention on nationwide issues, and indeed by itself first becoming a nationwide issue, would become a major force, perhaps *the* major force, in creating two great parties, and thus ironically making more probable the very majority coalition he so much feared; and, still more ironically, putting first Jefferson and then himself at the head of such a majority. What happened in due course, as it is so easy for us to see, was that our social pluralism made itself effective within each of the two major parties, a process that was strikingly evident in the Jeffersonian ranks by 1804, if not earlier. In our politics each major party has become a compound, a hodgepodge, of various and conflicting interests; and the imperatives of party struggle, the quest for victory and for offices, have forced the parties themselves to undertake the business of conciliation and compromise among such interests. This business goes on not merely in the legislative process, where Madison expected it would, but also in the internal processes of the great political parties themselves.

Madison's pluralism, then, had substantial merits as a generalized model, but as to the parties it was mislocated. Envisaging political parties as limited, homogeneous, fiercely aggressive, special interests, he failed to see that the parties themselves might become great, bland, enveloping coalitions, eschewing the assertion of firm principles and ideologies, embracing and muffling the struggles of special interests; or that they might forge the coalitions of majorities that are in fact necessary to effective government into forces sufficiently benign to avoid tyranny and sufficiently vulnerable to be displaced in time by the opposing coalition. Liberty, he had always understood, would sustain a political atmosphere in which a conflict of parties would take place. The reverse of that proposition, the insight that underlies our acceptance of the two-party system, that the conflict of parties can be made to reinforce rather than undermine liberty, was to be well understood only in the future.

INTRODUCTORY NOTE

The first American party system was perhaps less a party system than an experimental bridge between the previous no-party era and the evolution of the first modern party system in the world, centering around the dominant figure of Andrew Jackson. The squaring off of Whigs against Democrats followed a curious prelude, wherein the new nation came perilously close to shattering over sectional antagonism in 1814, then quickly fell into a decade of nonpartisan entropy that has been euphemistically labeled "The Era of Good Feelings." But when Jackson was denied the presidency by what his partisans called the "corrupt bargain" between John Quincy Adams and Henry Clay in 1824, the second American party system was launched.

Andrew Jackson is a curiously contradictory figure. A rags-to-riches Tennessee frontiersman who routed the Indians and slaughtered the British at New Orleans, Old Hickory, as President, is most dramatically remembered for crushing South Carolina's attempt at nullification in 1832. But in his first presidential address to Congress, on December 8, 1829 (part of which is reprinted here), Jackson enunciated the classical liberalism of his Madisonian faith, one that centered on Lord Acton's dictum that power corrupts—as it had allegedly corrupted Adams and Clay in 1824. From this remarkably candid message, and from Jackson's largely negative presidential record of extensive use of the veto power, his frequent removals from office, his attack upon the Second Bank of the United States, and his denial of the propriety of federal participation in internal improvements, the historian John William Ward has concluded that "Jackson's solution to the paradox of politics, the corruption of the selfless will of the people by the power necessary to enact that will, was no less than to dismiss the need for power in politics at all."[1]

[1]John William Ward, "Andrew Jackson: The Majority is to Govern," in Daniel J. Boorstin, ed., *An American Primer*, Chicago: The University of Chicago Press, 1966, p. 274.

First Presidential Address to Congress

ANDREW JACKSON

Fellow Citizens of the Senate, and
House of Representatives:

It affords me pleasure to tender my friendly greetings to you on the occasion of your assembling at the Seat of Government, to enter upon the important duties to which you have been called by the voice of our countrymen. The task devolves on me, under a provision of the Constitution, to present to you, as the Federal Legislature of twenty-four sovereign States, and twelve millions of happy people, a view of our affairs; and to propose such measures as, in the discharge of my official functions, have suggested themselves as necessary to promote the objects of our Union.

In communicating with you for the first time, it is, to me, a source of unfeigned satisfaction, calling for mutual gratulation and devout thanks to a benign Providence, that we are at peace with all mankind; and that our country exhibits the most cheering evidence of general welfare and progressive improvement. Turning our eyes to other nations, our great desire is to see our brethren of the human race secured in the blessings enjoyed by ourselves, and advancing in knowledge, in freedom, and in social happiness.

Our foreign relations, although in their general character pacific and friendly, present subjects of difference between us and other Powers, of deep interest, as well to the country at large as to many of our citizens. To effect an adjustment of these shall continue to be the object of my earnest endeavors; and notwithstanding the difficulties of the task, I do not allow myself to apprehend unfavorable results. Blessed as our country is with every thing which constitutes national strength, she is fully adequate to the maintenance of all her interests. In discharging the responsible trust confided to the Executive in this respect, it is my settled purpose to ask nothing that is not clearly right, and to submit to nothing that is wrong; and I flatter myself, that, supported by the other branches of the Government, and by the intelligence and patriotism of the People, we shall be able, under the protection of Providence, to cause all our just rights to be respected. . . .

I consider it one of the most urgent of my duties to bring to your attention the propriety of amending that part of our Constitution which relates to the election of President and Vice President. Our system of government was, by its framers, deemed an experiment; and they, therefore, consistently provided a mode of remedying its defects.

To the People belongs the right of electing their Chief Magistrate: it was never designed that their choice should, in any case, be defeated, either by the intervention of electoral colleges, or by the agency confided, under certain contingencies, to the House of Representatives. Experience proves, that, in proportion as agents to execute the will of the People are multiplied, there is danger of their wishes being frustrated. Some may be unfaithful: all are liable to err. So far, therefore, as the People can, with convenience, speak, it is safer for them to express their own will.

The number of aspirants to the Presidency, and the diversity of the interests which may influence their claims, leave little reason to expect a choice in the first instance: and, in that event, the election must devolve on the House of Representatives, where, it is obvious, the will of the People may not be always ascertained; or, if ascertained, may not be regarded. From the mode of voting by States, the choice is to be made by twenty-four votes; and it may often occur, that one of these will be controlled by an individual representative. Honors and offices are at the disposal of the successful candidate. Repeated ballotings may make it apparent that a single individual holds the cast in his hand. May he not be tempted to name his reward? But even without corruption—supposing the probity of the Representatives to be proof against the powerful motives by which it may be assailed—the will of the People is still constantly liable to be misrepresented. One may err from ignorance of the wishes of his constituents; another, from a conviction that it is his duty to be governed by his own judgment of the fitness of the candidates: finally, although all were inflexibly honest—all accurately informed of the wishes of their constituents—yet, under the present mode of election, a minority may often elect the President; and when this happens, it may reasonably be expected that efforts will be made on the part of the majority to rectify this injurious operation of their institutions. But although no evil of this character should result from such a perversion of the first principle of our system—*that the majority is to govern*—it must be very certain that a President elected by a minority cannot enjoy the confidence necessary to the successful discharge of his duties.

In this, as in all other matters of public concern, policy requires that as few impediments as possible should exist to the free operation of the public will. Let us, then, endeavor so to amend our system, that the office of Chief Magistrate may not be conferred upon any citizen but in pursuance of a fair expression of the will of the majority.

I would therefore recommend such an amendment of the Constitution as may remove all intermediate agency in the election of President and Vice President. The mode may be so regulated as to preserve to each State its present relative weight in the election; and a failure in the first attempt may be provided for, by confining the second to a choice between the two highest candidates. In connexion with such an amendment, it would seem advisable to limit the service of the Chief Magistrate to a single term, of either four or six years. If, however, it should not be adopted, it is worthy of consideration whether a provision disqualifying for office the Representatives in Congress on whom such an election may have devolved, would not be proper.

While members of Congress can be constitutionally appointed to offices of trust and profit, it will be the practice, even under the most conscientious adherence to duty, to select them for such stations as they are believed to be better qualified to fill than other citizens; but the purity of our Government would doubtless be promoted, by their exclusion from all appointments in the gift of the President in whose election they may have been officially concerned. The nature of the judicial office, and the necessity of securing in the Cabinet and in diplomatic stations of the highest rank, the best talents and political experience, should, perhaps, except these from the exclusion.

There are perhaps few men who can for any great length of time enjoy office and power, without being more or less under the influence of feelings unfavorable to the faithful discharge of their public duties. Their integrity may be proof against improper considerations immediately addressed to themselves; but they are apt to acquire a habit of looking with indifference upon the public interests, and of tolerating conduct from which an unpractised man would revolt. Office is considered as a species of property; and Government, rather as a means of promoting individual interests, than as an instrument created solely for the service of the People. Corruption in some, and, in others, a perversion of correct feelings and principles, divert Government from its legitimate ends, and make it an engine for the support of the few at the expense of the many. The duties of all public officers are, or, at least, admit of being made, so plain and simple, that men of intelligence may readily qualify themselves for their performance; and I cannot but believe that more is lost by the long continuance of men in office, than is generally to be gained by their experience. I submit therefore to your consideration, whether the efficiency of the Government would not be promoted, and official industry and integrity better secured, by a general extension of the law which limits appointments to four years.

In a country where offices are created solely for the benefit of the People, no one man has any more intrinsic right to official station than another. Offices were not established to give support to particular men, at the public expense. No individual wrong is therefore done by removal, since neither appointment to, nor continuance in, office, is a matter of right. The incumbent became an officer with a view to public benefits; and when these require his removal, they are not to be sacrificed to private interests. It is the People, and they alone, who have a right to complain, when a bad officer is substituted for a good one. He who is removed has the same means of obtaining a living, that are enjoyed by the millions who never held office. The proposed limitation would destroy the idea of property, now so generally connected with official station; and although individual distress may be sometimes produced, it would, by promoting that rotation which constitutes a leading principle in the republican creed, give healthful action to the system.

No very considerable change has occurred, during the recess of Congress, in the condition of either our Agriculture, Commerce, or Manufactures. . . .

. . . To regulate its conduct, so as to promote equally the

prosperity of these three cardinal interests, is one of the most difficult tasks of Government; and it may be regretted that the complicated restrictions which now embarass the intercourse of nations, could not by common consent be abolished; and commerce allowed to flow in those channels to which individual enterprise—always its surest guide—might direct it. . . . Frequent legislation in regard to any branch of industry, affecting its value, and by which its capital may be transferred to new channels, must always be productive of hazardous speculation and loss.

In deliberating, therefore, on these interesting subjects, local feelings and prejudices should be merged in the patriotic determination to promote the great interests of the whole. All attempts to connect them with the party conflicts of the day are necessarily injurious, and should be discountenanced. Our action upon them should be under the control of higher and purer motives. Legislation, subjected to such influences, can never be just; and will not long retain the sanction of a People, whose active patriotism is not bounded by sectional limits, nor insensible to that spirit of concession and forbearance, which gave life to our political compact, and still sustains it. Discarding all calculations of political ascendancy, the North, the South, the East, and the West, should unite in diminishing any burthen, of which either may justly complain.

The agricultural interest of our country is so essentially connected with every other, and so superior in importance to them all, that it is scarcely necessary to invite to it your particular attention. It is principally as manufactures and commerce tend to increase the value of agricultural productions, and to extend their application to the wants and comforts of society, that they deserve the fostering care of Government. . . .

[The] state of the finances exhibits the resources of the nation in an aspect highly flattering to its industry; and auspicious of the ability of Government, in a very short time, to extinguish the public debt. When this shall be done, our population will be relieved from a considerable portion of its present burthens; and will find, not only new motives to patriotic affection, but additional means for the display of individual enterprise. The fiscal power of the States will also be increased; and may be more extensively exerted in favor of education and other public objects: while ample means will remain in the

Federal Government to promote the general weal, in all the modes permitted to its authority.

After the extinction of the public debt, it is not probable that any adjustment of the tariff, upon principles satisfactory to the People of the Union, will, until a remote period, if ever, leave the Government without a considerable surplus in the Treasury, beyond what may be required for its current service. As then the period approaches when the application of the revenue to the payment of debt will cease, the disposition of the surplus will present a subject for the serious deliberation of Congress; and it may be fortunate for the country that it is yet to be decided. . . .

. . . It appears to me that the most safe, just, and federal disposition which could be made of the surplus revenue, would be its apportionment among the several States according to their ratio of representation; and should this measure not be found warranted by the Constitution, that it would be expedient to propose to the States an amendment authorizing it. I regard an appeal to the source of power, in cases of real doubt, and where its exercise is deemed indispensable to the general welfare, as among the most sacred of all our obligations. Upon this country, more than any other, has, in the providence of God, been cast the special guardianship of the great principle of adherence to written constitutions. If it fail here, all hope in regard to it will be extinguished. That this was intended to be a Government of limited and specific, and not general powers, must be admitted by all; and it is our duty to preserve for it the character intended by its framers. If experience points out the necessity for an enlargement of these powers, let us apply for it to those for whose benefit it is to be exercised; and not undermine the whole system by a resort to overstrained constructions. The scheme has worked well. It has exceeded the hopes of those who devised it, and become an object of admiration to the world. We are responsible to our country, and to the glorious cause of self-government, for the preservation of so great a good. The great mass of legislation relating to our internal affairs, was intended to be left where the Federal Convention found it—in the State Governments. Nothing is clearer, in my view, than that we are chiefly indebted for the success of the Constitution under which we are now acting, to the watchful and auxiliary operation of the State authorities. This is not the reflection of a day, but belongs to the most deeply rooted convictions of my mind. I cannot, therefore, too strongly or too earnestly, for my own sense of its importance, warn you against all encroachments upon the legitimate sphere of State sovereignty. Sustained by its healthful and invigorating influence, the Federal system can never fall. . . .

. . . I would suggest, also, an inquiry, whether the provisions of the act of Congress, authorizing the discharge of the persons of debtors to the Government, from imprisonment, may not, consistently with the public interest, be extended to the release of the debt, where the conduct of the debtor is wholly exempt from the imputation of fraud. Some more liberal policy than that which now prevails, in reference to this unfortunate class of citizens, is certainly due to them, and would prove beneficial to the country. The continuance of the liability, after the means to discharge it have been exhausted, can only serve to dispirit the debtor; or, where his resources are but partial, the want of power in the Government to compromise and release the demand, instigates to fraud, as the only resource for securing a support to his family. He thus sinks into a state of apathy, and becomes a useless drone in society, or a vicious member of it, if not a feeling witness of the rigor and inhumanity of his country. All experience proves, that oppressive debt is the bane of enterprise; and it should be the care of a Republic not to exert a grinding power over misfortune and poverty. . . .

The condition and ulterior destiny of the Indian Tribes within the limits of some of our States, have become objects of much interest and importance. It has long been the policy of Government to introduce among them the arts of civilization, in the hope of gradually reclaiming them from a wandering life. This policy has, however, been coupled with another, wholly incompatible with its success. Professing a desire to civilize and settle them, we have, at the same time, lost no opportunity to purchase their lands, and thrust them further into the wilderness. By this means they have not only been kept in a wandering state, but been led to look upon us as unjust and indifferent to their fate. Thus, though lavish in its expenditures upon the subject, Government has constantly defeated its own policy; and the Indians, in general, receding further and further to the West, have retained their savage habits. A portion, however, of the Southern tribes, having mingled much with the whites, and made some progress in the arts of civilized life, have lately attempted to erect an independent government, within the limits of Georgia and Alabama. These States, claiming to be the only Sovereigns within their territories, extended their laws over the Indians; which induced the latter to call upon the United States for protection.

Under these circumstances, the question presented was, whether the General Government had a right to sustain those people in their pretensions? The Constitution declares, that "no new State shall be formed or erected within the jurisdiction of any other State," without the consent of its legislature. If the General Government is not permitted to tolerate the erection of a confederate State within the territory of one of the members of this Union, against her consent; much less could it allow a foreign and independent government to establish itself there. Georgia became a member of the Confederacy which eventuated in our Federal Union, as a sovereign State, always asserting her claim to certain limits; which having been originally defined in her colonial charter, and subsequently recognised in the treaty of peace, she has ever since continued to enjoy, except as they have been circumscribed by her own voluntary transfer of a portion of her territory to the United States, in the articles of cession of 1802. Alabama was admitted into the Union on the same footing with the original States, with boundaries which were prescribed by Congress. There is no constitutional, conventional, or legal provision, which allows them less power over the Indians within their borders, than is possessed by Maine or New York. Would the People of Maine permit the Penobscot tribe to erect an Independent Government within their State? and unless they did, would it not be the duty of the General Government to support them in resisting such a measure? Would the People of New York permit each remnant of the Six Nations within her borders, to declare itself an independent people under the protection of the United States? Could the Indians establish a separate republic on each of their reservations in Ohio? and if they were so disposed, would it be the duty of this Government to protect them in the attempt? If the principle involved in the obvious answer to these questions be abandoned, it will follow that the objects of this Government are reversed; and that it has become a part of its duty to aid in destroying the States which it was established to protect.

Actuated by this view of the subject, I informed the Indians inhabiting parts of Georgia and Alabama, that their attempt to establish an independent government would not be countenanced by the Eexcutive of the United States; and advised them to emigrate beyond the Mississippi, or submit to the laws of those States.

Our conduct towards these people is deeply interesting to our national character. Their present condition, contrasted with what they once were, makes a most powerful appeal to our sympathies. Our ancestors found them the uncontrolled possessors of these vast regions. By persuasion and force, they have been made to retire from river to river, and from mountain to mountain; until some of the tribes have become extinct, and others have left but remnants, to preserve, for a while, their once terrible names. Surrounded by the whites, with their arts of civilization, which, by destroying the resources of the savage, doom him to weakness and decay; the fate of the Mohegan, the Narragansett, and the Delaware, is fast overtaking the Choctaw, the Cherokee, and the Creek. That this fate surely awaits them, if they remain within the limits of the States, does not admit of a doubt. Humanity and national honor demand that every effort should be made to avert so great a calamity. It is too late to inquire whether it was just in the United States to include them and their territory within the bounds of new States whose limits they could control. That step cannot be retraced. A State cannot be dismembered by Congress, or restricted in the exercise of her constitutional power. But the people of those States, and of every State, actuated by feelings of justice and a regard for our national honor, submit to you the interesting question, whether something cannot be done, consistently with the rights of the States, to preserve this much injured race?

As a means of effecting this end, I suggest, for your consideration, the propriety of setting apart an ample district West of the Mississippi, and without the limits of any State or Territory, now formed, to be guarantied to the Indian tribes, as long as they shall occupy it: each tribe having a distinct control over the portion designated for its use. There they may be secured in the enjoyment of governments of their own choice, subject to no other control from the United States than such as may be necessary to preserve peace on the frontier, and between the several tribes. There the benevolent may endeavor to teach them the arts of civilization; and, by promoting union and harmony among them, to raise up an interesting commonwealth, destined to perpetuate the race, and to attest the humanity and justice of this Government.

This emigration should be voluntary: for it would be as cruel as unjust to compel the aborigines to abandon the graves of their fathers, and seek a home in a distant land. But they should be distinctly informed that, if they remain within the limits of the States, they must be subject to their laws. In return for their obedience, as individuals, they will, without doubt, be protected in the enjoyment of those possessions which they have improved by their industry. But it seems to me visionary to suppose, that, in this state of things, claims can be allowed on tracts of country on which they have neither dwelt nor made improvements, merely because they have seen them from the mountain, or passed them in the chace. Submitting to the laws of the States, and receiving, like other citizens, protection in their persons and property, they will, ere long, become merged in the mass of our population. . . .

I now commend you, fellow-citizens, to the guidance of Almighty God, with a full reliance on his merciful providence for the maintenance of our free institutions; and with an earnest supplication, that, whatever errors it may be my lot to commit, in discharging the arduous duties which have devolved on me, will find a remedy in the harmony and wisdom of your counsels.

PART III

The Civil War and Reconstruction

The two-party system that evolved during the Jacksonian era was truly a wondrous creation, primarily because it was a *national* party system in which the democratic commitment to white manhood suffrage drove voter turnout in presidential elections from only 27 percent of the eligible electorate in 1824 to an average of 77 percent in the three heated elections of the 1840s. Moreover, the division of the two-party vote was consistently close, with the winners' margin during the 1840s averaging a modest 4 percent, in comparison to the 16 percent average margin for the two presidential elections of the 1830s. By the 1840s, the Whigs had learned both to accept and exploit the new mass base of political life, as the popular victories of Harrison in 1840 and Taylor in 1848 suggest.

But the very success of the second party system illustrated a fundamental dilemma, one that was to destroy the system on the eve of the Civil War. Critics of the American two-party system have long complained that despite the exaggerated campaign rhetoric, the parties were basically so similar in their constituencies and programs that the electoral choice involved only a contest between Tweedledum and Tweedledee—as compared with European party politics, which customarily pitted parties of the left against parties of the right; peasants and workers against gentry and aristocrats; socialists against tories; and communists against fascists. This fundamental division illustrates an abiding dilemma of democratic party systems. If, on the one hand, the parties become so aligned as to reflect crucial ideological, class, social, racial/ethnic, or sectional cleavages—as has been the European tendency—then the parties achieve great internal cohesiveness at the expense of disruptive strains on the political system as a whole, particularly at the level of government. If, on the other hand, each party is expected internally to mediate these conflicting interests by aggregating the broad spectrum of their competing claims—as has been the American tendency—the strains become disruptive of party itself. The transition from the second to the third American party system represents a transition from (or disintegration of) a broad-based two-party competition of the latter type into a multiparty donnybrook of the former type, and the result was electoral chaos and civil war. Part III examines the complex forces that shattered the second party system; the role of party competition as an independent variable in determining the outcome of the Civil War; the tortured evolution during the war of a commitment to the nationwide abolition of slavery; and the tragic failure of the Reconstruction in attempting to forge a new system of race relations that would extend beyond mere manumission.

INTRODUCTORY NOTE

Historians have argued endlessly about the causes of the Civil War, about whether it was an irrepressible conflict brought on by ineluctable historical forces or a repressible conflict caused by extremist propaganda and blundering politicians; about whether it was a second American revolution that replaced an agrarian with an industrial civilization. These disputes are important and revealing, but they often hinge upon what are ultimately unprovable philosophical assumptions about the nature of causation itself, or upon unanswerable hypothetical questions, such as what if the South had won, or what if Lincoln had not been assassinated.[1]

But we know that the Union shattered in 1861, and that during the preceding decade the fundamental ties of Union—whether attitudinal, as in conflicting nationalisms, or institutional, as in religious denominations—educational and economic institutions, the military, and ultimately government itself, all snapped under the increasing strains. In the following selection David M. Potter analyzes the collapse of the second party system under the extreme pressures of political, constitutional, and emotional polarization. The immediate background is the passage of the Kansas-Nebraska Act, which repealed the Missouri Compromise's ban on the introduction of slavery into the two territories. The first disastrous consequence was an outbreak of savage border warfare in Kansas, where rival pro- and antislavery factions warred for control of the government. The selection begins with Potter's discussion of the second consequence, the destruction of the second party system. The selection omits discussion of the events that transpired between Lincoln's election on November 6, 1860 and the Confederate firing on Fort Sumter on April 12, 1861, and it concludes with Potter's brilliantly concise analysis, "The Basic Issues Confounded."

[1]See generally Kenneth M. Stampp, ed., *The Causes of the Civil War,* Englewood Cliffs, N.J.: Prentice-Hall, 1959; Thomas J. Pressly, ed., *Americans Interpret Their Civil War,* Princeton, N.J.: Princeton University Press, 1954; and Roy Franklin Nichols, *The Disruption of the American Democracy,* New York: MacMillan, 1948.

Steps Toward Separation: Political, Constitutional, and Emotional Polarization

DAVID M. POTTER

THE CONSEQUENCE OF KANSAS-NEBRASKA: POLITICAL POLARIZATION

The second disastrous consequence of Kansas-Nebraska was the effect which it had on the system of political parties in the United States. At the time of Pierce's election there were two parties, both of which might be called national, in the sense that each had a strong northern wing and a strong southern wing, each wing dependent on the other to give it strength. In presidential elections, the winner, whether Whig or Democrat, usually won both in the North and in the South. This situation had an immensely moderating influence on sectional extremism in either party, for each wing needed allies in the other section to win against adversaries in its own section who belonged to the opposite party. In 1852 this delicate sectional balance began to weaken, and with the Kansas-Nebraska Act it almost collapsed.

THE WHIGS AND IMMIGRATION. The breakdown of the Whig party began visibly with the deep split in 1852 between the southern supporters of Fillmore and the northern supporters of Scott, who fought each other for forty-two ballots. The disastrous defeat of Scott, who carried only four states, caused northern Whigs to blame southern Whigs for saddling Scott with a platform which endorsed the compromise and thus made victory impossible in the North. Southern Whigs blamed northern Whigs for forcing the party to nominate Scott and then failing to carry any free states except Vermont and Massachusetts for him.

Further, the entire party was under a deep pall of gloom, because the stream of immigration was steadily increasing, and the mostly Irish Catholic immigrants affiliated overwhelmingly with the Democrats. Just why the Democratic party won the support of such a large proportion of the immigrants cannot be told with certainty. Probably, at the outset the Whigs, who were concentrated most heavily in New England, had a stronger Puritan tone than the Democrats. Puritanism was traditionally hostile to Catholicism; the Irish immigrants sensed this hostility among the Whigs and gravitated toward the Democrats. The Whigs, then, seeing that the immigrants were the allies of their political antagonists, began to demand laws unfavorable to immigrants, such as statutes requiring many years of residence before voting. The process then became cumulative: the more the immigrants became Democrats, the more the Whigs opposed them; and the more the Whigs opposed them, the more they became Democrats. By 1852 some Whigs had reached the conclusion that all Irishmen were Democrats, which was not far from the truth. This was a grim conclusion to reach because the stream of immigration was a flood in 1851.

As late as 1842, total immigration had never reached 100,-000 in a single year, but in the 1840's—the "hungry forties" as they have been called—Ireland experienced almost total failures of her potato crops, followed by acute famine and widespread starvation. Immense numbers emigrated—more to the United States than anywhere else. Three times in the four years between 1851 and 1855, total immigration to the United States exceeded 400,000. Later, in the decades around the turn of the century, the United States had considerably greater total immigration, but it never had so high a proportion of immigrants to the resident population, nor half so high a proportion from one country. In a decade when the population, excluding slaves, was 27 million, more than 1,200,000 immigrants arrived from Ireland. Total immigration in the four years preceding Winfield Scott's defeat in 1852 exceeded the total of Scott's popular vote.

After 1852 most Whigs felt that Whiggery was a losing proposition. Each sectional wing felt that its alliance with the other sectional wing—North or South as the case might be—cost more locally than it was worth nationally; and all recognized that continued immigration would be fatal to a party which failed to attract the immigrants and was rejected by them. Some wanted to fight the immigrants openly; some wanted to bail out of a party that had hopelessly antagonized them. All

were ready for new allies. But they were still a bisectional party
—Scott had carried 43 percent of the vote in the free states and
44 percent in the slave states. And they had no one to ally with.
The victorious Democrats certainly wanted no affiliation with
them.

Kansas-Nebraska offered the northern Whigs a way out,
for it bitterly antagonized northern antislavery Democrats. The
intensity of this opposition was shown by the losses sustained
by northern Democrats because of Kansas-Nebraska, which the
southern Democrats supported 57 to 2 in the House of Representatives. At the time of the vote northern Democrats held
ninety-one seats; after the storm of opposition that swept the
North in 1854, only twenty-five free state Democratic Congressmen survived after the November elections.

NEW ALIGNMENTS. As the antislavery Democrats swarmed out
of the Democratic party, the northern Whigs recognized the
potential allies whom they so badly needed. But they knew the
Whig label, already a liability, would be an obstacle to alliance.
Hence they abandoned the Whig organization, and in the elections of 1854 and 1855, an astonishing array of new parties appeared, varying from state to state.

Besides the old names, there were such new names as
Anti-Nebraskaites, Peoples Party, Republican Party, Temperance
Party, Rum Democrats, Hard Shell Democrats, Soft Shell Demo-
crats, Half Shells, Know Nothings, and Know Somethings.

THE KNOW NOTHINGS AND THE REPUBLICANS. In all this medley,
two focal points began to emerge. Antislavery sentiment began
to concentrate in the Republican party: anti-immigrant sentiment concentrated in a nativist organization that was partly a
political party and partly a secret society; the Order of the Star
Spangled Banner, whose members were called Know Nothings,
because they were pledged to say, "I know nothing," if questioned about the society's secrets.

If the Know Nothings had been strictly a political party
they would, of course, have consistently competed with other
parties, including the Republican, and every political candidate
or officeholder could have been classified as a Republican, a
Know Nothing, or as the member of some party. But since the
Know Nothings were partly a secret order, it was possible for

a person to be both a Know Nothing and a Republican. Not only was it possible, but in the Congress elected in 1854, a majority of the free state members were both Know Nothings and Republicans. There were almost enough to form a majority of the House. On one flank were twenty-odd Know Nothings who were not Republicans, and on the other twenty-odd Republicans who were not Know Nothings.

Historians since then have not recognized this curious dualism, perhaps in part because it was a complex and unconventional situation, perhaps even more because the tradition of antislavery is an honored one and the tradition of nativism is despised. Historians have been at a loss to deal with a situation where men who opposed the oppression of Negroes at the same time were ready to discriminate against Catholics and immigrants. They have been reluctant to see that there was even a certain affinity between the psychology of many of the abolitionists and many of the nativists. Both had a paranoid tendency to suspect an evil conspiracy against the republic, by the "slave power," or by the popish church. In an age when sexual inhibition prevented the expression of a direct interest in sex, both abolitionists and Know Nothings rationalized that they were exposing "moral evil" to justify an indulgence in fantasies about the sexual depravities practiced by priests with nuns or by southern planters with beautiful quadroon slave girls. To recognize this fact is not to deny that there was certainly sex exploitation in slavery; it is only to say that the injustice of this exploitation was not the only reason why antislavery men took such an excited interest in it. At any rate, regardless of any psychological kinship between antislavery and nativism, or of the profound philosophical differences between them, the fact is that a great number of people were sympathetic both to antislavery and to a nativism which was directed especially against Irish Catholic immigrants. Nativism was so strong that many observers expected the Know Nothings rather than the Republicans to become the second party in the two-party system and to win the election of 1856.

THE REPUBLICANS WIN OUT. The Republicans, of course, became the major party instead, and the Know Nothings faded away. The fact that the slavery question thus, in the long run, was uppermost, suggests that more people cared more deeply about it. But it must be added that in 1855 and 1856 the Republicans used some very adroit and even unethical tactics to gain the upper hand. First, in choosing a Speaker for the House of Representatives which was elected in 1854, they knew that they would have to accept someone who was both a Know Nothing and a Republican, as were a majority of the members, but they planned to bring about the election of a candidate whose nativism was secondary and whose commitment to antislavery was primary. For this purpose they chose Nathaniel P. Banks of Massachusetts. After inducing the Know Nothings to delay choosing a nominee for the Speakership, they moved to make Banks a nominee and manipulated the situation so that the candidate favored primarily by the Know Nothings was set aside. So, after a fierce struggle against the Democrats, Banks won the Speakership.

Later the Republicas completed their maneuver in the presidential campaign of 1856. They faced a dilemma because the Know Nothings had scheduled a nominating convention to precede the Republican convention. If the Know Nothings nominated first, the Republicans would either have to accept the Know Nothing nominee, which would make them appear disadvantageously to be junior partners in an alliance dominated by nativists, or they would have to choose a different nominee, which would split the anti-Democratic vote and almost assure a Democratic victory. They escaped this dilemma neatly by arranging for Banks to be nominated by the Know Nothings, for him to double-cross them by delaying his acceptance until the Republicans had made a nomination, and then for him to decline the Know Nothing nomination. This would force the Know Nothings to accept the Republican nominee or to make another nomination which would split the anti-Democratic vote. In short, with Banks playing a double game, they turned the tables completely on the Know Nothings and chose John C. Fremont, who was not a Know Nothing at all but who was reluctantly accepted by a majority in the Know Nothing convention. Thus the Republicans went into the election with the advantage of receiving Know Nothing votes, but without the stigma of being a nativist party. The details of this maneuver may seem excessive in a general history such as this one, but in fact it was a critical transformation point in the histroy of American politcal parties. It meant that Republicans rather than Know Nothings replaced Whigs as the second major party in a two-party system which has never had more than a temporary place for third parties. It meant also that the Republican party received a nativist infusion which has continued to make itself felt for more than a century, for the Democratic party has consistently had a disproportionate share of supporters who were Catholic in religion and of immigrant stock, while the Republican party supporters have been disproportionately Protestant and of British stock. Yet the Republican party has avoided any explicit or complete identification with nativism.

THE ELECTION OF 1856. In 1856 the Democrats nominated James Buchanan, with forty years of public service in the Cabinet, the Congress, and the diplomatic corps, to run against Fremont, with no public service except as an explorer of the Rocky Mountains and the Far West. The southern branch of the Know Nothing party nominated Millard Fillmore, and those who still clung to the Whig Party nominated Fillmore also.

The election almost resolved itself into two contests, with Buchanan running against Fillmore in the slave states and against Fremont in the free states. Buchanan won by carrying every slave state except Maryland (won by Fillmore) and five free states—Pennsylvania, New Jersey, Illinois, Indiana, and California. But Buchanan lost eleven free states to Fremont— all of the New England states, New York, Ohio, Michigan, Wisconsin, and Iowa.

What had happened was that, in place of two national political parties with bisectional wings and national strength, there were now two parties which were polarizing very heavily to become strictly sectional. The Democratic party drew two thirds of its strength from the slave states and in the House of Representatives, the southern Democrats usually outnumbered the northern Democrats by two to one (58 to 25 in 1854; 75 to 53 in 1856; and 68 to 34 in 1858). This meant that Southerners controlled the party caucus, the committee chairmanships, and the Congressional leadership. The Democratic party became and remained until Franklin Roosevelt's New Deal a southern party with a northern annex. Meanwhile, the Republican party became a northern party with no pretense of even an annex in the South. Fremont in 1856 and Lincoln in 1860 were not

even on the ticket in most of the southern states and received
few popular votes from that part of the Union. The Republicans
went for decades with almost no strength in the South and did
not win an electoral plurality there until Richard Nixon did so
in 1968. After Kansas-Nebraska the major political parties were
no longer a significant cohesive force with strong bisectional
strength. It was only Buchanan's success in carrying five
northern states which kept up the illusion that there was a
national party, and that illusion evaporated in 1860.

THE DRED SCOTT CASE: CONSTITUTIONAL POLARIZATION

THE POPULAR SOVEREIGNTY DOCTRINE. By the end of 1856, the
Missouri Compromise had been repealed, the strife in Kansas
had set a pattern of armed conflict, and the two major political
parties were heavily sectionalized. Moreover such events as the
publication in 1852 of *Uncle Tom's Cabin*, the classic fictional
indictment of slavery by Harriet Beecher Stowe; the assault
upon Senator Sumner; and the activities of abolitionists in
aiding fugitives and nullifying the Fugitive Slave Act all added
to the hostile feelings between the sections. At this stage of
acute sectional friction, much of the moderate ground had been
eroded away, and perhaps the only remaining hope of sectional
harmony was the "popular sovereignty" doctrine of Stephen A.
Douglas. Popular sovereignty had failed in Kansas, but perhaps
that was largely because one faction had been permitted to steal
a territorial election. If popular sovereignty were honestly administered, Douglas contended, it would localize the slavery
question, leave it to a democratic solution by those immediately
involved, and get it out of Congress. As late as the inauguration
of James Buchanan, this still seemed possible, though not likely.

Two days after Buchanan became President, however, the
Supreme Court handed down a decision in the case of a slave,
Dred Scott, which effectively killed the possibility of applying
popular sovereignty in the territories, and thus eroded away
almost all that was left of the ground on which moderates
might make a stand.

Popular sovereignty, as Douglas interpreted it, meant the
right of a territorial legislature to admit slavery to or exclude
it from a territory. But, as previously mentioned, from the time

when popular sovereignty was first proposed, southern leaders
had denied that Congress possessed power under the Constitution, either to exclude slavery from a territory (as in the Missouri Compromise north of 36°30′) or to give to a territorial
legislature, which was created by Act of Congress, power which
Congress itself did not have. According to the southern argument, the territories belonged not to the United States as one
sole owner but to all the states as joint owners, so a citizen of
any state had the right to carry property which was legal within
his own state (meaning slaves legally held as chattels in the
slave states) into a territory. Any act which denied this right,
so the southern argument ran, was unconstitutional. This argument is, to say the least, questionable, for the Constitution clearly
states: "The Congress shall have power to dispose of and make
all needful Rules and Regulations respecting the Territory or
other Property belonging to the United States." This clause
certainly lends itself to the interpretation that Congress might
itself exercise power over slavery or might delegate such power
to a territorial legislature. But since many Southerners denied
this power, political leaders had been hoping ever since 1848
for a judicial decision to settle the question. Congress had even
passed legislation which would make it easier to get a case
before the courts, but this proved unexpectedly difficult. The
courts could not decide until a concrete case arose, and no case
came to them from among the few dozens of slaves who had
been carried to New Mexico or Utah or Kansas.

THE SUPREME COURT RULING. The case which finally enabled
the Supreme Court to deal with the question concerned a slave,
Dred Scott, who had been taken from the slave state of Missouri
into the free territory of Minnesota more than twenty years
earlier and then about two years later had been taken back to
Missouri. Some eight years after his return to Missouri he
brought a suit in the Missouri courts, claiming his freedom on
the ground that his residence in Minnesota Territory had made
him a free man, since the territory was part of the Louisiana
Purchase north of 36°30′, from which Congress had barred
slavery by the Missouri Compromise. The case moved through
a contradictory series of rulings in the lower courts and was at
last appealed to the Supreme Court, where it was argued twice.

Finally, in March 1857, the Court handed down a ruling. All nine justices wrote opinions, and several points were left in confusion by this multiplicity of judgments.

One thing was clear: a majority of justices held that Scott was still a slave, but the ruling was badly confused by the curious relationship between two questions which the Court had before it: first, did the federal courts have jurisdiction—was this a case which properly came before the Supreme Court? And second, if they did have jurisdiction, how valid was Scott's claim that the Act of 1820 had made him a free man by making Minnesota a free territory? Superficially it would appear that the Court had no reason to consider the second question unless it decided affirmatively on the first. On the first question, Scott's lawyers argued that the case came before the federal courts because cases involving citizens of different states may be heard in the federal courts. Scott was from Missouri, and his owner at the time of the litigation lived in New York. Here was certainly a diversity of states, but it was not diversity of citizenship unless Scott was a citizen. Well, was Scott a citizen? The justices said he was not, *partly* (a) because a person could not acquire citizenship except by birth or by naturalization, and Scott, born a slave, had not acquired it in either way; and *partly* (b) because he was not even free—Congress had no constitutional power to exclude slavery from a territory. Minnesota Territory was therefore not a free territory, and no slave could acquire freedom by living there; if Scott was not free, he was certainly not a citizen and not in a position to claim diverse citizenship.

THE QUESTIONS BEFORE THE COURT. Now having decided that Scott was not a citizen and that jurisdiction was therefore lacking, the Court had no reason to rule on Scott's suit against the man who claimed to own him. But Chief Justice Roger B. Taney (pronounced Tawney) nevertheless went on to say that even if Scott could bring his case, he still could not win his freedom because the Act of 1820, on which he relied for his freedom, was unconstitutional. In saying that his plea was not valid, the Court was answering a question which it had ruled that Scott had no standing to ask—a question which really did not arise. Such comments by courts on questions not legally before them are not law but are just comments made in passing (*obiter dicta* in the terminology of lawyers). Antislavery men, obsessively eager to avoid recognizing that the Supreme Court had voided the power of Congress to exclude slavery from the territories, hastened to proclaim that this part of the ruling was *dicta*—mere gossip from the bench. Ironically, they flared up with denunciations of the Court for deciding a question which, during the previous decade, they had denounced it for failing to decide. Very little attention was directed to the much stronger contention that the Court had interpreted the Constitution incorrectly and that Congress *did* have power over slavery in the territories. But critics were more eager to make a case that the decision was not legally binding than that it was wrong. Hence their focus on a denunciation of the decision as *obiter dicta.*

Many historians have accepted the angry claim that the decision was *dicta,* but the case was extremely intricate, and when all angles are taken into consideration, it appears that the decision was not *dicta.* After deciding that the Court lacked jurisdiction, it is true that the justices did not have to decide whether the Missouri Compromise had made Scott *free,* but in the process of deciding whether the Court had jurisdiction, the justices did have to decide whether the Missouri Compromise might have made him a *citizen* which was, of course, linked with the question whether it had made him free. Paradoxically, the decision that the law had not made him a citizen for purposes of jurisdiction obviated the necessity of saying whether the law had made him free for purposes of his suit. But the Court had answered the question to which the suit sought a reply in the very process by which it decided that Scott could not bring the suit which asked the question.

EFFECTS OF THE DECISION. If all of this seems—and indeed is— a form of incredible hairsplitting, the point historically is that the intricacies of the decision lent themselves to the accusation that the judges were guilty of what, in a later generation, has been called "judicial usurpation"—of going against legislative enactments and deciding a question that did not have to be decided. Republicans attacked the decision savagely on this ground and also with accusations that the Court was overloaded with slave-state justices (five to four), that there had been an improper understanding about the decision between President Buchanan and some of the majority justices (many years later this accusation was proved to be true), and that the decision was part of a wicked conspiracy to spread slavery nationwide. In any circumstances, no doubt, a decision which deprived Congress of power over slavery in the territories would have caused a great increase in sectional antagonisms, but in this case the antagonism was made much worse by the widespread belief that the Court had gone entirely outside the judicial orbit to make a proslavery decision.

Also, apart from these special circumstances which accentuated the disruptive effect, the decision vastly sharpened sectional divisions for it weakened center positions. It did not especially matter that the Missouri Compromise was declared unconstitutional, because it had already been repealed by the Kansas-Nebraska Act. But it mattered a great deal that Congress could not regulate, nor authorize a territorial legislature to regulate, slavery in the territories. This destroyed the basis for popular sovereignty, and once that basis was destroyed, the opposing parties took completely polarized positions—that slavery should extend into all territories, or that the Court's decision should be ignored and slavery should be kept out of all the territories. The Dred Scott decision polarized the American people constitutionally, just as the party transformations of 1854–1856 had polarized them in terms of political parties. They were soon to be polarized emotionally as well. This emotional polarization was produced largely by the attempt of John Brown to lead a slave insurrection and by his subsequent hanging.

JOHN BROWN'S ROLE: EMOTIONAL POLARIZATION

After the killings at Pottawattomie, John Brown remained in Kansas for four months as a minor guerrilla leader in the antislavery forces, but he never received a post of any responsibility, partly because the antislavery people did not like what he had done, and they distrusted him as a trigger-happy, lone wolf who would get them all into trouble. As peace was restored in Kansas, Brown saw with increasing clarity that there was really no longer a place for him there. Having organized a small volunteer company of about two dozen young men, he conceived the idea of keeping this force together and using it as the nucleus for a small army that would march into Virginia and start a slave uprising, which might then spread throughout the entire South. To raise and equip such an army would require secrecy and also the raising of money, but these two were hard to reconcile, since no public appeals for funds could be made.

NORTHERN SUPPORTERS. Brown's plan evolved gradually, and underwent some changes during its evolution, but by 1859 he had enlisted some support from a wealthy antislavery man, Gerrit Smith, in New York, and from six well-to-do and intellectually very prominent Bostonians, including Theodore Parker, one of the most outstanding clergymen and intellectuals in the United States, and Samuel Gridley Howe, famous for his work with the blind and other philanthropies. Various other prominent people, including Henry D. Thoreau, Bronson Alcott, and Ralph W. Emerson, had met Brown, who understood instinctively how to play the role of a romantic hero of the Border War in Kansas. They admired him immensely and understood vaguely that he was up to something, but they did not know exactly what and probably preferred not to know.

Despite the help of Gerrit Smith and the "Secret Six," Brown's organizational efforts really must be regarded as a failure, though not through any fault of his own. He never raised more than $30,000 at the most, which is nothing in terms of financing an army, and he also failed in his efforts to recruit Negro followers. In April 1858 he went to Chatham, Ontario, where there was a large colony of Negroes—almost all fugitive slaves—and there, with reckless lack of secrecy, he revealed his plan for an "army of the North" and for a provisional government with a president (Brown), a congress, and a supreme court. But the Negroes of Chatham, more realistic than the intelligentsia of Boston, perceived that there was something peculiar about this man, and they would not follow him. He had really already failed before he moved to his base, a farm in Maryland, with twenty-two followers—seventeen whites and five blacks. Frederick Douglass, the most prominent and ablest Negro in the country, had refused to join him.

HARPER'S FERRY. After waiting in vain for three and a half months on the Maryland farm, hoping for money and recruits, Brown at last moved with his tiny force, on the night of October

16, 1859, to occupy the town of Harper's Ferry, Virginia. In many respects the operation was fantastically badly planned: Brown's men took no food with them, and they were hungry by the next morning; their objective, Harper's Ferry, was located at the convergence of the Shenandoah and the Potomac rivers, with high hills back of the town, and it formed a natural trap from which escape was almost impossible; Brown planned to seize a federal arsenal, which would bring the United States Army instantly into the picture; the area had a low proportion of slaves in its population; and because Brown feared betrayal, not one of the slaves had been informed that they were expected to join in an uprising. The whole idea of conquering the state of Virginia was so bizarre that it has led to the subsequent belief that Brown was insane. Yet it must be observed that his belief that the slaves were ready for instant revolt—that, as he expressed it, the "bees would swarm" as soon as he struck—was commonly believed in the North and commonly feared in the South. It is true that Brown was a strange sort of man—a loner, grim, rigid, preoccupied, obsessed with one idea, and given to alternations of inactivity and bursts of energy. It is also true that he combined rigorously high personal ideals with a record of financial irresponsibility which raises some questions, as does the sadism of the killings at Pottawattomie. Still, his "maddest" idea was one which he shared with countless antislavery men, including the best minds in Boston. The only difference was that he acted on the idea.

The complete surprise with which Brown struck enabled him easily to occupy Harper's Ferry and to seize the federal armory, with enough guns to equip a whole army of slaves. But no slaves came in—the bees did not swarm. Instead, local militia and federal troops converged on Harper's Ferry the next day and drove Brown's small force, with heavy losses, into an engine house which was part of the armory. On the second morning an assault party stormed the engine house and captured what was left of Brown's force. Brown himself was wounded in the final assault. Of his entire force, five had escaped the previous day, ten, including two of Brown's sons, were dead or dying, and seven were captured and later hanged by the state of Virginia.

THE AFTERMATH. If Brown himself had been killed, the whole affair might have been dismissed by the public as the crazy act of a mere desperado. But in his hour of failure—wounded, imprisoned, and on trial for his life—Brown surpassed himself, behaving with a dignity, composure, bravery, and faith in the rightness of his deed which won the admiration even of the Virginians. Gerrit Smith might seek refuge in an insane asylum and Samuel Gridley Howe might flee to Canada, but Brown himself did not flinch. He had failed many of the tests of life, and he knew he was about to face the grimmest test of all. But he also knew that this was one which he could successfully pass. He was stating a plan of action when he said "I am worth now infinitely more to die than to live."

Brown was put on trial while still suffering from his wounds. The trial lasted a week, and he was sentenced to death. During the trial he conducted himself with complete calmness and self-possession, and when sentenced he delivered a brief statement which stands as a classic. Expressing satisfaction with the fairness of his trial, he also said, "I feel no consciousness of guilt. . . . Now if it is deemed necessary that I should forfeit my life for the furtherance of the ends of justice and mingle my blood . . . with the blood of millions in this slave country whose rights are disregarded by wicked, cruel, and unjust enactments, I say let it be done."

It was done, after a delay mercifully much briefer than the delays which have awaited condemned men in the late twentieth century. On December 2, 1859, John Brown was hanged in the presence of a large force of troops at Charlestown, Virginia (now West Virginia). Outwardly, and perhaps inwardly, he was the calmest man at the hanging.

Elsewhere there was not much calm. Brown's raid had touched the slave South on the exposed nerve of its fear of slave insurrection. Worse still, the activities of the "Secret Six," and the unrestrained expressions of sympathy for Brown throughout the North (church bells tolling, Emerson writing that Brown had "made the gallows glorious like the cross") convinced many Southerners that they were in a Union with fellow citizens who would rejoice to see them slain in a bloody insurrection of slaves. They knew of a good many statements by Northerners like Congressman Joshua Giddings of Ohio who said that he looked forward to the day "when the torch of the incendiary shall light up the towns and cities of the South and blot out the last vestiges of slavery," and they did not usually pause to ask how typical Giddings might be. In the North, on the other hand, the hanging of Brown seemed an unspeakable atrocity. He had been put to death because he alone was willing to do more than just talk about the oppression of slaves. The society which could take his life was a brutal blot on American civilization. In short, Brown was a martyr. To the extent that these feelings prevailed in the South and in the North, respectively, the emotional polarization of the sections was complete.

On the day John Brown was hanged, the first of the nominating conventions for the presidential election of 1860 was little more than four months away.

THE 1860 ELECTION

PARTY ALIGNMENTS. As the 1860 campaign for the presidency opened, party alignments remained about as they had been in 1856. The old Whigs still had substantial strength in the border states and hoped to become a moderate center against the southern sectionalism of the Democratic party and the northern sectionalism of the Republican party. One of their leaders, Senator John J. Crittenden of Kentucky, had sought to revitalize them in a new organization, to be called the Constitutional Union party, where Whigs, Know Nothings, and, hopefully, moderate Republicans and moderate Democrats could meet on neutral ground. In December 1859, Crittenden and fifty other prominent men, mostly former Whigs, called for a convention of this party to meet in the following May.

The Republicans in 1860 had spent four years consolidating the organization which had been so new and so seriously jeopardized by its involvement with Know Nothingism in 1856; they were bouyed by the awareness that if they could hold the states which they had won in 1856 and carry three of the five free states previously won by Buchanan, they could win the election.

The Democrats held one great potential advantage: they were the only remaining party which could claim to be a national, bisectional party, and with fears of disunion becoming very widespread, this claim might have become a major asset. But they could not capitalize on it, because their Democratic party was itself profoundly divided. The bitter conflict over the Lecompton Constitution, in which Douglas and Buchanan fought each other with every weapon, was the foremost cause of this division, but Buchanan's whole policy as President had antagonized northern Democrats. Personally susceptible to southern influence, Buchanan had vetoed a tariff bill, a land grant college bill, and a homestead bill, all supported by northern Democrats and opposed by the southern elements in the party. The effect was to further weaken the Democratic party in the North and leave northern Democrats acutely conscious that they must throw off southern domination if they were to keep the party alive in their own states.

THE DEMOCRATIC PARTY CONVENTION. Against this background, the Democratic convention met (as if planned by a spiteful fate) in the stronghold of nullification, Charleston, South Carolina, in late April. In the party convention the northern states still held a majority, which they no longer had in the party's Congressional representation; in the convention, if nowhere else, the Democratic party was still a national party. Douglas, once the darling of the South because of Kansas–Nebraska, was now hated there both because of his fight against the Lecompton Constitution and because he refused freely to accept the Dred Scott decision and insisted that a territorial legislature could still keep slavery out of a territory simply by abstaining from the passage of any laws to enforce a slave system. In this political reversal he had again become the champion of the northern Democrats and was clearly the most impressive figure in the Democratic party. With their convention majority, the northern Democrats confidently expected to nominate him. It was true that they did not have the two-thirds majority required by the Democratic party rules, but usually, when a candidate had a majority, his opponents conceded the nomination. Douglas had done so to Buchanan in 1856.

THE DEMOCRATIC PARTY SPLITS. In relying on this practice, the northern Democrats failed to recognize the depth of southern bitterness. As the convention proceeded, bitter sectional hostility was expressed in the speeches. The northern delegates were reluctantly willing to leave out of a platform any disavowal of the Dred Scott decision, but they were immovably opposed to adopting a platform which explicitly accepted the Dred Scott ruling and sanctioned slavery in all territories. When they voted down such a platform, the delegations of seven states from the deep South (all except Georgia) walked out of the convention. This act may have been intended as a maneuver to put pressure on the party, and for months frantic efforts were made to heal the breach. Such efforts were in vain. Sectionalism had destroyed the only remaining national party and by doing so it threatened the national union.

The remaining delegates stayed in session, ballotted, and secured for Douglas a majority of the total votes (including those who had withdrawn) but they could not attain two thirds of the total, so finally they adjourned to meet later at Baltimore. The delegations which had walked out called another convention to meet at Richmond. At these meetings, further desperate efforts were made to reunite the party, but they failed. In the end the Baltimore covention nominated Douglas and the Richmond convention nominated the Vice-President, John C. Breckenridge of Kentucky. The last national party was now divided.

THE CONSTITUTIONAL UNION PARTY CONVENTION. One week after the Charleston convention voted to adjourn, the convention of the Constitutional Union party met in Baltimore, with delegates from only twelve of the fifteen slave states, and eleven of the eighteen free states, but with all large states represented. This convention nominated John Bell of Tennessee for President and Edward Everett for Vice-President. Instead of a platform it adopted with unanimity a statement pledging support to "the Constitution as it is, and the Union under it, now and forever. . . ."

THE REPUBLICAN PARTY CONVENTION. Exactly one week after that, the Republican convention met in Chicago. Most of the delegates thought they were meeting to nominate Senator William H. Seward of New York who was clearly the leader of the party. But some elements had a grudge against Seward and the more sagacious party leaders recognized that he had certain liabilities: (1) the Know Nothings hated him because he had been friendly to state support for Catholic parochial schools in New York; (2) he was identified with a strong antislavery position, largely because of two phrases that he had coined—"a higher law than the Constitution" and "irrepressible conflict"; and (3) his major appeal would not be to conservative states like Pennsylvania and Indiana which the Democrats had won in 1856 and which were precisely the ones the Republicans needed to concentrate on in order to win in 1860. Also, Horace Greeley, the powerful editor of the New York *Tribune,* who was publicly allied with Seward but privately held a personal grudge against him, was busily circulating the opinion that Seward could not win the election if he were nominated.

With the Democrats divided, the Republican managers perceived that they could certainly win if they avoided mistakes, and they made none. Broadening the party's policies to get away from a strictly antislavery position, they put planks into the platform for a protective tariff, a homestead act (160 free acres for anyone who would build a cabin and live on them), and a transcontinental railroad. Then, in the balloting they stopped Seward short of a majority, gradually wore him down, and on the third ballot nominated Abraham Lincoln of Illinois. Since Lincoln was an ex-Whig, they nominated an ex-Democrat, Hannibal Hamlin of Maine, for Vice-President.

THE CAMPAIGN AND ELECTION RESULTS. Although there were four candidates running for President, it was not really a four-cornered race, but rather a content between Lincoln and Douglas in the North, and between Bell and Breckenridge in the South. Lincoln's campaign stressed the issue of what would today be called the "containment" of slavery—it must not be extended beyond its existing limits—while Douglas stressed the danger of disunion and argued that the territorial issue was unrealistic because there was no economic basis for slavery to flourish in the territories in any case. In the South, Bell stressed the Union, as Douglas was doing in the North, while Breckenridge, although not yet a secessionist, stressed "southern rights" as defined by the Dred Scott decision.

On November 6, the dualism of the races in the two sections showed up very clearly. In the slave states, Bell and Breckenridge between them received 85 percent of the vote; in the free states, Lincoln and Douglas between them received 86 percent of the vote. This vote divided at 511,000 for Breckenridge and 500,000 for Bell in the slave states, but Bell was unlucky in the distribution of the vote and he carried only Virginia, Kentucky, and Tennessee. Douglas concentrated one third

of his entire slave state vote in Missouri, and carried the state
—it was the only state which he won clearly. Breckenridge
carried the remaining eleven slave states.

In the country as a whole, Lincoln received only 39 percent of the popular vote—the smallest percentage with which
any man has ever been elected to the presidency. This fact has
led to a widespread belief that Lincoln won only because his
opponents were divided. But in a statistical sense, at least, this
is not true. He won because his vote was distributed in such a
way as to pay off in electoral votes. With barely more than 1
percent of his vote in the fifteen slave states, and almost 99
percent of it concentrated in the eighteenth free states, he
carried all of the free states except New Jersey. In fifteen states,
wtih a majority of electoral votes, he won more than 50 percent
of the vote, and only in Oregon and California did his opponents have a vote which, if combined, would have been
greater than his. Thus, the nominee of a party which had
not existed seven years previously became President-elect of the
United States. . . .

THE BASIC ISSUES CONFOUNDED. Like most wars, the American
Civil War came about in a somewhat irrational fashion. For
four decades North and South had been increasingly antagonized
by the slavery question, and especially by the question of the
extension of slavery. But on the slavery issue, the North itself
was bitterly divided. While few Northerners really approved of
slavery, even fewer apparently approved of Negro equality. If
the North was antislavery, it was also to a great extent anti-
Negro. If the South had held strictly to the slavery issue, the
North would have been hopelessly divided in any confrontation
with the South.

But the South inadvertently changed the issue from the
question of slavery to the question of union. Abruptly, the
southern acts of secession pushed the slavery question into the
background and placed a focus upon the survival of the republic. To vast numbers of Northerners, the support of slavery was
wrong, but the support of secession was treason. Therefore, a
quarrel over slavery, on which the North was divided, suddenly
became converted into a quarrel over the Union, on which the
North was united—a war in which it was not even clear that
slavery was an issue.

Thus, in 1861 the American people stood on the eve of paying a great price for the solution of a problem which they had never clearly defined and which they could hardly expect to solve without defining it, no matter how great a price they paid. The problem concerned the relations of blacks and whites in the United States. But first, people had seen it too restrictively in terms of chattel servitude rather than of racial subordination, which would perpetuate the problem after chattel servitude was gone. Then further, they had seen it restrictively in terms of constitutional questions about slaves in the territories, placing so much emphasis upon this aspect at the expense of slavery in the states that Lincoln was willing to guarantee the servitude of four million slaves in the states as late as March 1861, but was adamant on the question of slavery in the territories, where there were no slaves. Finally, at the moment when historical forces brought the country to a point where one great era in the relations of the races must end and another era must begin, the surface events diverted the attention of most Americans and caused them to think that the problem was one of union and not of the relations of the races at all.

Even the South agreed in attaching high value to the Union. This is shown by the readiness with which the South came back to the Union after the war. But to say this is to say that North and South were about to fight the world's deadliest war between the Napoleonic Wars and World War I, without perceiving that the ostensible issue over which they fought—the issue of union—was one on which they did not basically disagree. Yet the root cause of the conflict—the issue of race relations—was so poorly perceived that they did not recognize the extent of either their agreement or disagreement, or the relation of the issue to the war which it had precipitated.

INTRODUCTORY NOTE

The war came, irrational or not, and the South lost. Hindsight makes clear the major reasons why the South lost: she was outnumbered more than two to one in population and about five to two in military manpower; the North had 1,300,000 industrial workers and the South only 110,000; the North had 22,000 miles of railroad and the South only 9,280 miles. Furthermore, the South erred fatally in assuming that wars were won primarily by valor on the battlefield, that cotton was still king, and that a defensive strategy was the best policy. But David Potter has suggested the possibility of the important intervention of another variable, one that has only recently been explored and that is consistent with the theme of this book. That was "the possibility that the Confederacy may have suffered real and direct damage from the fact that its political organization lacked a two-party system."[1] In the selection that follows, Eric McKitrick takes advantage of the unique opportunity afforded by the Civil War to make a comparative analysis of the differential impact of party structure and government in the Union and the Confederacy in determining the outcome of the Civil War.

[1] David M. Potter, "Jefferson Davis and the Political Factors in Confederate Defeat," in David Donald, ed., *Why the North Won the Civil War,* Baton Rouge: Louisiana State University Press, 1960, p. 113.

Party Politics and the Union and Confederate War Efforts

ERIC L. McKITRICK

The Civil War has always lent itself naturally and logically to the comparative method. Comparing the resources of the Union and the Confederacy in everything conceivable—manpower, brainpower, firepower—has been highly productive in helping us to understand the process whereby the North ultimately overwhelmed the South. But it is in the realm of government, where the process of historical comparison normally begins, that the results are on the whole least conclusive and least satisfying. The two sets of institutions exhibit a series of uncanny similarities. We may think we can detect in the Southern body politic a certain pallor, a lack of muscle tone that is in some contrast to the apparent resiliency of the North. But this is only a suspicion. We have not been very certain about how to get at such a subjective matter as the health of a metaphorical organism.

The Union and Confederate governments, as set down on paper, were almost identical. The Confederacy deliberately adopted the federal Constitution with very few changes, some of which might have been improvements had they been carried fully into effect. Cabinet members might sit in Congress, though few did; the executive had an itemized veto on appropriation bills, though it was a power he did not use; and bills for departmental appropriations had to be initiated with an estimate from the department concerned. The general welfare clause was dropped, but the "necessary and proper" clause—so useful for expanding national power—was kept. The states were "sovereign" but had no power to make treaties, which meant that they were in fact not sovereign. Nothing was said about the right of secession, and it was not as though no one had thought of it. The relations of the states to the central government would, in the course of things, reveal some crucial differences, but it is hard to find much evidence for this in the organic law of the two governments. A trend toward centralized power was perfectly possible within either of the two constitutions, and it could proceed just as far under the one as under the other. The co-ordinate branches of government were constitutionally the same, though in the election and term of office of the executive there were certain differences. As for the judiciary, the Confederacy too was to have had a Supreme Court, though it never actually got around to establishing one. In the Confederacy judicial review (with generous citations from *The Federalist*, as well as from the opinions of Marshall and Story) occurred in the states. How much difference this made may be debated, though historians have not in general made an issue of it. In any case, of the three branches of government on either side, the judiciary seems to have made the least impact on the waging of war. With regard to the two Congresses, the practices and procedures were strikingly similar. It might be said that even their membership overlapped, since a number of men had served in both.

The same executive departments were established in both governments, and with one exception the positions in each president's cabinet were the same. There has been some debate on the competence of the men who filled those positions. It is generally supposed that Lincoln's cabinet was the "better" one, though there is little clear agreement as to the reasons. One authority emphasizes the over-all deficiencies of the Confederate cabinet; another calls attention to its many merits. It is at least clear that both cabinets contained a mixed lot. Each had its good administrators, and on both sides there was incompetence. Leroy Pope Walker may have made a very poor Secretary of War, but the Union had to fight the first nine months of the war with Simon Cameron. Comparisons on this level, in short, are certainly enlightening, but they take one just so far. So much has been said about executive leadership that this almost constitutes a separate literature. It seems apparent that the leadership of Abraham Lincoln was superior to that of Jefferson Davis, though the fact of Northern victory is naturally quite helpful in making the case. Lincoln was "flexible," Davis "rigid."

And yet conditions may have been such, above and beyond the two men's personal characteristics, as to make Lincoln's flexibility and Davis's rigidity unavoidable political responses to the requirements of war as experienced in their respective sections.

But what were those conditions? What was the nature of the political setting, beyond the actual structure of government, within which the two leaders had to operate? Was it—a subject that has never been systematically investigated—affected by the presence or absence of political parties?

II

All such comparisons as those just surveyed, enlightening as they are, must be made within certain limits. Attention is always in some way directed to the formal structure of government and to the individuals occupying the formal positions established by that structure. But comparing these formal arrangements, even in the broadest and most extended way, still does not bring us a very clear idea of why the North won and where it drew the necessary energy for sustaining a long drawn out war effort. At this point one normally retreats to the "concrete realities" of military power and material resources, the logic of which has a reassuring finality. Military and economic organization—"in the last analysis," as we say—is what tells.

Still there may be, as I think, much more to be said for the way in which political organization, in and of itself, affected the respective war efforts. And if so, it is most likely to be found by moving to another level altogether: by turning from the formal to the informal functions of politics, from its official to its unofficial apparatus, from the explicit formulations to the implicit understandings. For at least a generation prior to the Civil War, the most salient unofficial structure in American public life was its system of political parties. No formal provision was ever made for such a system. Yet in this system of parties may be found historically the chief agency for mobilizing and sustaining energy in American government. It thus seems reasonable to consider how, as a matter of actual practice, the energies of government may have been affected by the workings of this unofficial system in waging the American Civil War.

In an essay published in 1960, David Potter suggested "the possibility that the Confederacy may have suffered real and direct damage from the fact that its political organization lacked a two-party system." This, with its implications, constitutes in my opinion the most original single idea to emerge from the mass of writing that has been done on the Civil War in many years. It implicitly challenges two of our most formidable and consistently held assumptions regarding political life of the time, assumptions which until recently have gone unquestioned. One is that Lincoln's leadership of the Union war effort was severely and dangerously hampered by political partisanship—that is, by obstructions put in his path by Democrats on the one hand and, on the other, by extremists within his own Republican party. The other assumption is that Davis and the Confederate government, by deliberately setting aside partisanship, avoided this difficulty. There were no parties in the Confederacy, and thus the South, in this respect at least, had the advantage.

In order to show these notions as fallacies, following Potter's cue, it should not be necessary to claim that the South "ought" to have encouraged the establishment of a party system. Even had such a system been seen as a positive value—which it was not, either North or South—there was probably a variety of reasons why an effort of that sort on the eve of war would have been out of the question. Such things must in any case grow naturally or they do not grow at all. Indeed it might better be wondered why the South did not put itself in an avowedly revolutionary posture and run its government as a kind of Committee of Public Safety, a procedure which could have given it maximum maneuverability for achieving what was in fact a set of revolutionary objectives. And yet this course was in reality even less thinkable; the mentality needed for it simply did not exist. The Confederates again and again insisted that they were not in rebellion, that it was not a civil war, that they were not truly engaged in a revolution. The South's ideological strategy was to declare, in effect, to the people of the United States: our constitutional title to exist is legally purer than yours. We are in fact the "true" United States; we are more faithful than you to the spirit of the Founders; it is you, not we, who have departed from it; it is you who are the rebels. The Confederates, in short, put an unusual amount of effort simply into behaving as a fully constituted nation, and they seemed to feel an almost obsessive need to clothe their government with as many of the symbols and minutiae of legitimacy as they could. They imagined themselves engaged not nearly so much in a revolutionary struggle for liberation as in a fully mounted war between two sovereign powers.

It is only necessary, then, to take the Confederates for the time being on their own terms: as a government possessing all the formal incidents of constitutional legitimacy, but lacking at least one of the informal ones—a system of political parties— possessed by their opponents. This discrepancy, it is here suggested, has much to tell us about the vigor of the respective war efforts. It is further suggested that the persistence of party contention in the North all through the war was on the whole salutary for Lincoln's government and the Union cause. The war was, of course, in addition to all else, one long political headache, tying up much of the executive's valuable time and attention. Obstacles of opposition were bound up again and again with the most annoying kind of partisan politics. Nobody at the time, so far as is known, ever explicitly thanked the Almighty for parties. But by the same token, it was partisan politics that provided the very framework within which these same obstacles could be contained and overcome. To Jefferson Davis's government such a framework was not available. Everything, to be sure, has its price; there were functions and dysfunctions. But it may well be that on balance the functions outweighed the dysfunctions, and that the price was worth paying.

III

The functions of party in the formation of a government seem to involve, on the face of it, something fairly direct and straightforward. But the process has its subtleties, which become apparent where there are two governments being formed at the same time, under comparable circumstances and by men sharing many of the same political traditions, but where, in one of the cases, the principle of party is not a factor.

The rapid growth of the Republican party in the brief span of five or six years prior to 1860 had generated certain byproducts. It had certainly dissipated the malaise of the early 1850's in which the expanding antislavery and free-soil sentiment of the North had been, for a time, without any clear vehicle for political organization. There were, moreover, established public men who had come to be identified with this sentiment, and whose careers could no longer be promoted without stultification amid the dissolution of the Whig party and the conservatism of the regular Democrats. Such men, of whom William H. Seward and Salmon P. Chase were conspicuous examples, now found in the Republican party a welcome field for their talents and leadership. In addition, the very effort required in organizing the new party in state after state brought to the fore hundreds of new men within the same short space of time. The very marching clubs which sprang up everywhere —the so-called "Wide Awakes"—amounted to much more than a freakish social phenomenon. They represented the "progressive" element of the community. That the Republicans by 1860 had elected governors in every Northern state, to say nothing of capturing the national government, is evidence of a vitality going far beyond the ordinary. The period was one of mounting public crisis; what has been less noticed is that precisely at this time public life began to present an expanding field for younger men of talent, ambition, and energy.

By the time the Confederacy was being established, politics was not attracting the South's best men to anywhere near this degree. An obvious immediate reason, of course, was that the war crisis naturally brought many of the Southern elite into the army, and many writers have commented on this. But antecedent factors were more pervasive. The chief mechanism for managing political talent and bringing it forward—party organizations—had in effect disintegrated in the South by the time the war began. The organizational stability of both the Whig and Democratic parties at local and state levels all over the country, ever since the emergence of such organizations in the 1830's, had depended on their maintaining some sort of national orientation and national interests. In the South, the growth of a sectional, state-centered ideology in defense of slavery had steadily undermined such interests, and with them, whatever stablity such organizations had once had. Thus the collapse in the South of the existing parties—the Whigs in the early 1850's and the Democrats in 1860—had created a setting in which the only real political issue came down to that of whether a man did or did not support secession. "Opposition" implied disloyalty, unless it could be based on state particularism—which was exactly the form opposition would in fact take. There was thus no national (that is, all-Confederate) basis on which a system of parties might be re-fashioned. Meanwhile those organizations which do so much to define political skill and political success, and to measure the satisfactions of politics for all from the humble to the high, had in most respects simply vanished.

How, then, would this affect the standards—of duty and commitment, as well as ability—to be used in the forming of a government?

The vice-presidency might be taken as a minor, though interesting example. The significance of Hannibal Hamlin has never inspired the historian; as with many a Vice-President of the nineteenth century, Hamlin does not even have a modern biographer. Yet in 1860 the man played a role whose specifications were clearly understood by all, especially by those most responsible for placing him in it. He represented an interest within the Republican party which might "balance" a national ticket, broaden its support, and thus help it to win an election. He had already served in Congress as a Democratic representative and senator, and he had been one of the chief organizers of the Republican party in the state of Maine. He could speak for the antislavery element of New England, having strong sympathies with abolition. As Vice-President, Hamlin hardly made a ripple on the surface of events, which is to say he played with unassuming perfection the role marked out for him. His one chance for fame—the presidency itself, which would have fallen to him upon Lincoln's death—was snatched away in 1864 when it was decided that the ticket of that year might be better balanced, in yet a different manner, by someone else, Andrew Johnson, a former Democrat from Tennessee. But in certain small ways Hamlin made himself useful from the first—for example, in the diplomacy of cabinet-making, in the choosing of officers for Negro regiments, and in testing the weather on emancipation. Despite his disappointment, he made no complaint at being superseded in 1864, supported the new ticket, and was eventually compensated in good party fashion with the Collectorship of Boston.

Had any such standards of choice governed the Confederate delegates at Montgomery, the last man they would have picked as Vice-President would have been the distinguished Alexander Stephens. The principal criterion in this case seems to have been the delegates' feeling that something was needed to placate the state of Georgia for having failed to elect a Georgian as President. Yet Stephens had strongly opposed secession, did not really believe in the Confederacy and hardly even pretended to, and had no inclination whatever to stay in Richmond and preside over the Confederate Senate. He spent most of his time at home in Georgia grumbling against his own government and actually attacking it in venomous letters and speeches for usurping the rights of citizens. Few men did more to undermine Davis's administration than his own Vice-President. Perhaps Stephens's one positive act, if such it may be called, was going to meet Lincoln on an unsuccessful peace mission. Davis himself once offered to resign, his one condition being the resignation of Alexander Stephens.

The choice in the one case had been a party matter; in the other, it had been made on a regional, "popular-front" basis. Hamlin's career was tied to the Republican party, and therefore to the success of the Lincoln administration; Stephens had been placed in the Confederate government mainly as a gesture toward the state of Georgia and to the former members of a political party (the Whigs) that no longer existed. He and his friends thus had no direct vested interest in the day-to-day success of the Davis administration.

How the unspoken assumptions of party politics might or might not govern men's behavior may be illustrated by another pair of cases, this time involving the runners-up for the presidency—the men who did not quite make it. When the supporters of William H. Seward arrived in Chicago for the Republican convention of 1860, they had every reason to be confident that their man, the new party's most prominent national figure, would receive the nomination. The most astute correspondents reported that Seward's candidacy was irresistible, and he was clearly preferred by a majority of the delegates. Seward led on the first two ballots, though he gained little ground on the second, and was overtaken on the third by the forces of Abraham Lincoln. Lincoln's views on the leading issues may in fact have been no less positive than Seward's but they, like Lincoln himself, had been considerably less exposed to the public in the years just preceding; he thus represented a principle then known, in the idiom of politics, as "availability." He also had an extraordinarily energetic and well-disciplined Republican organization in the state of Illinois. As the result was announced, Thurlow Weed, Seward's manager and friend of over thirty years, sat and wept.

The standards of party, as has been remarked more than once, generate a morality of their own. William H. Seward, with both his virtues and his foibles, and Weed with his, had been in some way governed by that morality ever since they had been young men together in the 1820's. Thurlow Weed could now act (if the thought does not seem ironically strained) as Seward's conscience, in case he needed one. "Whatever your ultimate purpose may be," he wrote to his heartbroken friend, "I cannot doubt that a prompt and cheerful acquiescence . . . is not only wise, but a duty." Seward knew his cue. "I wish that I was sure that your sense of the disappointment is as light as my own," he replied. "It ought to be equally so, for we have been equally thoughtful and zealous, for friends, party, and country. . . ." Weed, during the months that followed, made two trips to Springfield. No bargains were made, but Weed and Lincoln got on remarkably well, each recognizing in the other a man of ability, and each no doubt understanding that, owing to a certain shared fund of experience, communication did not always need to be on an absolutely explicit level. Communication on whatever level was made meaningful—indeed, possible —by what Weed represented, a party organization in New York state that already counted for a great deal in the way of power, influence, and a set of clear loyalties. William H. Seward entered the campaign wholeheartedly, making a number of very strong speeches for Lincoln all around the country. Rumors reached him that Lincoln was planning to invite him to become Secretary of State, and the evidence indicates that there was, for a time, much doubt in Seward's mind as to whether he really wanted it. Yet the offer was duly made, and Seward accepted. Throughout the entire war, whatever may have been his personal quirks, Seward's loyalty to the party, to the national cause, and to the administration were never in doubt.

In the Confederacy, Seward's counterpart was Robert Toombs. One of the ablest Southerners of his time, Toombs had served in Congress since 1844 as a Whig from the state of Georgia, first in the House and later in the Senate. He was genial and gregarious, a man of much practical knowledge, and a great debater and parliamentarian whose performances combined gusto, brilliance, and flourish. As a statesman and defender of Southern rights in the 1850's he had been ardent but certainly not foolish. Having once opposed the Mexican War, supported the Compromise of 1850, and defended the Union, he was carried by the events of that decade to the point where he could with perfect consistency stalk out of the Senate in January 1861, never to return, furiously denouncing Black Republicanism for all time: "Treason; bah!" He was, in short, rather an ideal Southerner and knew it, a man of both éclat and high intelligence, widely popular, and lionized by his friends. It has been said that when the delegates to the Confederate convention arrived in Montgomery in February 1861, the first choice of most of them for the presidency was Robert Toombs. He himself ached to be President, and would no doubt have made a good one, perhaps better than the man actually elected. Of that, too, he seems to have been convinced. The process by which he was passed over in favor of Davis was in certain ways not comparable to that whereby William H. Seward had lost out to Lincoln a few months before. It was not a "political" process, in the sense that it would have been with a party system, nor was there any desire that it should be. There was no trading in the usual sense, and virtually none of the sort of communication between delegations that characterizes a real nominating convention, because the group was obsessed with the notion that the choice should appear spontaneous and unanimous. As a result it was sufficiently haphazard that we are still not certain, except in a general way, how it was arrived at. Five of the six delegations present—each state with but one vote—apparently favored Toombs, but someone seems to have carried the untrue rumor that Georgia itself planned to present as its candidate not Toombs but Howell Cobb, the former Speaker of the House, Governor, and Secretary of the Treasury in Buchanan's cabinet. Under this misapprehension (Cobb being somewhat controversial) the other delegations in their separate conferences switched to Davis, a development of which the Georgians only learned through a messenger sent around at the last minute. The crestfallen Georgians thereupon felt they had no choice but to follow suit, not discovering the reason for the change until after the ballot was taken.

(Cobb's brother, it appeared, had been at the bottom of this.) So goes, at any rate, one story of Jefferson Davis's "unanimous" election as President of the Confederacy.

Toombs never swallowed his bitterness. He was duly offered the Secretaryship of State, which he accepted grudgingly. But he never tried to make anything of the office or to invest it with any distinction. Indeed, he held it rather in contempt, declaring on one occasion that he "carried the State department in his hat." He resigned after a few months for a brigadier's commission in the army, to the despair of his own brother, who, knowing Toombs had no military talents, whatever, vainly implored Alexander Stephens to talk him out of it. As a warrior he was hardly a success. (Once, while charging about on his horse, he was dumped, "purple with rage," before an aghast party of ladies.) Before quitting the army in disgust at not being promoted to major general, Toombs was elected by his legislature to the Confederate Senate. Since the election was not nearly unanimous, and thus not the mandate he wanted for opposing the administration, he refused to go. His hatred of Davis, whose "incapacity" he called "lamentable" and whom he characterized as "that scoundrel," grew ever hotter with the passing of time. None of the once-great "Georgia Triumvirate" —Stephens, Toombs, and Cobb—ever came close to lending his immense talents and prestige to the success of the Confederate government. And one of Alexander Stephens's closest allies, in his unrelating warfare upon the administration, was Robert Toombs. Of his President, Toombs declared, "I shall be justified in any extremity to which the public interest would allow me to go in hostility to his illegal and unconstitutional course." In the absence of party platforms and party morality, there could be as many separate versions of "the public interest" as there were contentious men who thought themselves qualified to say what it was. By the same token, there were far fewer checks on purely "personal" politics.

A further contrast between the Federal and Confederate governments, looking now at their formation from still another viewpoint, might consist in the standards whereby the cabinets as a whole were organized. For Davis, the chief concern was that each state had to be represented. For Lincoln also, geography counted as a strong consideration, but for him, both merit and geography as factors in choice had to operate within the limits of another criterion, which gave the problem a certain focus and required a certain precision. His cabinet had to be primarily a party alliance, which was its true functioning character, and its character as a coalition of state interests was thus quite secondary. He wanted every shade of commitment within the party, from border-state conservative to antislavery radical —and the influence they commanded—represented in his cabinet and, as it were, under his eye. A further nicety was that, owing to the comparative newness of the party, considerations of present and future support required that a man's antecedents also be weighed: there should be some balance between former Whigs and former Democrats. On the other hand, Davis had no choice but to follow the principle of state representation, and had he not done so he would undoubtedly have suffered even more general dissension and public attacks on his cabinet than he did. But judging both from this and from the cabinet's own instability, the political symbolism of a coalition of states, just in itself, as a focus for loyalty was somehow abstract, lacking in sharpness, and not very compelling. In the Union cabinet such men as Seward, Chase, Gideon Welles, Edward Bates, and Montgomery Blair represented the most powerful elements that made up the party alliance, which was exactly how they were seen both in the party councils and in the country at large. It was understood that the state of the cabinet reflected the state of the party. Thus the chronic tug-of-war which ensued over the relative standing of Seward, Chase, and Blair should be read not primarily as a matter of individuals and their capacities, as such cases would tend to be in the Confederacy. The struggle was over the party influence those individuals represented in the administration, and how, or whether, the balance ought to be altered. Correspondingly, the changes Lincoln made, as well as the ones he refused to make, were on the whole governed not by the official's performance of his duties but by what the result would reflect in the way of party unity. Except in the case of Simon Cameron, which involved both incompetence and corruption, Lincoln's major moves in the management of his cabinet were made for studied party reasons.

The Seward-Chase crisis in the winter of 1862–63 furnishes an outstanding example. During this time Seward became the target of many Republican senators, who had been persuaded by stories that his influence was preventing a sufficiently vigorous war policy and causing dissension within the cabinet. Chase had done much to encourage these rumors. A delegation of senators met with Lincoln to demand that he reorganize the cabinet in order to end the dissension. Sizing this up, Lincoln perceived that what they really wanted was to force Seward's resignation and have the cabinet reconstituted with Chase as a sort of prime minister; he also knew that Seward's resignation would split the party. He thereupon executed what amounted to a virtuoso maneuver to keep the cabinet intact. Seward had already offered his resignation. The President invited the delegation to come back the next evening, and when they arrived the entire cabinet, except for Seward, was waiting for them. In the presence of all, Lincoln blandly asserted that full harmony prevailed and asked Chase whether in his opinion, the rumors of dissension were true. Chase was trapped between the choice of supporting the senators' claims and thus showing himself as a talebearer, or of upholding the President—which he shamefacedly did—and losing prestige with the senators. Next day the smarting Chase brought in his resignation—to Lincoln's delight, since that was the way he had planned it—and the President, with both resignations now in his pocket, knew that if the senators still demanded Seward's dismissal they would lose Chase too. He refused to accept either one. "If I had yielded to that storm and dismissed Seward," he later remarked with something of a connoisseur's relish, "the thing would all have slumped over one way, and we would have been left with a scanty handful of supporters. When Chase gave in his resignation I saw that the game was in my hands. . . ." Lincoln's patience with Chase lasted through five resignations, which came to be offered quite regularly. But by 1864 the secretary's activities and ambitions had created a threat to Lincoln's own renomination, which was quite another matter. By keeping him in the cabinet until the nomination was secure, the President inhibited the scope of Chase's mischief and at the same time retained the use of his talents and influence, but as soon as that danger was over he decided that he had had enough. Chase's sixth offer to resign, over a matter of patronage, was happily accepted, much to Chase's own consternation. Chase's usefulness had been calculated with some nicety just to the point of diminishing returns. He was later

made Chief Justice of the Supreme Court, but this was not until
after the election, and after he had done his duty in the
campaign.

And yet Chase's removal created a new kind of party imbalance which would hardly solve itself, since Chase's bitterest
enemies, the conservative followers of Postmaster-General Montgomery Blair, took this as a triumphant vindication of themselves. The fact was that Blair's influence in the party at large
had been steadily diminishing, and a radical movement for
Blair's head thereupon became, in Lincoln's judgment, too
dangerous to resist. Though both the personal and official
relations between the two had always been characterized by
great warmth, Lincoln judiciously decided to cut Blair adrift in
September 1864. (Jefferson Davis, as many instances show,
would never have played that sort of trick on a loyal subordinate.) Yet this did not prevent Blair from working vigorously
for the President's re-election. He was not prepared to sacrifice
his claim on the party, which he would have done had he
refused to campaign, nor was he willing to risk a Democratic
victory.

There were relatively few changes in Lincoln's cabinet, and
they were all made under circumstances firmly controlled by
Lincoln himself. The historian of Jefferson Davis's cabinet is
unable to account satisfactorily for its lack of stability, except
to chronicle a long series of resignations, most of them under
fire. (There were six secretaries of war, five attorneys-general,
and four secretaries of state.) The legislative branch of government has no constitutional right to interfere in the business
of the President's cabinet, and in this light Lincoln would have
been quite justified in refusing to deal with the senatorial delegation that challenged him on Seward. But constitutional for-
mality was only one of the guidelines. These men confronted
him in at least two capacities, as senators and as leaders of the
party, and in their latter capacity, as Lincoln well knew, they
could not safely be turned away. The resulting adjustment,
though exhausting and worrisome, brought rich dividends in the
repair of morale. Davis was not required to adjust to any such
principle. He too was harassed by informal groups of legislators
on similar missions. In February 1865, with the Confederacy
rapidly deteriorating, the legislative delegation of Virginia urged
him to make certain changes in his cabinet. He thought it

proper to declare, as he had on other occasions: "The relations between the President and the Heads of the Executive Departments are . . . of the closest and most intimate character . . . and it is not a Constitutional function of the Legislative Department to interfere with these relations. . . ." Lincoln's cabinet represented an ever-uneasy alliance, which is why it required so much of his attention. But in the very process of managing it he was, in effect, at the same time managing the party and fashioning it into a powerful instrument for waging war. In reference to that cabinet, it is not too much to say that the choice of its members, its stability, its management, and the major changes made in it, are all to be understood largely with reference to a single principle, the exigencies of party politics.

The whole corps of federal officeholders may be understood in much the same light. We have no full study of Jefferson Davis's patronage policies, which is probably symptomatic; there may never be much of a basis for generalizing about them. But there certainly was one striking, self-evident difference between Lincoln's and his, which was clarity of standards. Davis wanted merit, zeal, and loyalty. (As one writer puts it, he "favored civil service reform.") Lincoln also, naturally, wanted merit, zeal, and loyalty. But he also had some very straightforward criteria for determining in a hurry what those qualities actually meant and how they were to be found. The appointee had to be a Republican—which was at least helpful in narrowing a swarming field by roughly half—and the most dependable general standard for assessing loyalty and zeal was services to the party. It was within this category that he made his choices on "merit." The rules of procedure were also quite precise. For example:

> The appointments of postmasters, with salaries less than $1000 per annum, will be made upon the recommendations of the [Republican] members of Congress in the different districts. Applications addressed to them will receive attention earlier than if sent to the Department, and save much delay and trouble.

Lincoln was, moreover, very meticulous about "senatorial courtesy."

Though Davis, as might naturally be supposed, accepted the recommmendations of others, he does not seem to have felt bound by any given rule in acting upon them. For example, by insisting on having his own way over the postmastership of Montgomery, Davis deeply alienated both the senators from Alabama. Wrote Senator Clement Clay to the equally outraged Senator Yancey: "He did not recognize the duty to respect the wishes of the Senators and Representatives, even when the office was in the town of a Senator and a Representative." And Davis loftily declared: "I am not aware of the existence of any such usage. . . . I must add that the Senate is no part of the *nominating* power, and that according, as I do, the highest respect to the opinions of Senators when they recommend applicants, I decline to yield to any dictation from them on the subject of nominations."

Patronage is a care and a worry; it is also a cherished prerogative, with gratifications for those who give as well as those who receive. They are all part of the same sensitive network. The responsiveness and *espirit* of such a network thus require that both the giving and the receiving be widely shared, and on some understood basis. We have no way of measuring the energy with which the men who made up these two patronage systems supported their respective administrations and worked to carry out their purposes. But we do know that one administration had an intricate set of standards for appraising energy and rewarding it—in addition always, of course, to standards of patriotism—which was not available to the other.

IV

The field of comparison in which contrasts between the two governments are perhaps most grossly striking is that of state-federal relations. In both cases there was a set of natural fault-lines, inherent in a federal structure, between the state and national governments. In the Confederacy, these cracks opened ever more widely as the war went on. Toward the end, indeed, some states were in a condition of virtual rebellion against the Confederate government. In the North, the very opposite occurred. The states and the federal government came to be bound more and more closely in the course of the four years, such that by the end of that time the profoundest change had been effected in the character of their relations. In the course of things, moreover, the people themselves would come to be more closely bound to their national government. But the mechanisms are by no means self-evident. It cannot be taken for granted that in the nature of things such a process was bound to occur.

For the Confederacy, one very good way to tell this story is in terms of states' rights. The late Frank Owsley made a seminal contribution to historical thought on just these lines when he published his *State Rights in the Confederacy* over forty years ago. With a number of impressive examples, Owsley asserted that it was the mystique of state sovereignty, the inability of the South to overcome the states' rights mentality in order to operate as a nation, that ultimately did in the Confederacy. Most subsequent writers, including the present one, agree that the argument is essentially sound. For comparative purposes, however, something more is required. There was, after all, considerable states' rights sentiment in the North as well. Yet there, states' rights pressure came to be counterbalanced over time by other pressures. What kind? What was the process? How did it work?

There are two areas in which this may be observed most aptly. One is that of control and recruitment of troops; the other, of dealing with disaffection and disloyalty.

For the Confederacy, the great problem in raising and organizing armies was far less a matter of insufficient manpower than it was of divided authority. The various efforts of the Confederate government to get full access to and control over military manpower in the states were successfully obstructed throughout the war by the state governors. The patriotic ardor of the governors for mobilizing troops need not in itself be doubted. The perpetual question was rather how it ought to be managed and how troops were to be used; state resistance to Confederate policy always came down to one of two principles: local defense, or the dangers of a centralized military despotism. Referring to Confederate recruiting in his state, one of the most co-operative of the governors, John Milton of Florida, wrote angrily to Davis in December, 1861: "These troops have been raised by authority of the War Department in disrespect to State authority . . . and I do most solemnly protest, the tendency of the assumption and exercise of such power by the Confederate Government is to sap the very foundation of the rights of the States and . . . to [promote] consolidation."

The organization of the army in the spring and summer of 1861 was held up by shortages not of men but of arms, substantial amounts of which were in possession of the state governments. They were held back partly for what were seen as local needs, and partly in pique at the War Department's receiving of volunteers raised without the intermediary of the governor. Efforts of the states to control the appointment of field officers led them either to hold back regiments until they were fully formed—instead of sending them forward by companies—or else by tendering "skeleton regiments" with a full complement of state-commissioned officers and only a few privates. Their insistence on controlling the clothing and supply of their own state troops in Confederate service led to consequences that were almost disastrous. Resources being not only unequal but at the very best limited, the maximum co-ordination of both purchasing and distribution was imperative. Yet as it was, Confederate purchasing agents had to engage everywhere in the most ruinous competition with agents from the states for sources of supply at home and abroad, while at the same time the output of state-controlled factories was kept consistently out of general reach. Governor Zebulon B. Vance of North Carolina actually boasted that, at the time of Robert E. Lee's surrender (of a tattered and starving army), he himself had huge stores of uniforms, blankets, cloth, leather, overcoats, and bacon in his state warehouses.

Conscription was adopted in the Confederacy in April 1862, a full year before the same step was taken in the North. One of the objects was to reorganize the twelve-months' volunteers whose terms were then running out; the other was to get control of the aggregations of militia which had been built up during the previous year and held in the states for local defense. This latter purpose was never properly achieved. State guards were once again built up, the condition of whose discipline and training made them worthless for almost any purpose so long as they were withheld from general service; and conscription itself, especially after the Act of February 1864, was resisted by the governors in a variety of ways. The chief device was that of exemptions, wherein wide categories of persons were sweepingly redefined as "state officers."

In all such respects, Governor Joseph E. Brown of Georgia stands as an almost incredible Confederate legend. Units of

Georgia men who had volunteered directly for the Confederate service (rather than being mustered by the state) were forbidden by Brown in the spring of 1861 to take any arms, whether from state arsenals or even owned by themselves, beyond the borders of Georgia. He organized and fully equipped a brigade—though Confederate law would not allow the Secretary of War to accept such a unit—and then kept it idle during the first Manassas campaign because the War Department wanted him to send it by regiments and would not let him commission a brigadier for it. In order to keep eligible Georgians away from Confederate conscription officers, and his state militia out of Confederate service, he proceeded in 1864 to exempt as "indispensable state officers" a total of about 15,000 men, including everyone remotely connected with the state and county governments as well as factory and railroad employees and some 3000 newly commissioned "officers" of the state militia. When Sherman began his Atlanta campaign, Brown raised 10,000 men for local defense and insisted on their being used as militia. He "loaned" them to General John B. Hood (subject to withdrawal at any time), but when it appeared that the War Department was about to requisition the whole force into general service, he declared that the "emergency" was over and sent them all home on thirty-day furlough to harvest their crops. This was a week after the fall of Atlanta, and at the very time Sherman was preparing for his march to the sea. Brown's endless quarrels with Davis and his attacks on the "tyranny" of the central government were grimly abetted and assisted throughout by the Stephens brothers and Robert Toombs. Indeed, one of the governor's most vicious messages to his legislature was virtually ghost-written by the Confederate Vice-President.

In the North, the story of the recruitment and control of the army was, at least by comparison, relatively straightforward. The raising of troops was at the outset fully in the hands of the state governors, and so in a nominal sense it remained throughout. And yet by a series of steps the actual initiative tended to pass increasingly to the national government. By calling for three-year volunteer enlistments during the first month of hostilities and enlarging the regular army without the authority of law before the assembling of Congress, Lincoln took clear control of the national forces. Through most of the first year the recruiting activities of the governors proceeded with the utmost energy. The first major shift in initiative occurred after the failure of the Peninsular Campaign, when patriotic fervor began wearing thin and volunteers became increasingly harder to find. At this point Secretary Seward persuaded all the governors to unite in memorializing the President to call for 150,000 more volunteers, whereupon Lincoln promptly called for twice that many, together with 300,000 nine-months' militia. Both calls were more than met. Under the threat of a militia draft, the governors threw themselves with renewed zeal into a very aggressive campaign of recruiting. After the Emancipation Proclamation, the administration agreed to the enrolling of Negro troops. Aside from the raising of a few independent regiments, this recruiting was done directly by field commanders, entirely outside the control of any state government, and approximately 186,000 men were thus added to the national army. A further step was the adoption of conscription with the National Enrollment Act of March 1863, which gave the President full power to raise and support armies without state assistance. The unpopular Act was not fully exploited, and conscription as such accounted for not more than about 6 per cent of the total Union forces. It was successfully used, however, from 1863 to the end of the war, as a device for filling deficiencies in state volunteer quotas and for encouraging the governors to see that such deficiencies did not occur. In the mobilization of military manpower the state governors on the whole performed their function with exceptional vigor, even while becoming—as one writer somewhat extravagantly puts it—"mere agents" of the national government.

The energy of the Union government may be seen with even greater clarity in its actions against disaffection and disloyalty. Without any special legislation, Lincoln immediately assumed executive authority to suspend the writ of habeas corpus and make summary arrests in areas particularly endangered by disloyal activities; and in handling such cases the government made very little use of the courts. A blanket proclamation of September 24, 1862 (previous ones had designated specific localities), made "all persons discouraging volunteer enlistments, resisting militia drafts, or guilty of any disloyal practice . . . subject to martial law and liable to trial and punishment by Courts Martial or Military Commission," anywhere in the country and at any time "during the existing insurrection." Congress made some effort to define the President's powers in the Habeas Corpus Act of March 3, 1863, but whether the Act intended to grant these powers for the first time or to recognize powers he had exercised all along was not clear, and in any event executive policy and practice proceeded unaltered. For such activities as aiding desertion, circulating disloyal literature, bushwhacking, bridge-burning, forming and promoting disloyal secret societies, and so on, the State and War Departments with their network of provost-marshals and other agents made thousands of arrests throughout the war. The exact number will never be known. The chief voices of opposition to these policies came from the Democratic party; the chief supporters were the Republican governors, especially in the Midwest.

No such freedom or directness of action was ever permitted to Jefferson Davis. He could make no summary moves against practices whose effect was to obstruct the war effort until the badly unsettled conditions of early 1862 finally persuaded the Confederate Congress that something needed to be done. The Act passed on February 27 thereupon permitted the executive to suspend habeas corpus and apply martial law to places threatened by invasion. But though Davis used his power in a very restricted way, the resulting hostility to martial law as imposed on Richmond and certain other places was such that Congress in April felt constrained to put further limits on the executive and to amend the law by giving it a fixed date of expiration. A second Act was also limited to a fixed term—it was passed on October 13, 1862, and expired five months later—and did not authorize trials of civilians by military courts. During this time, the writ of habeas corpus was suspended in fewer places than before. But despite Davis's urgings the law was allowed to lapse, and for a year nothing was enacted to take its place. A third Act, in force from the middle of February to the end of July 1864, contained many limits on executive discretion, and after that time the most desperate pleas by the Confederate President could not induce his Congress to pass another. The reason which the Congress gave for its refusal was the opposition of the states. That opposition had, indeed, been so bitter that Confederate law was in many places rendered practically unenforceable. Governor Brown insisted that the people of Georgia had "more to apprehend from military despotism than from subjugation by the enemy," and when Alexander Stephens harangued the Georgia legislature in March 1864 on the government's "despotic" suspension of habeas corpus, Brown had the speech printed and mailed to the company officers of every Georgia regiment and to every county clerk and county sheriff in Confederate territory. The legislature of North Carolina passed an Act making it compulsory for state judges to issue the writ, in effect nullifying Confederate law. A meeting of governors in October 1864 adopted a resolution "virtually condemning" the suspension of habeas corpus.

One result was a serious weakening of the South's military system. State judges in Virginia, Texas, North Carolina, and elsewhere issued writs of habeas corpus indiscriminately to persons accused of desertion or evading military service, and Governor Vance used his militia to enforce them. Robert E. Lee complained to the Secretary of War that the drain on the army thus caused by the use of habeas corpus was "more than it can bear." Moreover, the deterioration of civil government in many areas made a wide field for lawless bands, disloyal secret societies, and trading with the enemy. Persons arrested for such activities were again and again freed by habeas corpus on grounds of insufficient evidence. All this despite Davis's plea that "the suspension of the writ is not simply advisable and expedient, but almost indispensable to the successful conduct of the war."

The chief mechanism that prevented such centrifugal tendencies from developing in the Northern states, as William B. Hesseltine pointed out some years ago, was the Republican party. It was the energy of the Republican party that established the political structure with which the North began the war, and through which the war was prosecuted to the end. More specifically, the governors of every Northern state in 1861 had been put there through the efforts of that party, and these men represented both the state organizations and the national coalition responsible for bringing a Republican administration to Washington. They were politically committed from the very first to positive measures for suppressing disunion. With remarkable unanimity they invited Lincoln at the outset to take steps—indeed, they insisted he take them—which could only draw more and more power into his hands, leaving them with

less and less initiative. As with the raising of armies, there
was something cumulative about this process; it came to take
on a life of its own.

In turn, the various state administrations—especially after
the resurgence of the Democratic party with the reverses of
1862—came more and more, despite their traditions of particularism, to realize their growing dependence on the federal
government for political support. There are numerous examples
of this. One is the famous case of Governor Oliver Morton of
Indiana, whom the elections of 1862 had confronted with a
Democratic legislature. These Democrats, denouncing Morton,
Lincoln, conscription, emancipation, and arbitrary arrests, tried
to remove the state's military affairs from Morton's control and
successfully held up appropriation bills until the session expired, leaving the governor without money to run the state.
The distraught Morton, not wanting to call a special session
and at the same time convinced that treasonable Copperhead
conspiracies were about to engulf the entire Northwest, appealed in his extremity to the President, who was no more
anxious than he to have Indiana's Democrats crippling the state's
war effort. Funds were found in the War Department, which,
together with private subscriptions, enabled Morton to steer
through a critical period without state appropriations.

The state elections of 1863—notably those in Connecticut,
Ohio, and Pennsylvania, where the full resources of the federal
government were exerted for the Republican candidates—show
even more clearly this process of growing dependence. In
Connecticut, Governor Buckingham was running for re-election
against the Democrat Thomas H. Seymour, who flatly opposed the war. Buckingham's 3000-vote victory was assisted by
the Secretary of War, who got as many of the state's Republican
soldiers furloughed home as the armies could spare; by the
President, who wielded the federal patronage where it could
best influence the result; and by the Ordnance Department,
which let it be understood that Connecticut's arms manufacturers would do well to see that all their workers turned out
and voted—for Buckingham. The Democrats of Pennsylvania
nominated Judge George W. Woodward, who held that federal
conscription was unconstitutional, to run against Governor
Andrew G. Curtin; and in Ohio the Republican candidate John
Brough was opposed by Clement L. Vallandigham, who had

recently been arrested by military authorities for seditious utterances tending to discourage enlistments. Lincoln gave both campaigns his fullest attention. Government clerks from the two states were given free railroad passes, sent home on leave to vote, and assessed one per cent of their salaries for campaign expenses. Secretary Chase, assisted by governors Morton of Indiana and Yates of Illinois, made rousing speeches in Ohio. Workers at the Philadelphia arsenal were marched to the polls on election day "like cattle to the slaughter." Field commanders were again authorized to furlough troops, who thereupon performed the double service of voting themselves and encouraging the whole citizenry to do the right thing. Curtin defeated Woodward by 15,000 votes in Pennsylvania; Brough, who had barely received the Republican nomination, beat Vallandigham by over 100,000 in Ohio.

In the broadest sense the dependence of the state and national administrations was mutual, and was mutually acknowledged; but in any case the binding agency and energizing force was the Republican party. And this in turn was maintained—indeed, made possible—through the continued existence of the Democrats.

V

There is certainly no need here to discuss the beneficial functions of a "loyal opposition." But something might be said about the functions of an opposition which is under constant suspicion of being only partly loyal. The Northern Democratic party during the Civil War stood in precisely this relation to the Union war effort, and its function in this case was of a double nature. On the one hand, its legitimacy as a quasi-formal institution would remain in the last analysis unchallenged, so long as it kept its antiwar wing within some sort of bounds. But by the same token there was the rough and ready principle that "every Democrat may not be a traitor, but every traitor is a Democrat."

Thus, the very existence of the Democratic party provided the authorities (who badly needed some standard) with a ready-made device for making the first rough approximation in the identification of actual disloyalty. It also provided a kind of built-in guarantee against irrevocable personal damage should the guess turn out to be wrong. When in doubt they could always round up the local Democrats, as many a time they did, and in case of error there was always a formula for saving face all around: it was "just politics." There was, in short, a kind of middle way, an intermediate standard that had its lighter side and alleviated such extremes in security policy as, on the one hand, the paralysis and frustration of doing nothing, and, on the other, the perversions of power that accompany political blood-baths. For example, elections in the doubtful border states were always accompanied by rioting, skulduggery, and various kinds of dirty work; a familiar technique for preventing this was to make wholesale arrests of Democrats just beforehand. Or, in the case of Clement L. Vallandigham, the man was arrested in 1863 by order of General Ambrose Burnside, convicted by military commission, and lodged in a Cincinnati military prison for expressing sympathy with the enemy and speaking with intent to hinder the war effort. Vallandigham's prominence in the Democratic party of Ohio both created a dilemma and provided for its solution. On the one hand, it would hardly seem safe to have such a man in high public office; on the other hand a shade might be established somewhere between "treason" and "mere politics." Lincoln's solution, without exactly repudiating General Burnside's, was to commute Vallandigham's sentence to deportation through the Confederate lines.

Two state governments, those of New York and New Jersey, actually did fall into Democratic hands for a time during the war. But despite much talk of states' rights and arbitrary central authority, neither of these administrations did anything that materially hindered the war effort. Both, in fact, did much to promote it, and it was not as though either state was lacking in Democrats ready for almost any measure which might tie up the federal government. But a strong stimulus to the Democratic governors, as well as to the state Democratic organizations, for keeping such elements in check was the existence in each state of a formidable Republican organization which was watching their every move.

Meanwhile Jefferson Davis also had opposition, in his Congress as well as in the states, and it grew ever larger. But it was not "an" opposition in any truly organized sense. It was far more toxic, an undifferentiated bickering resistance, an unspecified something that seeped in from everywhere to soften the very will of the Confederacy. Davis could not move against this; he had no real way of getting at it. He had no way, for example, without either an organized opposition party or an organized administration party, of dealing with a man like Joseph E. Brown. Had there been such organizations, and had Brown himself been at the head of either the one or the other of them in the state of Georgia, the administration forces would have had some sort of check on him. As it was, Brown could claim expansively and with the fullest justice that he simply represented the whole people of Georgia; and had Davis directly challenged Brown's loyalty he would have challenged the good faith of an entire state. Not being held to the administration and the other states by party ties, Brown and others like him were without any continuing mode of instruction in the requirements and interests of the Confederacy as a whole. His supreme parochialism and reluctance to co-operate need not be seen as a matter of mere spite. The world's history is full of political elites—such as the Polish nobles of the eighteenth century, unwilling to give up their *liberum veto* to a king to achieve a strong Polish state—that literally did not know their own best interests. Although Brown could not see beyond the borders of Georgia, it ought to be said for him that what he did see he saw very clearly. His whole sense and image of power was tied up in the relation between himself and the population of his state. Thus to him, Davis's efforts to mobilize the total resources of the Confederacy were as great a threat as was the Union army—Brown as much as said so—and they intruded, in any case, an element of uncertainty into his own political world so gross as to be intolerable. Unlike the Northern governors, Brown had no formal national structure with a clear set of organizational interests, and on which his own power depended, to persuade him otherwise.

If Abraham Lincoln could be said to have any sort of counterpart to Davis's Brown, perhaps the man who came closest to filling that role was Horatio Seymour, the Democratic governor of New York. Seymour was a man of strong intelligence who had been elected in 1862, at a time when the administration's prestige had suffered a number of setbacks. He spoke vigorously for states' rights and individual liberties, attacked conscription, emancipation, arbitrary arrests, suspension of habeas corpus, and the consolidation of national power. His sayings gave much anxiety to the administration, and much heart to its enemies everywhere. And yet the structure of political parties provided every element needed for containing what mischief Seymour might make, in case he ever intended any. Lincoln's technique for handling Seymour was to keep him off balance by receiving all his high pronouncements of principle —though with elaborate politeness—as the utterances of a man who, as a matter of course, wanted to be the next Democratic President. Seymour was treated, in short, as a partisan political schemer. At the same time, there was in Seymour's own state an alert and powerful Republican organization ready to pick up the faintest treasonable echoes that might be coming out of Albany. They would catch at the governor's every word—as with his innocent blunder of addressing an antidraft mob in New York City as "my friends"—in an effort to make the charge stick. The man's leeway was not very wide. He tried without success to have the draft suspended in New York, yet was as energetic as anyone in raising the state's quota of volunteers. He was defeated for re-election in 1864 by Republican Congressman Reuben E. Fenton.

A further note on "opposition" might involve the relations of Lincoln with the "Radical" faction of his own party. This question has produced some strong debate among historians, though the principal issues appear by now to have been largely settled. One side of it was opened by the publication in 1941 of T. Harry Williams's *Lincoln and the Radicals,* which represented the President's greatest political burdens as having been heaped on him not so much by the Democrats as by extremists within the Republican ranks. This determined phalanx of "Radicals," or "Jacobins" as John Hay first called them, hounded Lincoln without mercy. Their Committee on the Conduct of the War, with its investigations into military policy and its eternal pressure for changes of generals, was a serious hindrance to the administration. Their insistence on emancipation, Negro troops, and confiscation of rebel property embarrassed Lincoln in his policy of moderation toward the border states during the early stage of the war. They tried to refashion his cabinet; they tried to force his hand on reconstruction; they even tried to replace him as the Republican candidate in 1864 with someone more forceful. On every issue but the last, the Radicals "conquered" Lincoln. Nor was Williams seeing mirages. It may be, indeed, that he saw things in much the way Lincoln himself must at times have seen them. There *were* Radicals; they did harass him constantly; more than once they drove him virtually to despair. It might even be said that in the end they "won." But whether this should mean that Lincoln "lost" is another question. How fundamental, really, was the "struggle"? Williams was eventually challenged on just this ground by David Donald in 1956, and as a result the entire tone of the matter has since become much altered. Donald pointed out that "presidents are always criticized by members of their own parties," but that this is hardly the same as out-and-out warfare. The Radicals were not in fact a very cohesive or disciplined group; they were far from agreed among themselves on a great many things; and they were certainly not inveterate enemies of the President. He wanted their support, and at the most critical points he did not fail to get it. Personal relations were always reasonably good; with one of the leaders, Charles Sumner, they were excellent. As Donald says, "to picture Lincoln at swords' points with the Radical leaders of his own party, then, is an error."

The one point which may need further emphasis is that these Radicals, whatever may have been their many differences, represented the most articulate, most energetic, most militant wing of the Republican party. The one thing that did unite such men as Trumbull, Wade, Greeley, Chandler, Fessenden, Julian, and the rest was their implacable insistence that the war be prosecuted with ever more vigor, and that the President use the national power to the utmost in doing it. There is every evidence that in this over-all objective they and the President were at one, inasmuch as the war was, in the end, so prosecuted. Whether Lincoln welcomed his tormentors is doubtful. But whether he or anyone else would have moved as decisively without them is equally doubtful, and what the Union war effort as a whole would have been without the energy they represented is more doubtful still. The tensions and conflicts of the Lincoln administration—such as those having to do with emancipation, the use of Negro troops, and the complexion of the government that was to stand for re-election in 1864—were,

as we know, considerable. But without a party apparatus to
harness and direct them, they would surely have been un-
manageable.

In any event, we might imagine Jefferson Davis as being
quite willing to exchange this sort of "opposition" for the one
he had. In the Confederate Congress there seem to have been
some who pressed for greater vigor than Davis's in fighting the
war; a much larger number inclined to measures that would
have resulted in less. But perhaps more fundamental was that
these men were all mixed in together. There was no recognized
way of segregating or defining them, no basis of expectations,
no clear principle for predicting what they might do. "There were
no political organizations seeking undivided loyalty," as the
historian of that Congress puts it, "nor was there consistent
pressure from the electorate. Conditions changed, opinions
changed, consequently administration sympathies changed." This
lack of sharpness seems to have been accompanied by a certain
lack of initiative which is quite noticeable when contrasted with
the wartime federal Congress, and it is apparent that lack of
party responsibility had much to do with it. Davis's Congress
for the most part was not violently obstructive, in the sense
that groups within it confronted him with formidable alternatives in policy to which he had to adjust. Much of his legislation, indeed, was rather passively enacted, which is to say that
at best he could drag his Congress along. At the worst, however,
it ended by being a drag on him. Perhaps his snappishness and
rigidity were, after all, only appropriate to the circumstances.
Professor Yearns mildly concludes:

> He despaired at Congress's amendments, delays, and occasional
> rejections. Only subservience satisfied him, and, as his influence
> with Congress was based primarily on an agreement of ideas,
> not on party discipline, he ultimately lost some of this influence.

Certainly Davis had no counterpart of Lincoln's "Radicals" to
spur him on. Could the rabid secessionists of the 1850's, the
so-called Southern "fire-eaters," the Robert Barnwell Rhetts, the
William Lowndes Yanceys, the Edmund Ruffins, have made
such a counterpart? There is little evidence that they could,
or would. Such men are quite absent from the roll of the Confederacy's leading statesmen. The most dynamic "fire-eaters"

who came into their own in the war years were two obstruction-
ist state governors, already mentioned, Zebulon Vance and
Joseph E. Brown.

VI

It has been asserted throughout this essay that the Republican
party, in the presence of an organized party of opposition, performed a variety of functions in mobilizing and managing the
energies needed for sustaining the Union war effort. These were
carried on both inside and outside the formal structure of
government, and by men active in party affairs whether they
held office or not. The absence of such a system in the Confederacy seems to have had more than a casual bearing on the
process whereby Southern energies, over and beyond the course
of military events, became diffused and dissipated. National
commitments in the North were given form and direction by
an additional set of commitments, those of party. This hardly
means that the Republican party is to be given sole credit for
the success of the war effort, which was in fact supported by
overwhelming numbers of Democrats. But it does mean, among
other things, that there were political sanctions against the
Democrats' *not* supporting it, sanctions which did not exist in
the Confederacy. When Democratic leaders were inclined to
behave irresponsibly they could not, like Brown and Vance,
play the role of state patriots. A hint of Democratic disloyalty
anywhere tightened the Republican organization everywhere.

The emphasis hitherto has been upon leadership, upon
how the process of politics affected the workings of government,
but a final word should be said about how that process affected
the body of citizenry. What may have been the function of a
party system as a vehicle of communication? What did it do
toward making popular elections a mode whereby the people
were in effect called upon to define and reaffirm their own
commitment to the national cause? In 1862, 1863, and 1864,
through a series of elections which made the heaviest psychological demands on the entire country, the North had annually
to come to terms with the war effort. The Republicans, with
varying degrees of success, everywhere made attempts to
broaden their coalition by bringing as many Union Democrats
into it as possible, and naturally tried to attract as many Demo-

cratic voters to it as they could. The national party even changed its name in 1864, calling itself the "Union" party to dramatize the breadth of its appeal. And yet the result was in no true sense an all-party front or bipartisan coalition; rather it was a highly successful device for detaching Democrats from their regular party loyalties. The distinction is of some importance. The initiative for this effort remained throughout in Republican hands, and the Democrats everywhere maintained their regular organizations. The structure of parties was therefore such that every election became, in a very direct way, a test of loyalty to the national government.

The tests were by no means consistently favorable. In the fall of 1862, the time of the mid-term elections, the Republicans were significantly divided on the President's policy of emancipation, and a heavy majority of Democrats opposed it. This was reflected in the state and congressional election results, which were deeply depressing to the administration. The Democrats elected governors in two states and majorities in the legislatures of several, and substantially increased their numbers in Congress. This had several important consequences. One was that, inasmuch as the Republicans still maintained their control of Congress, the weakened state organizations were brought a step farther in that progress, already described, of growing dependency on the national party and the national administration for leadership and support. Another was that the Republicans were inspired to great exertions in justifying emancipation as an integral feature of the party program and in minimizing the Democrats' claim that the purposes of the war had been altered to make it an abolition crusade. Still a further consequence was that the Democrats were sufficiently emboldened by their successes that in a number of places they overstepped themselves. The "peace" theme in the Democrats' case against the administration emerged with a clarity that had hitherto been muted, making them much more vulnerable than before to the Republicans' "treason" theme, and drawing clear lines for the state elections of 1863. Ohio in that year was something of a showcase, with the entire country watching. Vallandigham's "martyrdom" at the hands of General Burnside had delivered Ohio's Democratic party over to the "Peace" men, who had made Vallandigham their nominee for governor. The crisis which thus confronted the Republicans called forth their utmost efforts, not only in Ohio but in neighboring states and even in the national capital. Brough, the "Union" candidate, insisted again and again that the people had to choose between treason and disunion on the one hand, and Lincoln, emancipation, and a final crushing of the rebellion on the other. James G. Blaine of Maine, himself an anxious observer, later wrote his own history of the period, and when he noted the importance of this election he did not even mention the name of the winning candidate. He simply said that the people gave "a majority of one hundred and one thousand for the Administration."

Once again in 1864, the Democrats, amid the military discouragements of the summer, assisted in clarifying the choices by writing a peace plank into their national platform and nominating a general, George B. McClellan, who had been dismissied for the failure of the operations of 1862 in the Eastern theater. The re-election of Lincoln was accompanied by the restoration of Republican majorities to every legislature and every congressional delegation, and of Republican governors to every state.

The people of the Confederacy, of course, continued to hold elections. Yet we know surprisingly little—indeed, almost nothing—about these elections. No study has ever been made of them, which is some measure of how comparatively little importance was attached to them at the time. The people were asked in November 1861 to choose Davis and Stephens as heads of the "permanent" government. The election "was marked, however, by general apathy." The first elections to Congress, according to Professor Yearns, "went off quietly." There was virtually no campaigning, and "balloting everywhere was light, as is usual when issues are absent." The elections of 1863, from what little glimpse we have of them, seem aggressive only by contrast. The increased activity at that time was principally a product of increased dissatisfaction with Davis's government. Yet even here the opposition was unorganized and unfocused, and candidates "failed to offer any clear substitute for policies they denigrated." "Mixed with rodomontade was the familiar state rights ingredient which gave much criticism a respectable flavor. All of the strong war measures were condemned as evidence of centralized despotism which was abusing the states."

The sluggishness of communication in the Confederacy has

often been commented on, and yet here the contrast with the North is one which the disparity in technology does not quite fully account for. There was no counterpart in the South of the resonance which party elections provided for the Northern cause. The historian of Confederate propaganda asserts that official efforts in this direction were very deficient, which is not surprising when it is recalled how preponderantly such efforts in the North were handled through party agencies. We have a description of how such activities were carried on in Washington with the heartiest co-operation of the national government during the fall of 1864:

> The National Republican Committee have taken full possession of all the Capitol buildings, and the committee rooms of the Senate and House of Representatives are filled with clerks, busy in mailing Lincoln documents all over the loyal States. . . .
> The Post Office Department, of course, is attending to the lion's share of this work. Eighty bags of mail matter, all containing Lincoln documents, are daily sent to Sherman's army.

Not long after this time, a measure was timidly offered in the Confederate Congress whereby the government frank might be used for mailing newspapers to soldiers in the field. The Confederate Postmaster-General was distressed. His department was required by law to be self-supporting, and he was very proud of its being the only one to show a surplus, which he had achieved by doing away with all but the bare minimum services. He spoke to the President about this new bill, and the latter solemnly vetoed it as being unconstitutional.

Whether Northern wartime elections served to give refinement and precision to the issues is perhaps less important than that they served to simplify and consolidate them. When the people of Indiana were urged in 1863 to vote for Republicans in their local elections, they were really being asked to do more than elect a few county officers. And by the same token the candidate for such an office accepted, along with his nomination, a whole train of extraordinary responsibilities: Governor Morton, President Lincoln, emancipation, arbitrary arrests, and war to the end. There was no separating them; under the circumstances of war, the voter who took the Republican candidate took them all. And the candidate, if successful in his debates with his Democratic opponent, would have enacted something akin to the principle of the self-fulfilling prophecy. He defined his position, he defended the administration, he persuaded his audience, and in the process he repersuaded and recommitted himself. It may be quite proper to say that it was, after all, the Union's military success that made political success possible. The fall of Atlanta in September 1864, for example, certainly rescued Lincoln's chances for re-election. But conceivably it was not that simple, and short-term correlations may be deceiving. How was the Northern will sustained for the three and a half years that were needed before it could reap successes of any kind in late 1864? A continual affirmation and reaffirmation of purpose was built into the very currents of political life in the Northern states. It is altogether probable that the North's political energies and its military will were, all along, parts of the same process.

Every election, moreover, was a step in nationalizing the war. The extension of local and state loyalties into national loyalties during this period was something of a revolution, and it did not occur easily. This profound change cannot be taken for granted, nor is it best understood simply by examining the formal federal structure through which it began. It is revealed rather through the far less formal political process whereby the national government in the Civil War was able to communicate its purposes, to persuade, and to exercise its will directly upon individuals in state, city, town, and local countryside.

INTRODUCTORY NOTE

Given the confounding of the basic issues, as Potter has elucidated them on page 192, Lincoln enjoyed the advantage of fighting a war primarily to save the Union, rather than fighting a war to destroy slavery (a cause that found powerful support in the North, in the crucial border states, and even in the rim and highland parts of the South). Indeed, in his first inaugural address Lincoln had offered the South a constitutional amendment, already passed by Congress as an amendment not subject to repeal, that would guarantee slavery in the states where it existed against any future interference by the federal government. Hell-bent for secession, the South rejected this extraordinary concession—probably foolishly, given the South's objectives. Even after the war had begun, the Congress (with the southern delegations of course absent) overwhelmingly passed a resolution that declared that "this war is not waged . . . for any purpose . . . of overthrowing or interfering with the rights or established institutions of those states [that had seceded], but to defend and maintain the supremacy of the Constitution and to preserve the Union, with all the dignity, equality, and rights of the several states unimpaired, and . . . as soon as these objects are accomplished, the war ought to cease." Lincoln accepted this position, which amounted to an affirmation that victory in the war should not be used to deal with the underlying issue that had caused the war to break out!

Ever the astute politician, Lincoln's extreme reluctance to confront the slavery question flowed from a blend of personal convictions and political sensitivity. On the question of freeing the slaves and making them "politically and socially our equals," Lincoln admitted that "my own feelings will not admit of this, and if mine would, we well know that those of the great mass of white people will not. Whether this feeling accords with justice and sound judgment is not the sole question, if indeed it is any part of it. A universal feeling, whether well- or ill-founded cannot be safely disregarded." Lincoln never lost sight of the fact that he was fighting a war supported by an unstable coalition of con-

servative Unionists and radical antislavery men, and if the coalition ever broke down, he would lose the war. Furthermore, he
knew that a direct attack upon slavery would likely drive the
border states into the Confederacy, in which case he would surely
lose the war. Hence he tenaciously resisted emancipation until
a combination of military, diplomatic, and radical congressional
pressures became overwhelming. Then, on September 22, 1862,
on the heels of the limited Union victory at Antietam, he gave
preliminary notice that on the first of January 1863, he would
emancipate all slaves in the areas still in rebellion against the
United States. Abolitionist critics were quick to point out that if
the Confederate states ceased their rebellion before January 1,
they could keep their slaves, and even if they did not, no slaves
would be freed anyway, because the proclamation applied only
to areas where the Union government had no control. The London
Spectator commented bitterly, "The principle is not that a human
being cannot justly own another, but that he cannot own him
unless he is loyal to the United States." Richard Hofstadter has
observed that the celebrated proclamation, justified as a "war
measure," had "all the moral grandeur of a bill of lading."

The Emancipation Proclamation

ABRAHAM LINCOLN

January 1, 1863

By the President of the United States of America:
A Proclamation.

Whereas, on the twenty-second day of September, in the year of our Lord one thousand eight hundred and sixty two, a proclamation was issued by the President of the United States, containing, among other things, the following, to wit:

> That on the first day of January, in the year of our Lord one thousand eight hundred and sixty-three, all persons held as slaves within any State or designated part of a State, the people whereof shall then be in rebellion against the United States, shall be then, thenceforward, and forever free; and the Exccutive Government of the United States, including the military and naval authority thereof, will recognize and maintain the freedom of such persons, and will do no act or acts to repress such persons, or any of them, in any efforts they may make for their actual freedom.
>
> That the Executive will, on the first day of January aforesaid, by proclamation, designate the States and parts of States, if any, in which the people thereof, shall on that day be, in good faith, represented in the Congress of the United States by members chosen thereto at elections wherein a majority of the qualified voters of such State shall have participated, shall in the absence of strong countervailing testimony, be deemed conclusive evidence that such State, and the people thereof, are not then in rebellion against the United States.

Now, therefore, I, Abraham Lincoln, President of the United States, by virtue of the power in me invested as Commander-in-Chief, of the Army and Navy of the United States in time of actual armed rebellion against authority and government of the United States, and as a fit and necessary war measure for suppressing said rebellion, do, on this first day of January, in the year of our Lord one thousand eight hundred and sixty-three, and in accordance with my purpose so to do publicly proclaimed for the full period of one hundred days, from the day first above mentioned, order and designate as the States and parts of States wherein the people thereof respectively, are this day in rebellion against the United States, the following to wit:

Arkansas, Texas, Louisiana, (except the Parishes of St. Bernard, Plaquemines, Jefferson, St. Johns, St. Charles, St. James, Ascension, Assumption, Terrebone, Lafourche, St. Mary, St. Martin, and Orleans, including the City of New-Orleans) Mississippi, Alabama, Florida, Georgia, South-Carolina, North-Carolina, and Virginia (except the forty-eight counties designated as West Virginia, and also the counties of Berkley, Accomac, Northampton, Elizabeth-City, York, Princess Ann, and Norfolk, including the cities of Norfolk and Portsmouth, and which excepted parts are, for the present, left precisely as if this proclamation were not issued.

And by virtue of the power, and for the purpose aforesaid, I do order and declare that all persons held as slaves within said designated States, and parts of States, are, and henceforward shall be free; and the Executive government of the United States, including the military and naval authorities thereof, will recognize and maintain the freedom of said persons.

And I hereby enjoin upon the people so declared to be free to abstain from all violence, unless in necessary self-defence; and I recommend to them that, in all cases when allowed, they labor faithfully for reasonable wages.

And I further declare and make known that such persons of suitable condition, will be received into the armed service of the United States to garrison forts, positions, stations, and other places, and to man vessels of all sorts in said service.

And upon this act, sincerely believed to be an act of justice, warranted by the Constitution, upon military necessity, I invoke the considerate judgment of mankind, and the gracious favor of Almighty God.

In witness whereof, I have hereunto set my hand and caused the seal of the United States to be affixed.

Done at the City of Washington, the first day of January,

in the year of our Lord one thousand eight hundred and sixty-three, and of the Independence of the United States of America the eighty-seventh.

By the President: ABRAHAM LINCOLN
WILLIAM H. SEWARD, *Secretary of State.*

The odds against a radical reconstruction of race relations in postbellum America were truly formidable. The central problem was the racial subordination of the black population. For decades Americans had argued the issue in terms of the institutional form that subordination took—chattel slavery—and they argued about an abstraction—slavery in the territories, where there were essentially no slaves. Then, when the war came, the predominant issue became transformed from the question of slavery or race to the question of Union. Even when the exigencies of war pressed hard on the Union leadership, emancipation was delayed, and instead Lincoln called enthusiastically for a gradual and compensated form of emancipation that would last until 1900 and would be linked to colonization of all American Negroes—in Haiti, Panama or elsewhere—an utterly fanciful proposal in the face of a black birthrate of 500 infants a day and a massive reluctance on the part of 4 million blacks to leave the land of their birth, particularly when freedom was possible. Once committed to emancipation, however, Lincoln followed through with consistency and force, and when in June of 1864 the House failed to cast the required two-thirds vote for the proposed Thirteenth Amendment, Lincoln exerted powerful administration influence, and the amendment to outlaw slavery passed on January 31, 1865, only ten weeks before Lincoln's death (it was not ratified until the December following the war).

But even emancipation was only preliminary to the real question, which was the racial subordination of American Negroes, and throughout the war the dreams of colonization and the delicate and imperative necessities of holding together an unstable coalition of Unionists and antislavery men had muted any serious discussion of what sort of new social system should follow the war. Then, with monumental irony, the victory of the coalition put an abrupt end to its reason for existence. Although the Union had been restored and slavery abolished, the Confederate surrender did what secession had done, but in reverse: it transformed the central question from one of union back to one of the status of

Negroes, who on this question had far fewer supporters in the North as freedmen than they ever had as slaves. The nub of the problem, as it had been all along, was the deep entrenchment of racist attitudes among northern and southern whites alike. It is small wonder, although it is a sad commentary, that when pressed to choose between two conflicting values—the restoration of a voluntary Union, or the reorganization by federal authority of southern society—the nation chose the former at the expense of the latter.

From this perspective it is remarkable that Reconstruction achieved as much as it did and in so brief a time, for the next real burst of reformist activity in race relations had to wait almost a century. In the essay that follows, C. Vann Woodward assesses the seeds of failure in the racial aspects of Radical Reconstruction, which were intricately entwined with the political and economic aspects of Reconstruction. The tortured evolution of the Republican Party toward an ambiguous commitment to racial equality, which was so fatally compromised by the contrary thrust of white public opinion and the exigencies of politics, tragically illustrates the historic tension between the democratic commitment to majority rule and the equalitarian commitment to minority rights under the Constitution.

Seeds of Failure in
Radical Race Policy

C. VANN WOODWARD

The Republican leaders were quite aware in 1865 that the
issue of Negro status and rights was closely connected with
the two other great issues of Reconstruction—who should reconstruct the South and who should govern the country. But
while they were agreed on the two latter issues, they were
not agreed on the third. They were increasingly conscious that
in order to reconstruct the South along the lines they planned
they would require the support and the votes of the freedmen.
And it was apparent to some that once the reconstructed states
were restored to the Union, the Republicans would need the
votes of the freedmen to retain control over the national government. While they could agree on this much, they were far
from agreeing on the status, the rights, the equality, or the
future of the Negro.

The fact was that the constituency on which the Republican congressmen relied in the North lived in a race-conscious,
segregated society devoted to the doctrine of white supremacy
and Negro inferiority. "In virtually every phase of existence,"
writes Leon Litwack with regard to the North in 1860, "Negroes
found themselves systematically separated from whites. They
were either excluded from railway cars, omnibuses, stage
coaches, and steamboats or assigned to special 'Jim Crow' sections; they sat, when permitted, in secluded and remote corners
of theatres and lecture halls; they could not enter most hotels,
restaurants, and resorts, except as servants; they prayed in
'Negro pews' in the white churches. . . . Moreover, they were
often educated in segregated schools, punished in segregated
prisons, nursed in segregated hospitals, and buried in segregated
cemeteries." Ninety-four percent of the Northern Negroes in

1860 lived in states that denied them the ballot, and the six percent who lived in the five states that permitted them to vote were often disfranchised by ruse. In many Northern states, discriminatory laws excluded Negroes from interracial marriage, from militia service, from the jury box, and from the witness stand when whites were involved. Ohio denied them poor relief, and Indiana, Illinois, and Iowa had laws carrying severe penalties against Negroes settling in those states. Everywhere in the free states, the Negro met with barriers to job opportunities and in most places he encountered severe limitations to the protection of his life, liberty, and property.

One political consequence of these racial attitudes was that the major parties vied with each other in their professions of devotion to the dogma of white supremacy. Republicans were especially sensitive on the point because of their antislavery associations. Many of them, like Senator Lyman Trumbull of Illinois, found no difficulty in reconciling antislavery with anti-Negro views. "We are for free white men," said Senator Trumbull in 1858, "and for making white labor respectable and honorable, which it can never be when negro slave labor is brought into competition with it." Horace Greeley the following year regretted that it was "the controlling idea" of some of his fellow Republicans "to prove themselves 'the white man's party,' or else all the mean, low, ignorant, drunken, brutish whites will go against them from horror of 'negro equality.'" Greeley called such people "the one-horse politicians," but he could hardly apply that name to Lyman Trumbull, nor for that matter to William H. Seward, who in 1860 described the American Negro as "a foreign and feeble element like the Indians, incapable of assimilation," nor to Senator Henry Wilson of Massachusetts, who firmly disavowed any belief "in the mental or the intellectual equality of the African race with this proud and domineering white race of ours." Trumbull, Seward, and Wilson were the front rank of Republican leadership and they spoke the mind of the Middle West, the Middle Atlantic states, and New England. There is much evidence to sustain the estimate of W. E. B. Du Bois that "At the beginning of the Civil War probably not one white American in a hundred believed that Negroes could become an integral part of American democracy."

When the war for Union began to take on the character of a war for Freedom, Northern attitudes toward the Negro, as demonstrated in the previous chapter, paradoxically began to harden rather than soften. This hardening process was especially prominent in the Middle Western states where the old fear of Negro invasion was intensified by apprehensions that once the millions of slaves below the Ohio River were freed they would push northward—this time by the thousands and tens of thousands, perhaps in mass exodus, instead of in driblets of one or two who came furtively as fugitive slaves. The prospect filled the whites with alarm and their spokesmen voiced these fears with great candor. "There is," Lyman Trumbull told the Senate, in April 1862, "a very great aversion in the West—I know it to be so in my state—against having free negroes come among us." And about the same time, John Sherman, who was to give his name to the Radical Reconstruction acts five years later, told Congress that in Ohio "we do not like negroes. We do not disguise our dislike. As my friend from Indiana [Congressman Joseph A. Wright] said yesterday, the whole people of the northwestern States are, for reasons whether correct or not, opposed to having many negroes among them and the principle or prejudice has been engrafted in the legislation of nearly all the northwestern States."

So powerful was this anti-Negro feeling that it almost overwhelmed antislavery feeling and seriously imperiled the passage of various confiscation and emancipation laws designed to free the slave. To combat the opposition, Republican leaders such as George W. Julian of Indiana, Albert G. Riddle of Ohio, and Treasury Secretary Salmon P. Chase advanced the theory that emancipation would actually solve Northern race problems. Instead of starting a mass migration of freedmen northward, they argued, the abolition of slavery would not only put a stop to the entry of fugitive slaves but would drain the Northern Negroes back to the South. Once slavery were ended, the Negro would flee Northern race prejudice and return to his natural environment and the congenial climate of the South.

The official answer of the Republican party to the Northern fear of Negro invasion, however, was deportation of the freedmen and colonization abroad. The scheme ran into opposition from some Republicans, especially in New England, on the ground that it was inhumane as well as impractical. But with the powerful backing of President Lincoln and the support of Western Republicans, Congress overcame the opposition. Lin-

coln was committed to colonization not only as a solution to
the race problem but as a means of allaying Northern opposition
to emancipation and fears of Negro exodus. To dramatize his
solution, the President took the unprecedented step of calling
Negro leaders to the White House and addressing them on the
subject. "There is an unwillingness on the part of our people,"
he told them on August 14, 1862, "harsh as it may be, for you
free colored people to remain with us." He told them that "your
race suffer very greatly, many of them by living among us,
while ours suffer from your presence. . . . If this be admitted,
it affords a reason at least why we should be separated."

The fall elections following the announcement of the
Emancipation Proclamation were disastrous for the Republican
party. And in his annual message in December the President
returned to the theme of Northern fears and deportation. "But
it is dreaded that the freed people will swarm forth and cover
the whole land?" he asked. They would flee the South, he suggested, only if they had something to flee from. "*Heretofore,*" he
pointed out, "colored people to some extent have fled North
from bondage; and *now,* perhaps, from both bondage and
destitution. But if gradual emancipation and deportation be
adopted, they will have neither to flee from." They would cheerfully work for wages under their old masters "till new homes
can be found for them in congenial climes and with people
of their own blood and race." But even if this did not keep the
Negroes out of the North, Lincoln asked, "in any event, can
not the north decide for itself, whether to receive them?" Here
the President was suggesting that the Northern states might
resort to laws such as several of them used before the war to
keep Negroes out.

During the last two years of the war Northern states began to modify or repeal some of their anti-Negro and discriminatory laws. But the party that emerged triumphant from the
crusade to save the Union and free the slave was not in the
best political and moral position to expand the rights and assure the equality of the freedman. It is difficult to identify any
dominant organization of so-called "Radical Republicans" who
were dedicated to the establishment of Negro equality and
agreed on a program to accomplish their end. Both Southern
conservatives and Northern liberals have long insisted or assumed that such an organization of radicals existed and de-

terminedly pursued their purpose. But the evidence does not seem to support this assumption. There undoubtedly *did* emerge eventually an organization determined to overthrow Johnson's policies and take over the control of the South. But that was a different matter. On the issue of Negro equality the party remained divided, hesitant, and unsure of its purpose. The historic commitment to equality it eventually made was lacking in clarity, ambivalent in purpose, and capable of numerous interpretations. Needless to say, its meaning has been debated from that day to this.

The Northern electorate that the Republicans faced in seeking support for their program of reconstruction had undergone no fundamental conversion in its wartime racial prejudices and dogmas. As George W. Julian told his Indiana constituents in 1865, "the real trouble is that *we hate the negro.* It is not his ignorance that offends us, but his color."

In the years immediately following the war every Northern state in which the electorate was given the opportunity to express its views on issues involving racial relations reaffirmed, usually with overwhelming majorities, its earlier and conservative stand. This included the states that reconsidered—and reaffirmed—their laws excluding Negroes from the polls, and others that voted on such questions as office holding, jury service, and school attendance. Throughout these years, the North remained fundamentally what it was before—a society organized upon assumptions of racial privilege and segregation. As Senator Henry Wilson of Massachusetts told his colleagues in 1867, "There is today not a square mile in the United States where the advocacy of the equal rights of those colored men has not been in the past and is not now unpopular." Whether the Senator was entirely accurate in his estimate of white opinion or not, he faithfully reflects the political constraints and assumptions under which his party operated as they cautiously and hesitantly framed legislation for Negro civil and political rights—a program they knew had to be made acceptable to the electorate that Senator Wilson described.

This is not to suggest that there was not widespread and sincere concern in the North for the terrible condition of the freedmen in the South. There can be no doubt that many Northern people were deeply moved by the reports of atrocities, peonage, brutality, lynchings, riots, and injustices that filled the press. Indignation was especially strong over the Black Codes adopted by some of the Johnsonian state legislatures, for they blatantly advertised the intention of some Southerners to substitute a degrading peonage for slavery and make a mockery of the moral fruits of Northern victory. What is sometimes overlooked in analyzing Northern response to the Negro's plight is the continued apprehension over the threat of a massive Negro invasion of the North. The panicky fear that this might be precipitated by emancipation had been allayed in 1862 by the promises of President Lincoln and other Republican spokesmen that once slavery was abolished, the freedmen would cheerfully settle down to remain in the South, that Northern Negroes would be drawn back to the South, and that deportation and colonization abroad would take care of any threat of Northern invasion that remained. But not only had experiments with deportation come to grief, but Southern white persecution and abuse combined with the ugly Black Codes had produced new and powerful incentives for a Negro exodus while removal of the shackles of slavery cleared the way for emigration.

The response of the Republican Congress to this situation was the Civil Rights Act of 1866, later incorporated into the Fourteenth Amendment. Undoubtedly part of the motivation for this legislation was a humanitarian concern for the protection of the Negro in the South, but another part of the motivation was less philanthropic and it was concerned not with the protection of the black man in the South but the white man in the North. Senator Roscoe Conkling of New York, a member of the Joint Committee of Fifteen who helped draft the Civil Rights provisions, was quite explicit on this point. "Four years ago," he said in the campaign of 1866, "mobs were raised, passions were roused, votes were given, upon the idea that emancipated negroes were to burst in hordes upon the North. We then said, give them liberty and rights at the South, and they will stay there and never come into a cold climate to die. We say so still, and we want them let alone, and that is one thing that this part of the amendment is for."

Another prominent member of the Joint Committee who had a right to speak authoritatively of the meaning of its racial policy was George Boutwell of Massachusetts. Addressing his colleagues in 1866, Boutwell said: "I bid the people, the working people of the North, the men who are struggling for subsistence, to beware of the day when the southern freedmen shall swarm over the borders in quest of those rights which should be secured to them in their native states. A just policy on our part leaves the black man in the South where he will soon become prosperous and happy. An unjust policy in the South forces him from home and into those states where his rights will be protected, to the injury of the black man and the white man both of the North and the South. Justice and expediency are united in indissoluble bonds, and the men of the North cannot be unjust to the former slaves without themselves suffering the bitter penalty of transgression." The "bitter penalty" to which Boutwell referred was not the pangs of a Puritan conscience. It was an invasion of Southern Negroes. "Justice and expediency" were, in the words of a more famous states-man of Massachusetts, "one and inseparable."

The author and sponsor of the Civil Rights Act of 1866 was Senator Lyman Trumbull, the same man who had in 1858 described the Republicans as "the white man's party," and in 1862 had declared that "our people want nothing to do with the negro." Trumbull's bill was passed and, after Johnson's veto, was repassed by an overwhelming majority. Limited in application, the Civil Rights Act did not confer political rights or the franchise on the freedmen.

The Fourteenth Amendment, which followed, was even more equivocal and less forthright on racial questions and freedmen's rights. Rejecting Senator Sumner's plea for a guarantee of Negro suffrage, Congress left that decision up to the Southern states. It also left Northern states free to continue the disfranchisement of Negroes, but it exempted them from the penalties inflicted on the Southern states for the same decision. The real concern of the franchise provisions of the Fourteenth Amendment was not with justice to the Negro but with justice to the North. The rebel states stood to gain some twelve seats in the House if all Negroes were counted as a basis of representation and to have about eighteen fewer seats if none were counted. The Amendment fixed apportionment of representation according to enfranchisement.

There was a great deal of justice and sound wisdom in the Fourteenth Amendment, and not only in the first section conferring citizenship on the Negro and protecting his rights, but in the other three sections as well. No sensible person could contend that the rebel states should be rewarded and the loyal states penalized in apportionment of representation by the abolition of slavery and the counting of voteless freedmen. That simply made no sense. Nor were there many, in the North at least, who could object to the temporary disqualification for office and ballot of such Southern officeholders of the old regime as were described in the third section. The fourth section asserting the validity of the national debt and avoiding the Confederate debts was obviously necessary. As it turned out these were the best terms the South could expect—for better than they eventually got—and the South would have been wise to have accepted them.

The tragic failure in statesmanship of the Fourteenth Amendment lay not in its terms but in the equivocal and pusillanimous way it was presented. Had it been made a firm and clear condition for readmission of the rebel states, a lot of anguish would have been spared that generation as well as later ones, including our own. Instead, in equivocal deference to states rights, the South was requested to approve instead of being compelled to accept. In this I think the moderates were wrong and Thaddeus Stevens was right. As W. R. Brock put it, "The onus of decision was passed to the Southern states at a moment when they were still able to defy Congress but hardly capable of taking a statesmanlike view of the future." It was also the fateful moment when President Johnson declared war on Congress and advised the South to reject the Amendment. Under the circumstances, it was inevitable that the South should reject it, and it did so with stunning unanimity. Only thirty-two votes were cast for ratification in all the Southern legislatures. This spelled the end of any hope for the moderate position in the Republican leadership.

After two years of stalling and fumbling, of endless committee work and compromise, the First Reconstruction Act was finally adopted in the eleventh hour of the expiring Thirty-ninth Congress. Only after this momentous bill was passed, was it realized that it had been drastically changed at the last moment by amendments that had not been referred to or considered by committees and that had been adopted without debate in the House and virtually without debate in the Senate. In a panicky spirit of urgency, men who were ordinarily clear-headed yielded their better judgment to the demand for anything-better-than-nothing. Few of them liked what they got, and fewer still understood the implications and the meaning of what they had done. Even John Sherman, who gave his name to the bill, was so badly confused and misled on its effect that he underestimated by some 90 percent the number who would be disqualified from office and disfranchised. And this was one of the key provisions of the bill. It was, on the whole, a sorry performance and was far from doing justice to the intelligence and statesmanship and responsibility of the men who shaped and passed the measure.

One thing was at least clear, despite the charges of the Southern enemies and the Northern friends of the act to the contrary. It was not primarily devised for the protection of Negro rights and the provision of Negro equality. Its primary purpose, however awkwardly and poorly implemented, was to put the Southern states under the control of men loyal to the Union or men the Republicans thought they could trust to control those states for their purposes. As far as the Negro's future was concerned, the votes of the Congress that adopted the Reconstruction Act speak for themselves. Those votes had turned down Stevens' proposal to assure an economic foundation for Negro equality and Sumner's resolutions to give the Negro equal opportunity in schools, in homesteads, and full civil rights. As for the Negro franchise, its provisions, like those for civil rights, were limited. The Negro franchise was devised for the passage of the Fourteenth Amendment and setting up the new Southern state constitutions. But disfranchisement by educational and property qualifications was left an available option, and escape from the whole scheme was left open by permitting the choice of military rule. No guarantee of proportional representation for the Negro population was contemplated, and no assurance was provided for Negro officeholding.

A sudden shift from defiance to acquiescence took place in the South with the passage of the Reconstruction Act of March 2, 1867. How deep the change ran it would be hard to say. The evidence of it comes largely from public pronouncements of the press and conservative leaders, and on the negative side from the silence of the voices of defiance. The mood of submission and acquiescence was experimental, tentative, and precarious at best. It can not be said to have predominated longer than seven months, from spring to autumn of 1867.

That brief period was crucial for the future of the South and the Negro in the long agony of Reconstruction.

Southerners watched intently the forthcoming state elections in the North in October. They were expected to reflect Northern reactions to Radical Reconstruction and especially to the issue of Negro suffrage. There was much earnest speculation in the South. "It may be," said the Charleston *Mercury*, "that Congress but represents the feelings of its constituents, that it is but the moderate mouthpiece of incensed Northern opinion. It may be that measures harsher than any . . . that confiscation, incarceration, banishment may brood over us in turn! But all these things will not change our earnest belief—that *there will be a revulsion of popular feeling in the North.*"

Hopes were aroused first by the elections in Connecticut on April 1, less than a month after the passage of the Reconstruction Act. The Democrats won in almost all quarters. The radical *Independent* taunted the North for hypocrisy. "Republicans in all the great states, North and West, are in a false position on this question," it said. "In Congress they are for impartial suffrage; at home they are against it." In only six states outside the South were Negroes permitted to vote, and in none with appreciable Negro population. The *Independent* thought that "it ought to bring a blush to every white cheek in the loyal North to reflect that the political equality of American citizens is likely to be sooner achieved in Mississippi than in Illinois—sooner on the plantation of Jefferson Davis than around the grave of Abraham Lincoln!" Election returns in October seemed to confirm this. Republican majorities were reduced throughout the North. In the New England states and in Nebraska and Iowa, they were sharply reduced, and in New York, New Jersey, and Maryland, the party of Reconstruction went down to defeat. Democrats scored striking victories in Pennsylvania and Ohio. In Ohio, Republicans narrowly elected the Governor by 8,000 votes but overwhelmed a Negro suffrage amendment by 40,000. In every state where the voters expressed themselves on the Negro suffrage issue, they turned it down.

Horace Greeley read the returns bluntly, saying that "the Negro question lies at the bottom of our reverses. . . . Thousands have turned against us because we purpose to enfranchise the Blacks. . . . We have lost votes in the Free States by daring to be just to the Negro." The *Independent* was quite as frank. "Negro suffrage, as a political issue," it admitted, "never before was put so squarely to certain portions of the Northern people as during the late campaigns. The result shows that the Negro is still an unpopular man." Jay Cooke, the conservative financier, wrote John Sherman that he "felt a sort of intuition of coming disaster—probably growing out of a consciousness that other people would feel just as I did—disgust and mortification at the vagaries into which extremists in the Republican ranks were leading the party."

To the South, the Northern elections seemed a confirmation of their hopes and suspicions. The old voices of defiance and resistance, silent or subdued since March, were lifted again. They had been right all along, they said. Congress did not speak the true sentiment of the North on the Negro and Reconstruction. President Johnson had been the true prophet. The correct strategy was not to seek the Negro vote but to suppress it, not to comply with the Reconstruction Acts but to subvert them. The New York *Times* thought that "the Southern people seem to have become quite beside themselves in consequence of the *quasi* Democratic victories" in the North, and that there was "neither sense nor sanity in their exultations." Moderates such as Governor James W. Throckmorton of Texas, who declared he "had advocated publicly and privately a compliance with the Sherman Reconstruction Bill," were now "determined to defeat" compliance and to leave "no stone unturned" in their efforts.

The standard Southern reply to Northern demands was the endlessly reiterated charge of hypocrisy. Northern radicals, as a Memphis conservative put it, were "seeking to fasten what they themselves repudiate with loathing upon the unfortunate people of the South." And he pointed to the succession of Northern states that had voted on and defeated Negro suffrage. A Raleigh editor ridiculed Republicans of the Pennsylvania legislature who voted 29 to 13 against the franchise for Negroes, "This is a direct confession, by Northern Radicals," he added, "that they refuse to grant in Pennsylvania the '*justice*' they would enforce on the South. . . . And this is Radical meanness and hypocrisy—this their love for the negro."

There was little in the Republican presidential campaign of 1868 to confute the Southern charge of hypocrisy and much to support it. The Chicago Platform of May on which General

Grant was nominated contained as its second section this formulation of the double standard of racial morality: "The guaranty by Congress of equal suffrage to all loyal men at the South was demanded by every consideration of public safety, of gratitude, and of justice, and must be maintained; while the question of suffrage in all the loyal [i.e., Northern] States properly belongs to the people of those States." Thus Negro *dis*franchisement was assured in the North along with enfranchisement in the South. No direct mention of the Negro was made in the entire platform, and no mention of schools or homesteads for freedmen. Neither Grant nor his running-mate Schuyler Colfax was known for any personal commitment to Negro rights, and Republican campaign speeches in the North generally avoided the issue of Negro suffrage.

Congress acted to readmit seven of the reconstructed states to the Union in time for them to vote in the presidential election and contribute to the Republican majority. In attaching conditions to readmission, however, Congress deliberately refrained from specifying state laws protecting Negroes against discrimination in jury duty, officeholding, education, intermarriage, and a wide range of political and civil rights. By a vote of 30 to 5, the Senate defeated a bill attaching to the admission of Arkansas the condition that "no person on account of race or color shall be excluded from the benefits of education, or be deprived of an equal share of the moneys or other funds created or used by public authority to promote education. . . ."

Not until the election of 1868 was safely behind them did the Republicans come forward with proposals of national action on Negro suffrage that were to result in the Fifteenth Amendment. They were extremely sensitive to Northern opposition to enfranchisement. By 1869, only seven Northern states had voluntarily acted to permit the Negro to vote, and no state with a substantial Negro population outside the South had done so. Except for Minnesota and Iowa, which had only a handful of Negroes, every postwar referendum on the subject had gone down to defeat.

As a consequence moderates and conservatives among Republicans took over and dominated the framing of the Fifteenth Amendment and very strongly left their imprint on the measure. Even the incorrigibly radical Wendell Phillips yielded to their sway. Addressing other radicals, he pleaded, ". . . for the first time in our lives we beseech them to be a little more *politicians* and a little less *reformers*." The issue lay between the moderates and the radicals. The former wanted a limited, negative amendment that would not confer suffrage on the freedmen, would not guarantee the franchise and take positive steps to protect it, but would merely prohibit its denial on the grounds of race and previous condition. Opposed to this narrow objective were the radicals who demanded positive and firm guarantees, federal protection, and national control of suffrage. They would take away state control, North as well as South. They fully anticipated and warned of all the elaborate devices that states might resort to—and eventually did resort to—in order to disfranchise the Negro without violating the proposed amendment. These included such methods—later made famous—as the literacy and property tests, the understanding clause, the poll tax, as well as elaborate and difficult registration tricks and handicaps. But safeguards against them were all rejected by the moderates. Only four votes could be mustered for a bill to guarantee equal suffrage to all states, North as well as South. "This amendment," said its moderate proponent, Oliver P. Morton, "leaves the whole power in the State as it exists, now, except that colored men, shall not be disfranchised for the three reasons of race, color, or previous condition of slavery." And he added significantly, "They may, perhaps, require property or educational tests." Such tests were already in existence in Massachusetts and other Northern states, and the debate made it perfectly apparent what might be expected to happen later in the South.

It was little wonder that Southern Republicans, already faced with aggression against Negro voters and terribly apprehensive about the future, were intensely disappointed and unhappy about the shape the debate was taking. One of their keenest disappointments was the rejection of a clause prohibiting denial or abridgment of the right of officeholding on the ground of race. It is also not surprising that Southern white conservatives, in view of these developments, were on the whole fairly relaxed about the proposed Fifteenth Amendment. The shrewder of them, in fact, began to realize that the whole thing was concerned mainly, not with the reconstruction of the South, but with maneuvers of internal politics in the Northern states. After all, the Negroes were already fully enfranchised and voting regularly and solidly in all the Southern states, their suffrage built into state constitutions and a condition of readmission to the Union.

Were there other motives behind the Fifteenth Amendment? The evidence is somewhat inferential, but a recent study has drawn attention to the significance of the closely divided vote in such states as Indiana, Ohio, Connecticut, New York, and Pennsylvania. The Negro population of these states was small, of course, but so closely was the white electorate in them divided between the two major parties that a small Negro vote could often make the difference between victory and defeat. It was assumed, of course, that this potential Negro vote would be reliably Republican. Enfranchisement by state action had been defeated in all those states, and federal action seemed the only way. There is no doubt that there was some idealistic support for Negro enfranchisement, especially among antislavery people in the North. But it was not the antislavery idealists who shaped the Fifteenth Amendment and guided it through Congress. The effective leaders of legislative action were moderates with practical political considerations in mind—particularly that thin margin of difference in partisan voting strength in certain Northern states. They had their way, and they relentlessly voted down all measures of the sort the idealists, such as Senator Sumner, were demanding.

For successful adoption the amendment required ratification by twenty-eight states. Ratification would therefore have been impossible without support of the Southern states, and an essential part of that had to come by requiring ratification as a condition of readmission of Virginia, and perhaps of Mississippi and Georgia as well.

The Fifteenth Amendment has often been read as evidence of renewed notice to the South of the North's firmness of purpose, as proof of its determination not to be cheated of its idealistic war aims, as a solemn rededication to those aims. Read more carefully, however, the Fifteenth Amendment reveals more deviousness than clarity of purpose, more partisan needs than idealistic aims, more timidity than boldness.

Signals of faltering purpose in the North, such as the Fifteenth Amendment and state elections in 1867, were not lost on the South. They were assessed carefully and weighed for their implications for the strategy of resistance. The movement of counter-reconstruction was already well under way by the time the amendment was ratified in March 1870, and in that year, the reactionary movement took on new life in several quarters. Fundamentally it was a terroristic campaign of underground organizations, the Ku Klux Klan and several similar ones, for the intimidation of Republican voters and officials, the overthrow of their power, and the destruction of their organization. Terrorists used violence of all kinds, including murder by mob, by drowning, by torch; they whipped, they tortured, they maimed, they mutilated. It became perfectly clear that federal intervention of a determined sort was the only means of suppressing the movement and protecting the freedmen in their civil and political rights.

To meet this situation, Congress passed the Enforcement Act of May 30, 1870, and followed it with the Second Enforcement Act and the Ku Klux Klan Act of 1871. These acts on the face of it would seem to have provided full and adequate machinery for the enforcement of the Fifteenth Amendment and the protection of the Negro and white Republican voters. They authorized the President to call out the army and navy and suspend the writ of habeas corpus; they empowered federal troops to implement court orders; and they reserved the federal courts' exclusive jurisdiction in all suffrage cases. The enforcement acts have gone down in history with the stereotypes "infamous" and "tyrannical" tagged to them. As a matter of fact, they were consistent with tradition and with democratic principle. Surviving remnants of them were invoked in recent years to authorize federal intervention at Little Rock and at Oxford, Mississippi. They are echoed in the Civil Rights Acts of 1957 and 1960, and they are greatly surpassed in the powers conferred by the Civil Rights Act of 1964 and the Voting Rights Act of 1965.

Surely this impressive display of federal power and determination, backed by gleaming steel and judicial majesty, might be assumed to have been enough to bring the South to its senses and dispel forever the fantasies of Southern intransigents. And in fact, historians have in the main endorsed the assumption that the power of the Klan was broken by the impact of the so-called Force Bills.

The truth is that, while the Klan was nominally dissolved, the campaign of violence, terror, and intimidation went forward virtually unabated, save temporarily in places where federal power was displayed and so long as it was sustained. For all the efforts of the Department of Justice, the deterioration of the freedman's status and the curtailment and denial of his suffrage continued steadily and rapidly. Federal enforcement officials met with impediments of all sorts. A close study of their efforts reveals that "in virtually every Southern state . . . federal deputy marshals, supervisors of elections, or soldiers were arrested by local law-enforcement officers on charges ranging from false arrest or assault and battery to murder."

The obvious course for the avoidance of local passions was to remove cases to federal courts for trial, as provided under a section of the First Enforcement Act. But in practice this turned out to be "exceedingly difficult." And the effort to find juries that would convict proved often to be all but impossible, however carefully they were chosen, and in whatever admixture of color composed them. The most overwhelming evidence of guilt proved unavailing at times. Key witnesses under intimidation simply refused to testify, and those that did were known to meet with terrible reprisals. The law authorized the organization of the *posse comitatus* and the use of troops to protect juries and witnesses. But in practice the local recruits were reluctant or unreliable, and federal troops were few and remote and slow to come, and the request for them was wrapped in endless red tape and bureaucratic frustration.

All these impediments to justice might have been overcome had sufficient money been made available by Congress. And right at this crucial point, once again, the Northern will and purpose flagged and failed the cause they professed to sustain. It is quite clear where the blame lies. Under the new laws, the cost of maintaining courts in the most affected districts of the South soared tremendously, quadrupled in some. Yet Congress starved the courts from the start, providing only about a million dollars a year—far less than was required. The Attorney General had to cut corners, urge economy, and in 1873 instruct district attorneys to prosecute no case "unless the public interest imperatively demands it." An antiquated judicial structure proved wholly inadequate to handle the extra burden and clear their dockets. "If it takes a court over one month to try five offenders," asked the Attorney General concerning 420 indictments in South Carolina, "how long will it take to try four hundred, already indicted, and many hundreds more who deserve to be indicted?" He thought it "obvious that the attempt to bring to justice even a small portion of the guilty in that state must fail" under the circumstances. Quite apart from the inadequacy and inefficiency of the judicial structure, it is of significance that a majority of the Department of Justice officers in the South at this time, despite the carpetbagger infusion, were Southern-born. A study by Everette Swinney concludes that "some marshals and district attorneys were either sensitive to Southern public opinion or in substantial agreement with it." The same has been found true of numbers of federal troops and their officers on duty in the South. Then in 1874 an emasculating opinion of the Supreme Court by Justice Joseph P. Bradley in *United States* v. *Cruikshank et al.* cast so much doubt on the constitutionality of the enforcement acts as to render successful prosecutions virtually impossible.

There is also sufficient evidence in existence to raise a question about how much the Enforcement Acts were intended all along for application in the policing of elections in the South, as against their possible application in other quarters of the Union. As it turned out, nearly half of the cost of policing was applied to elections in New York City, where Democratic bosses gave the opposition much trouble. Actually the bulk of federal expenditures under the Enforcement Acts was made in the North, which leads one student to conclude that their primary object from the start was not the distraught South under reconstruction, but the urban strongholds of the Democrats in the North. Once again, as in the purposes behind the Fifteenth Amendment, one is left to wonder how much Radical Reconstruction was really concerned with the South and how much with the party needs of the Republicans in the North.

Finally, to take a longer view, it is only fair to allow that if ambiguous and partisan motives in the writing and enforcing of Reconstruction laws proved to be the seeds of failure in American race policy for the earlier generations, those same laws and constitutional amendments eventually acquired a wholly different significance for the race policy of a later generation. The laws outlasted the ambiguities of their origins. While the logic that excuses and vindicates the failures of one generation by reference to the successes of the next has always left something to be desired, it is, nevertheless, impossible to account fully for such limited successes as the Second Reconstruction can claim without acknowledging its profound indebtedness to the First.

PART IV

Twentieth-Century Reform

The failure of Reconstruction to create a new social order of race relations in America illustrates a tendency—not an immutable principle, but an historical inclination —in the American political order to resist radical change through state coercion. This kind of inertia is of course identifiable in all social orders, but in the United States it has been powerfully reinforced by the hostility of classical liberalism toward power and hence by the diffusion of power that was purposely structured into the original design of the federal system. In the latter nineteenth century conservative theoreticians, most notably William Graham Sumner, attempted to elevate this tendency to the status of a social law by applying the dynamics of Darwinian evolution to society and concluding that the social order, like the natural order, was a constant struggle in which only the fittest should survive, and consequently that stateways could not change folkways.

Against this background modern Americans who called themselves progressive reformers attempted with considerable success to forge a political doctrine that would divorce modern liberalism from its classical links to laissez-faire by attaching the principle of aggressive national intervention to egalitarian goals. They argued that the power of government should be used to intervene in the marketplace in order to redistribute income, protect the rights of labor, and regulate commerce and industry in the interest of consumers. They advocated a nonradical intervention that would not displace the primacy of capitalism but would operate through the traditional channels of government and party. (These channels included third parties, which were also traditional, if short-lived, political phenomena that customarily functioned as bellwethers to telegraph the swelling discontents that were symptomatic of a looming political explosion.) Thus far, the twentieth century has witnessed three such major bursts of reform activity: Progressivism; the New Deal; and the aggregation of reformist activities associated with the post-World War II civil rights movement, the war on poverty, and the movement against the war in Indochina. It is striking how, on all three occasions, the indignation and zeal of reformers captured national power and translated much of their reformist programs into national law, only to witness the engulfment of much of that idealism, or at least the absorption of much of that energy, into an international war that preempted the reform effort and brought bitterness, disillusionment, and even reaction in its wake.

This is to suggest no inevitabilities about the relationship between reform and war, no iron law of Thermidor that dooms reform and mocks the American dream. But the readings in Part IV that bear on these great reform efforts focus less on the undeniable political and economic achievements of reform than on their intellectual assumptions and social base, on their internal paradoxes, and on what their failures as well as their achievements tell us about ourselves.

Herbert Croly's name scarcely ranks in the informed popular mind with such luminaries of progressive thought as Theodore Roosevelt, John Dewey, Woodrow Wilson, and Walter Lippmann, but the man who published *The Promise of American Life* in 1909, and who in 1914 joined Lippmann and Walter Weyl in founding *The New Republic,* has been called by intellectual historian Cushing Strout "the most seminal mind" of the Progressive movement. Convinced that the abundant corruption of political bosses, the untaxed fortunes of the "robber barons" of industry and commerce, the suffering of industrial workers, and the burgeoning inequity in the distribution of income in urban-industrial America were an avoidable affront to the American dream and a dangerous invitation to radicals, Croly directly confronted the crippling historical legacy of Jeffersonian liberalism that enshrined a society of individuals with natural rights anterior to society and government. Sensitive, like Tocqueville, to the fundamental antagonism between liberty and equality, Croly insisted that democracy's paramount principle of popular sovereignty required active discrimination and intervention by the national government in behalf of disadvantaged groups because in an industrial society individuals and groups are never equal in their opportunities for exercising their rights. Hence the notion that the state could be an impartial umpire of a fair fight was a fiction. He admired not Jefferson and Jackson, but Hamilton, Lincoln, and Theodore Roosevelt.

The bulk of *The Promise of American Life* is an historical analysis of the failures of Jeffersonian and Jacksonian individualism, and it reveals both erudition and a finely analytical mind, and some of the warts of progressivism as well. Like most progressives, Croly was a racist. In condemning slavery, he observed that the southern slaveowners were "estimable if somewhat quick-tempered and irascible gentlemen, who did much to mitigate the evils of negro servitude" and who "were right, moreover, in believing that the negroes were a race possessed of moral and intellectual qualities inferior to those of the white men." Similarly, Croly shared with many progressives a jingoism that approved the colonial extension of Christian civilization, and a conservative conviction that effective reform was an imperative counterthrust to growing radicalism. But his major concern was the reformist goal of linking Jeffersonian ends to Hamiltonian means, and this was a monumental and crucial intellectual battle in which he was a giant.

The Promise of American Life

HERBERT CROLY

THE LOGIC OF REFORM

The prevailing preconception of the reformers, that the existing evils and abuses have been due chiefly to the energy and lack of scruple with which businessmen and politicians have taken advantage of the good but easy-going American, and that a general increase of moral energy, assisted by some minor legal changes, will restore the balance,—such a conception of the situation is less than half true. No doubt, the "plain people" of the United States have been morally indifferent, and have allowed unscrupulous special interests to usurp too much power; but that is far from being the whole story. The unscrupulous energy of the "Boss" or the "tainted" millionaire is vitally related to the moral indifference of the "plain people." Both of them have been encouraged to believe by the nature of our traditional ideas and institutions that a man could be patriotic without being either public-spirited or disinterested. The democratic state has been conceived as a piece of political machinery, which existed for the purpose of securing certain individual rights and opportunities—the expectation being that the greatest individual happiness would be thereby promoted, and one which harmonized with the public interest. Consequently when the "Boss" and the "tainted" millionaire took advantage of this situation to secure for themselves as unusually large amount of political and economic power, they were putting into practice an idea which traditionally had been entirely respectable, and which during the pioneer period had not worked badly. On the other hand, when the mass of American voters failed to detect the danger of such usurpation until it had gone altogether too far, they, too, were not without warrant for their lethargy and callousness. They, too, in a smaller way had considered the American political and economic system chiefly as a system framed for their individual benefit; and it did not seem sportsmanlike to turn and rend their more successful competitors, until they were told that the "trusts" and the "Bosses" were violating the sacred principle of equal rights. Thus the abuses of which we are complaining are not weeds which have been allowed to spring up from neglect, and which can be eradicated by a man with a hoe. They are cultivated plants, which, if not precisely specified in the plan of the American political and economic garden, have at least been encouraged by traditional methods of cultivation.

The fact that this dangerous usurpation of power has been accomplished partly by illegal methods has blinded many reformers to two consderations, which have a vital relation to both the theory and the practice of reform. Violation of the law was itself partly the result of conflicting and unwise state legislation, and for this reason did not seem very heinous either to its perpetrators or to public opinion. But even if the law had not been violated, similar results would have followed. Under the traditional American system, with the freedom permitted to the individual, with the restriction placed on the central authority, and with its assumption of a substantal identity between the individual and the public interest—under such a system unusually energetic and unscrupulous men were bound to seize a kind and an amount of political and economic power which was not entirely wholesome. They had a license to do so; and if they had failed to take advantage thereof, their failure would have been an indication, not of disinterestedness or moral impeccability, but of sheer weakness and inefficiency.

How utterly confusing it is, consequently, to consider reform as equivalent merely to the restoration of the American democracy to a former condition of purity and excellence! Our earlier political and economic condition was not at its best a fit subject for any great amount of complacency. It cannot be restored, even if we would; and the public interest has nothing to gain by its restoration. The usurpation of power by "trusts" and "Bosses" is more than anything else an expression of a desirable individual initiative and organizing ability—which have been allowed to become dangerous and partly corrupt, because of the incoherence and the lack of purpose and responsibility in the traditional American political and economic system. A "purification" might well destroy the good with the evil; and even if it were successful in eradicating certain abuses, would only prepare the way for the outbreak in another form of the tendency towards individual aggrandizement and social classification. No amount of moral energy, directed merely towards the enforcement of the laws, can possibly avail to accomplish any genuine or lasting reform. It is the laws themselves which are partly at fault, and still more at fault is the group of ideas and traditional practices behind the laws.

Reformers have failed for the most part to reach a correct diagnosis of existing political and economic abuses, because they are almost as much the victim of perverted, confused, and routine habits of political thought as is the ordinary politician. They have eschewed the tradition of partisan conformity in reference to controverted political questions, but they have not eschewed a still more insidious tradition of conformity—the tradition that a patriotic American citizen must not in his political thinking go beyond the formulas consecrated in the sacred American writings. They adhere to the stupefying rule that the good Fathers of the Republic relieved their children from the necessity of vigorous, independent, or consistent thinking in political matters,—that it is the duty of their loyal children to repeat the sacred words and then await a miraculous consummation of individual and social prosperity. Accordingly, all the leading reformers begin by piously reiterating certain phrases about equal rights for all and special privileges for none, and of government of the people, by the people, and for the people. Having in this way proved their fundamental political orthodoxy, they proceed to interpret the phrases according to their personal, class, local, and partisan preconceptions and interests. They have never stopped to inquire whether the principle of equal rights in its actual embodiment in American institutional and political practice has not been partly responsible for some of the existing abuses, whether it is either a safe or sufficient platform for a reforming movement, and whether its continued proclamation as the fundamental political principle of a democracy will help or hinder the higher democratic consummation. Their unquestioning orthodoxy in this respect has made them faithless both to their own personal interest as reformers and to the cause of reform. Reform exclusively as a moral protest and awakening is condemned to sterility. Reformers exclusively as moral protestants and purifiers are condemned to misdirected effort, to an illiberal puritanism, and to personal self-stultification. Reform must necessarily mean an intellectual as well as a moral challenge; and its higher purposes will never be accomplished unless it is accompanied by a masterful and jubilant intellectual awakening.

All Americans, whether they are professional politicians or reformers, "predatory" millionaires or common people, political philosophers or schoolboys, accept the principle of "equal rights for all and special privileges for none" as the absolutely sufficient rule of an American democratic political system. The platforms of both parties testify on its behalf. Corporation lawyers and their clients appear frequently to believe in it. Tammany offers tribute to it during every local political campaign in New York. A Democratic Senator, in the intervals between his votes for increased duties on the products of his state, declares it to be the summary of all political wisdom. The fact that Mr. Bryan incorporates it in most of his speeches does not prevent Mr. Hearst from keeping it standing in type for the purpose of slowing how very American the *American* can be. The fact that Mr. Hearst has appropriated it with the American flag as belonging peculiarly to himself has not prevented Mr. Roosevelt from explaining the whole of his policy of reform as at bottom an attempt to restore a "Square Deal"—that is, a condition of equal rights and non-existing privileges. More radical reformers find the same principle equally useful for their own purposes. Mr. Frederic C. Howe, in his "Hope of Democracy," bases an elaborate scheme of municipal socialism exclusively upon it. Mr. William Smythe, in his "Constructive Democracy," finds warrant in the same principle for the immediate purchase by the central government of the railway and "trust" franchises. Mr. Henry George, Jr., in his "Menace of Privilege," asserts that the plain American citizen can never enjoy equality of rights as long as land, mines, railroad rights of way and terminals, and the like remain in the hands of private owners. The collectivist socialists are no less certain that the institution of private property necessarily gives some men an unjust advantage over others. There is no extreme of radicalism or conservatism, of individualism or socialism, of Republicanism or Democracy, which does not rest its argument on this one consummate principle.

In this respect the good American finds himself in a situation similar to that with which he was confronted before the Civil War. At that time, also, Abolitionist and slave-holder, Republican and pioneer Democrat, each of them declared himself to be the interpreter of the true democratic doctrine; and no substantial progress could be made towards the settlement of the question, until public opinion had been instructed as to the real meaning of democracy in relation to the double-headed problem of slavery and states' rights. It required the utmost intellectual courage and ability to emancipate the conception of democracy from the illusions and confusions of thought which enabled Davis, Douglas, and Garrison all to pose as impeccable democrats; and at the present time reformers need to devote as much ability and more courage to the task of framing a fitting creed for a reformed and reforming American democracy.

The political lessons of the anti-slavery and states' rights discussions may not be of much obvious assistance in thinking out such a creed; but they should at least help the reformers to understand the methods whereby the purposes of a reformed democracy can be achieved. No progress was made towards the solution of the slavery question until the question itself was admitted to be national in scope, and its solution a national responsibility. No substantial progress had been made in the direction of reform until it began to be understood that here, also, a national responsibility existed, which demanded an exercise of the powers of the central government. Reform is both meaningless and powerless unless the Jeffersonian principle of non-interference is abandoned. The experience of the last generation plainly shows that the American economic and social system cannot be allowed to take care of itself, and that the automatic harmony of the individual and the public interest, which is the essence of the Jeffersonian democratic creed, has proved to be an illusion. Interference with the natural course of individual and popular action there must be in the public interest; and such interference must at least be sufficient to accomplish its purposes. The house of the American democracy is again by way of being divided against itself, because the national interest has not been consistently asserted as against special and local interests; and again, also, it can be reunited only by being partly reconstructed on better foundations. If reform does not and cannot mean restoration, it is bound to mean reconstruction.

The reformers have come partly to realize that the Jeffersonian policy of drift must be abandoned. They no longer expect the American ship of state by virtue of its own righteous framework to sail away to a safe harbor in the Promised Land. They understand that there must be a vigorous and conscious assertion of the public as opposed to private and special interests, and that the American people must to a greater extent than they have in the past subordinate the latter to the former. They behave as if the American ship of state will hereafter require careful steering; and a turn or two at the wheel has given them some idea of the course they must set. On the other hand, even the best of them have not learned the name of its ultimate destination, the full difficulties of the navigation, or the stern discipline which may eventually be imposed upon the ship's crew. They do not realize, that is, how thoroughly Jeffersonian individualism must be abandoned for the benefit of a genuinely individual and social consummation; and they do not realize how dangerous and fallacious a chart their cherished principle of equal rights may well become. In reviving the practice of vigorous national action for the achievement of national purpose, the better reformers have, if they only knew it, been looking in the direction of a much more trustworthy and serviceable political principle. The assumption of such a responsibility implies the rejection of a large part of the Jeffersonian creed, and a renewed attempt to establish in its place the popularity of its Hamiltonian rival. On the other hand, it involves no less surely the transformation of Hamiltonianism into a thoroughly democratic political principle. None of these inferences have, however, as yet been generally drawn, and no leading reformer has sought to give reform its necessary foundation of positive political principle.

Only a very innocent person will expect reformers to be convinced of such a novel notion of reform by mere assertion, no matter how emphatic, or by argument, no matter how conclusive. But if, as I have said, reform actually implies a criticism of traditional American ideas, and a more responsible and more positive conception of democracy, these implications will necessarily be revealed in the future history of the reforming agitation. The reformers who understand will be assisted by the logic of events, whereas those who cannot and will not understand will be thwarted by the logic of events. Gradually (it may be anticipated) reformers, who dare to criticise and who are not afraid to reconstruct will be sharply distinguished from reformers who believe reform to be a species of higher conservatism. The latter will be forced where they belong into the ranks of the supporters and beneficiaries of the existing system; and the party of genuine reform will be strengthened by their departure. On the other hand, the sincere and thorough-going reformers can hardly avoid a division into two divergent groups. One of these groups will stick faithfully to the principle of equal rights and to the spirit of the true Jeffersonian faith. It will seek still further to undermine the representative character of American institutions, to deprive official leadership of any genuine responsibility, and to cultivate individualism at the expense of individual and national integrity. The second group, on the other hand, may learn from experience that the principle of equal rights is a dangerous weapon in the hands of factious and merely revolutionary agitators, and even that such a principle is only a partial and poverty-stricken statement of the purpose of a democratic polity. The logic of its purposes will compel it to favor the principle of responsible representative government, and it will seek to forge institutions which will endow responsible political government with renewed life. Above all, it may discover that the attempt to unite the Hamiltonian principle of national political responsibility and efficiency with a frank democratic purpose will give a new meaning to the Hamiltonian system of political ideas and a new power to democracy. . . .

RECONSTRUCTION: ITS CONDITIONS AND PURPOSES

The best method of approaching a critical reconstruction of American political ideas will be by means of an analysis of the meaning of democracy. A clear popular understanding of the contents of the democratic principle is obviously of the utmost practical political importance to the American people. Their loyalty to the idea of democracy, as they understand it,

THE PROMISE OF AMERICAN LIFE

cannot be questioned. Nothing of any considerable political importance is done or left undone in the United States, unless such action or inaction can be plausibly defended on democratic grounds; and the only way to secure for the American people the benefit of a comprehensive and consistent political policy will be to derive it from a comprehensive and consistent conception of democracy.

Democracy as most frequently understood is essentially and exhaustively defined as a matter of popular government; and such a definition raises at once a multitude of time-honored, but by no means superannuated, controversies. The constitutional liberals in England, in France, and in this country have always objected to democracy as so understood, because of the possible sanction it affords for the substitution of a popular despotism in the place of the former royal or oligarchic despotisms. From their point of view individual liberty is the greatest blessing which can be secured to a people by a government; and individual liberty can be permanently guaranteed only in case political liberties are in theory and practice subordinated to civil liberties. Popular political institutions constitute a good servant, but a bad master. When introduced in moderation they keep the government of a country in close relation with well-informed public opinion, which is a necessary condition of political sanitation; but if carried too far, such institutions compromise the security of the individual and the integrity of the state. They erect a power in the state, which in theory is unlimited and which constantly tends in practice to dispense with restrictions. A power which is theoretically absolute is under no obligation to respect the rights either of individuals or minorities; and sooner or later such power will be used for the purpose of oppressing the individual. The only way to secure individual liberty is, consequently, to organize a state in which the Sovereign power is deprived of any rational excuse or legal opportunity of violating certain essential individual rights.

The foregoing criticism of democracy, defined as popular government, may have much practical importance; but there are objections to it on the score of logic. It is not a criticism of a certain conception of democracy, so much as of democracy itself. Ultimate responsibility for the government of a community must reside somewhere. If the single monarch is practically dethroned, as he is by these liberal critics of democracy, some Sovereign power must be provided to take his place. In England Parliament, by means of a steady encroachment on the royal prerogatives, has gradually become Sovereign; but other countries, such as France and the United States, which have wholly dispensed with royalty, cannot, even if they would, make a legislative body Sovereign by the simple process of allowing it to usurp power once enjoyed by the Crown. France did, indeed, after it had finally dispensed with Legitimacy, make two attempts to found governments in which the theory of popular Sovereignty was evaded. The Orleans monarchy, for instance, through the mouths of its friends, denied Sovereignty to the people, without being able to claim it for the King; and this insecurity of its legal framework was an indirect cause of a violent explosion of effective popular Sovereignty in 1848. The apologists for the Second Empire admitted the theory of a Sovereign people, but claimed that the Sovereign power could be safely and efficiently used only in case it were delegated to one Napoleon III—a view the correctness of which the results of the Imperial policy eventually tended to damage. There is in point of fact no logical escape from a theory of popular Sovereignty—once the theory of divinely appointed royal Sovereignty is rejected. An escape can be made, of course, as in England, by means of a compromise and a legal fiction; and such an escape can be fully justified from the English national point of view; but countries which have rejected the royal and aristocratic tradition are forbidden this means of escape—if escape it is. They are obliged to admit the doctrine of popular Sovereignty. They are obliged to proclaim a theory of unlimited popular powers.

To be sure, a democracy may impose rules of action upon itself—as the American democracy did in accepting the Federal Constitution. But in adopting the Federal Constitution the American people did not abandon either its responsibilities or rights as Sovereign. Difficult as it may be to escape from the legal framework defined in the Constitution, that body of law in theory remains merely an instrument which was made for the people and which if necessary can and will be modified. A people, to whom was denied the ultimate responsibility for its welfare, would not have obtained the prime condition of genuine liberty. Individual freedom is important, but more important still is the freedom of a whole people to dispose of its own destiny; and I do not see how the existence of such an ultimate popular political freedom and responsibility can be denied by any one who has rejected the theory of a divinely appointed political order. The fallibility of human nature being what it is, the practical application of this theory will have its grave dangers; but these dangers are only evaded and postponed by a failure to place ultimate political responsibility where it belongs. While a country in the position of Germany or Great Britain may be fully justified from the point of view of its national tradition in merely compromising with democracy, other countries, such as the United States and France, which have earned the right to dispense with these compromises, are at least building their political structure on the real and righteous source of political authority. Democracy may mean something more than a theoretically absolute popular government, but it assuredly cannot mean anything less.

If, however, democracy does not mean anything less than popular Sovereignty, it assuredly does mean something more. It must at least mean an expression of the Sovereign will, which will not contradict and destroy the continuous existence of its own Sovereign power. Several times during the political history of France in the nineteenth century, the popular will has expressed itself in a manner adverse to popular institutions. Assemblies have been elected by universal suffrage, whose tendencies have been reactionary and undemocratic, and who have been supported in this reactionary policy by an effective public opinion. Or the French people have by means of a plebiscite delegated their Sovereign power to an Imperial dictator, whose whole political system was based on a deep suspicion of the source of his own authority. A particular group of political institutions or course of political action may, then, be representative of the popular will, and yet may be undemocratic. Popular Sovereignty is self-contradictory, unless it is expressed in a manner favorable to its own perpetuity and integrity.

The assertion of the doctrine of popular Sovereignty is, consequently, rather the beginning than the end of democracy. There can be no democracy where the people do not rule; but government by the people is not necessarily democratic. The popular will must in a democratic state be expressed somehow in the interest of democracy itself; and we have not traveled very far towards a satisfactory conception of democracy until this democratic purpose has received some definition. In what way must a democratic state behave in order to contribute to its own integrity?

The ordinary American answer to this question is contained in the assertion of Lincoln, that our government is "dedicated to the proposition that all men are created equal." Lincoln's phrasing of the principle was due to the fact that the obnoxious and undemocratic system of negro slavery was uppermost in his mind when he made his Gettysburg address; but he meant by his assertion of the principle of equality substantially what is meant to-day by the principle of "equal rights for all and special privileges for none." Government by the people has its natural and logical complement in government for the people. Every state with a legal framework must grant certain rights to individuals; and every state, in so far as it is efficient, must guarantee to the individual that his rights, as legally defined, are secure. But an essentially democratic state consists in the circumstance that all citizens enjoy these rights equally. If any citizen or any group of citizens enjoys by virtue of the law any advantage over their fellow-citizens, then the most sacred principle of democracy is violated. On the other hand, a community in which no man or no group of men are granted by law any advantage over their fellow-citizens is the type of the perfect and fruitful democratic state. Society is organized politically for the benefit of all the people. Such an organization may permit radical differences among individuals in the opportunities and possessions they actually enjoy; but no man would be able to impute his own success or failure to the legal framework of society. Every citizen would be getting a "Square Deal."

Such is the idea of the democratic state, which the majority of good Americans believe to be entirely satisfactory. It should endure indefinitely, because it seeks to satisfy every interest essential to associated life. The interest of the individual is protected, because of the liberties he securely enjoys. The general social interest is equally well protected, because the liberties enjoyed by one or by a few are enjoyed by all. Thus the individual and the social interests are automatically harmonized. The virile democrat in pursuing his own interest "under the law" is contributing effectively to the interest of society, while the social interest consists precisely in the promotion of these individual interests, in so far as they can be equally exercised. The divergent demands of the individual and the social interest can be reconciled by grafting the principle of equality on the thrifty tree of individual rights, and the ripe fruit thereof can be gathered merely by shaking the tree.

It must be immediately admitted, also, that the principle of equal rights, like the principle of ultimate popular political responsibility is the expression of an essential aspect of democracy. There is no room for permanent legal privileges in a democratic state. Such privileges may be and frequently are defended on many excellent grounds. They may unquestionably contribute for a time to social and economic efficiency and to individual independence. But whatever advantage may be derived from such permanent discriminations must be abandoned by a democracy. It cannot afford to give any one class of its citizens a permanent advantage or to others a permanent grievance. It ceases to be a democracy, just as soon as any permanent privileges are conferred by its institutions or its laws; and this equality of right and absence of permanent privilege is the expression of a fundamental social interest.

But the principle of equal rights, like the principle of ultimate popular political responsibility, is not sufficient; and because of its insufficiency results in certain dangerous ambiguities and self-contradictions. American political thinkers have always repudiated the idea that by equality of rights they meant anything like equality of performance or power. The utmost varieties of individual power and ability are bound to exist and are bound to bring about many different levels of individual achievement. Democracy both recognizes the right of the individual to use his powers to the utmost, and encourages him to do so by offering a fair field and, in case of success, an abundant reward. The democratic principle requires an equal start in the race, while expecting at the same time an unequal finish. But Americans who talk in this way seem wholly blind to the fact that under a legal system which holds private property sacred there may be equal rights, but there cannot possibly be any equal opportunities for exercising such rights. The chance which the individual has to compete with his fellows and take a prize in the race is vitally affected by material conditions over which he has no control. It is as if the competitor in a Marathon cross country run were denied proper nourishment or proper training, and was obliged to toe the mark against rivals who had every benefit of food and discipline. Under such conditions he is not as badly off as if he were entirely excluded from the race. With the aid of exceptional strength and intelligence he may overcome the odds against him and win out. But it would be absurd to claim, because all the rivals toed the same mark, that a man's victory or defeat depended exclusively on his own efforts. Those who have enjoyed the benefits of wealth and thorough education start with an advantage which can be overcome only by very exceptional men,—men so exceptional, in fact, that the average competitor without such benefits feels himself disqualified for the contest.

Because of the ambiguity indicated above, different people with different interests, all of them good patriotic Americans, draw very different inferences from the doctrine of equal rights. The man of conservative ideas and interests means by the rights, which are to be equally exercised, only those rights which are defined and protected by the law—the more fundamental of which are the rights to personal freedom and to private property. The man of radical ideas, on the other hand, observing, as he may very clearly, that these equal rights cannot possibly be made really equivalent to equal opportunities, bases upon the same doctrine a more or less drastic criticism of the existing economic and social order and sometimes of the motives of its beneficiaries and conservators. The same principle, differently interpreted, is the foundation of American political orthodoxy and American political heterodoxy. The same measure of reforming legislation, such as the new Interstate Commerce Law, seems to one party a wholly inadequate attempt to make the exercise of individual rights a little more equal, while it seems to others an egregious violation of the principle itself. What with reforming legislation on the one hand and the lack of it on the other, the once sweet air of the American political mansion is soured by complaints. Privileges and discriminations seem to lurk in every political and economic corner. The "people" are appealing to the state to protect them against the usurpations of the corporations and the Bosses. The government is appealing to the courts to protect the shippers against the railroads. The corporations are appealing to the Federal courts to protect them from the unfair treatment of state legislatures. Employers are fighting trades-unionism, because it denies equal rights to their employees. The unionists are entreating public opinion to protect them against the unfairness of "government by injunction." To the free trader the whole protectionist system seems a flagrant discrimination on behalf of a certain portion of the community. Everybody seems to be clamoring for a "Square Deal" but nobody seems to be getting it.

The ambiguity of the principle of equal rights and the resulting confusion of counsel are so obvious that there must be some good reason for their apparently unsuspected existence. The truth is that Americans have not readjusted their political ideas to the teaching of their political and economic experience. For a couple of generations after Jefferson had established the doctrine of equal rights as the fundamental principle of the American democracy, the ambiguity resident in the application of the doctrine was concealed. The Jacksonian Democrats, for instance, who were constantly nosing the ground for a scent of unfair treatment, could discover no example of political privileges, except the continued retention of their offices by experienced public servants; and the only case of economic privilege of which they were certain was that of the National Bank. The fact is, of course, that the great majority of Americans were getting a "Square Deal" as long as the economic opportunities of a new country had not been developed and appropriated. Individual and social interest did substantially coincide as long as so many opportunities were open to the poor and untrained man, and as long as the public interest demanded first of all the utmost celerity of economic development. But, as we have seen in a preceding chapter, the economic development of the country resulted inevitably in a condition which demanded on the part of the successful competitor either increasing capital, improved training, or a larger amount of ability and energy. With the advent of comparative economic and social maturity, the exercise of certain legal rights became substantially equivalent to the exercise of a privilege; and if equality of opportunity was to be maintained, it could not be done by virtue of non-interference. The demands of the "Higher Law" began to diverge from the results of the actual legal system. . . .

Hence it is that continued loyalty to a contradictory principle is destructive of a wholesome public sentiment and opinion.

A wholesome public opinion in a democracy is one which keeps a democracy sound and whole; and it cannot prevail unless the individuals composing it recognize mutual ties and responsibilities which lie deeper than any differences of interest and idea. No formula whose effect on public opinion is not binding and healing and unifying has any substantial claim to consideration as the essential and formative democratic idea. Belief in the principle of equal rights does not bind, heal, and unify public opinion. Its effect rather is confusing, distracting, and at worst, disintegrating. A democratic political organization has no immunity from grievances. They are a necessary result of a complicated and changing industrial and social organism. What is good for one generation will often be followed by consequences that spell deprivation for the next. What is good for one man or one class of men will bring ills to other men or classes of men. What is good for the community as a whole may mean temporary loss and a sense of injustice to a minority. All grievances from any cause should receive full expression in a democracy, but, inasmuch as the righteously discontented must be always with us, the fundamental democratic principle should, above all, counsel mutual forbearance and loyalty. The principle of equal rights encourages mutual suspicion and disloyalty. It tends to attribute individual and social ills, for which general moral, economic, and social causes are usually in large measure responsible, to individual wrong-doing; and in this way it arouses and intensifies that personal and class hatred, which never in any society lies far below the surface. Men who have grievances are inflamed into anger and resentment. In claiming what they believe to be their rights, they are in their own opinion acting on behalf not merely of their interests, but of an absolute democratic principle. Their angry resentment becomes transformed in their own minds into rightous indignation; and there may be turned loose upon the community a horde of self-seeking fantasies—like unto those soldiers in the religious wars who robbed and slaughtered their opponents in the service of God.

DEMOCRACY AND DISCRIMINATION

The principle of equal rights has always appealed to its more patriotic and sensible adherents as essentially an impartial rule of political action—one that held a perfectly fair balance between the individual and society, and between different and hostile individual and class interests. But as a fundamental principle of democratic policy it is as ambiguous in this respect as it is in other respects. In its traditional form and expression it has concealed an extremely partial interest under a formal proclamation of impartiality. The political thinker who popularized it in this country was not concerned fundamentally with harmonizing the essential interest of the individual with the essential popular or social interest. Jefferson's political system was intended for the benefit only of a special class of individuals, viz., those average people who would not be helped by any really formative rule or method of discrimination. In practice it has proved to be inimical to individual liberty, efficiency, and distinction. An insistent demand for equality, even in the form of a demand for equal rights, inevitably has a negative and limiting effect upon the free and able exercise of individual opportunities. From the Jeffersonian point of view democracy would incur a graver danger from a violation of equality than it would profit from a triumphant assertion of individual liberty. Every opportunity for the edifying exercise of power, on the part either of an individual, a group of individuals, or the state, is by its very nature also an opportunity for its evil exercise. The political leader whose official power depends upon popular confidence may betray the trust. The corporation employing thousands of men and supplying millions of people with some necessary service or commodity may reduce the cost of production only for its own profit. The state may use its great authority chiefly for the benefit of special interests. The advocate of equal rights is preoccupied by these opportunities for the abusive exercise of power, because from his point of view rights exercised in the interest of inequality have ceased to be righteous. He distrusts those forms of individual and associated activity which give any individual or association substantial advantages over their associates. He becomes suspicious of any kind of individual and social distinction with the nature and effects of which he is not completely familiar.

A democracy of equal rights may tend to encourage certain expressions of individual liberty; but they are few in number and limited in scope. It rejoices in the freedom of its citizens, provided this freedom receives certain ordinary expressions. It will follow a political leader, like Jefferson or Jackson, with a blind confidence of which a really free democracy would not be capable, because such leaders are, or claim to be in every respect, except their prominence, one of the "people." Distinction of this kind does not separate a leader from the majority. It only ties them together more firmly. It is an acceptable assertion of individual liberty, because it is liberty converted by its exercise into a kind of equality. In the same way the American democracy most cordially admired for a long time men who pursued more energetically and successfully than their fellows, ordinary business occupations, because they believed that such familiar expressions of individual liberty really tended towards social and industrial homogeneity. Herein they were mistaken; but the supposition was made in good faith, and it constitutes the basis of the Jeffersonian Democrat's illusion in reference to his own interest in liberty. He dislikes or ignores liberty, only when it looks in the direction of moral and intellectual emancipation. In so far as his influence has prevailed, Americans have been encouraged to think those thoughts and to perform those acts which everybody else is thinking and performing.

The effect of a belief in the principle of "equal rights" on freedom is, however, most clearly shown by its attitude toward Democratic political organization and policy. A people jealous of their rights are not sufficiently afraid of special individual efficiency and distinction to take very many precautions against it. They greet it oftener with neglect than with positive coercion. Jeffersonian Democracy is, however, very much afraid of any examples of associated efficiency. Equality of rights is most in danger of being violated when the exercise of rights is associated with power, and any unusual amount of power is usually derived from the association of a number of individuals for a common purpose. The most dangerous example of such association is not, however, a huge corporation or a labor union; it is the state. The state cannot be bound hand and foot by the law, as can a corporation, because it necessarily possesses some powers of legislation; and the power to legislate inevitably escapes the limitation of the principle of equal rights. The power to legislate implies the power to discriminate; and the best way consequently for a good democracy of equal rights to avoid the danger of discrimination will be to organize the state so that its power for ill will be rigidly restricted. The possible preferential interference on the part of a strong and efficient government must be checked by making the government feeble and devoid of independence. The less independent and efficient the several departments of the government are permitted to become, the less likely that the government as a whole will use its power for anything but a really popular purpose.

In the foregoing type of political organization, which has been very much favored by the American democracy, the freedom of the official political leader is sacrificed for the benefit of the supposed freedom of that class of equalized individuals known as the "people," but by the "people" Jefferson and his followers have never meant all the people or the people as a whole. They have meant a sort of apotheosized majority—the people in so far as they could be generalized and reduced to an average. The interests of this class were conceived as inimical to any discrimination which tended to select peculiarly efficient individuals or those who were peculiarly capable of social service. The system of equal rights, particularly in its economic and political application *has* worked for the benefit of such a class, but rather in its effect upon American intelligence and morals, than in its effect upon American political and economic development. The system, that is, has only partly served the purpose of its founder and his followers, and it has failed because it did not bring with it any machinery adequate even to its own insipid and barren purposes. Even the meager social interest which Jefferson concealed under cover of his demand for equal rights could not be promoted without some effective organ of social responsibility; and the Democrats of to-day are obliged, as we have seen, to invoke the action of the central government to destroy those economic discriminations which its former inaction had encouraged. But even so the traditional democracy still retains its dislike of centralized and socialized responsibility. It consents to use the machinery of the government only for a negative or destructive object. Such must always be the case as long as it remains true to its fundamental principle. That principle defines the social interest merely in the terms of an indiscriminate individualism—which is the one kind of individualism murderous to both the essential individual and the essential social interest.

The net result has been that wherever the attempt to dis-

criminate in favor of the average or indiscriminate individual
has succeeded, it has succeeded at the expense of individual
liberty, efficiency, and distinction; but it has more often failed
than succeeded. Whenever the exceptional individual has been
given any genuine liberty, he has inevitably conquered. That is
the whole meaning of the process of economic and social development traced in certain preceding chapters. The strong and
capable men not only conquer, but they seek to perpetuate their
conquests by occupying all the strategic points in the economic
and political battlefield—whereby they obtain certain more or
less permanent advantages over their fellow-democrats. Thus in
so far as the equal rights are freely exercised, they are bound
to result in inequalities; and these inequalities are bound to
make for their own perpetuation, and so to provoke still further
discrimination. Wherever the principle has been allowed to mean
what it seems to mean, it has determined and encouraged its
own violation. The marriage which it is supposed to consecrate
between liberty and equality gives birth to unnatural children,
whose nature it is to devour one or the other of their parents.

The only way in which the thorough-going adherent of the
principle of equal rights can treat these tendencies to discrimination, when they develop, is rigidly to repress them; and this
tendency to repression is now beginning to take possession of
those Americans who represent the pure Democratic tradition.
They propose to crush out the chief examples of effective individual and associated action, which their system of democracy has encouraged to develop. They propose frankly to destroy,
so far as possible, the economic organization which has been
built up under stress of competitive conditions; and by assuming such an attitude they have fallen away even from the
pretense of impartiality, and have come out as frankly representative of a class interest. But even to assert this class interest efficiently they have been obliged to abandon, in fact if
not in word, their correlative principle of national irresponsibility. Whatever the national interest may be, it is not to be
asserted by the political practice of non-interference. The hope
of automatic democratic fulfillment must be abandoned. The
national government must step in and discriminate; but it must
discriminate, not on behalf of liberty and the special individual,
but on behalf of equality and the average man.

Thus the Jeffersonian principle of national irresponsibility can no longer be maintained by those Democrats who sincerely believe that the inequalities of power generated in the American economic and political system are dangerous to the integrity of the democratic state. To this extent really sincere followers of Jefferson are obliged to admit the superior political wisdom of Hamilton's principle of national responsibility, and once they have made this admission, they have implicitly abandoned ther contention that the doctrine of equal rights is a sufficient principle of democratic political action. They have implicitly accepted the idea that the public interest is to be asserted, not merely by equalizing individual rights, but by controlling individuals in the exercise of those rights. The national public interest has to be affirmed by positive and aggressive action. The nation has to have a will and a policy as well as the individual; and this policy can no longer be confined to the merely negative task of keeping individual rights from becoming in any way privileged.

Croly and his progressive associates were largely successful in divorcing liberal reform from Jeffersonian individualism, but the rhetoric of indignation that was essential to this transformation convinced the progressives themselves, and subsequent generations of mostly sympathetic historians, that the epic contest pitted the enlightened and humane against the selfish and debased. Yet the progressives knew that they were not a monolithic group, that those who paraded under the New Nationalism banner of Theodore Roosevelt were convinced that the giant corporations were natural and efficient organizations whose abuses should best be rectified by regulation, whereas the Wilsonians of the New Freedom persuasion preferred trustbusting and a return to the competition of smaller units. But historians have only relatively recently become aware of the wide variety of progressive concerns and mentalities and the considerable degree to which their thrusts could and did conflict. Many of the regulatory reforms so celebrated by the progressives as triumphs over selfish business were in fact shrewdly engineered by the businesses to be regulated, and many of the reform crusades, such as campaigns for prohibition, immigration restriction by national origins quota, eugenics, and racial segregation were "reforms" that contemporary liberals would scarcely recognize as such.

In the selection that follows, Otis L. Graham, Jr., analyzes the convolutions of a progressive impulse that ostensibly combined three rather distinctly different sources of concern and activity. Most noticeable, yet not really central to the dominant concerns of the era, were the social justice progressives, whose campaigns for the regulation of child labor, minimum wages, workmen's compensation, and decent housing more often than not led to empty victories and broken hearts. Also noticeable, yet backward-looking and often decidedly illiberal, were the efforts of the "return progressives," often small town and rural, to restore the small-scale enterprise and nineteenth-century moral code of a confused and nostalgic America. Most important (and from the viewpoint of their own concerns, most successful) were those progressives, often in business and the professions, who sought to submit social processes and governmental institutions to the discipline of technology and industrialism—to rationalize and modernize the chaotic welter of modern urban life through bureaucratic procedures. All these fascinating and often contradictory efforts, and importantly, the powerful resistance of the entrenched conservatives, are skillfully and sensitively analyzed in the following essay.

Progressive Reform

OTIS L. GRAHAM, JR.

How may progressivism be summarized, its various forms and
extended history managed in the fewest generalizations? Historians must mediate between the untidy details of the movement and the desire of their readers for generalization. Scholars,
as did contemporaries, strike out for two or three categories—
more would be an intolerable mental burden—into which they
may fit all the complex facts of an historical era such as this
one. The oldest set of categories into which progressives have
been put was one established by progressives themselves. It
is the New Freedom–New Nationalism distinction, arising out
of the political struggles of 1912. For all its flaws this is a
useful division. A considerable number of reformers may be
described as citizens who were primarily or even solely worried
about large industrial and financial combinations, who wished
them broken into competitive units, and who were uneasy with
a powerful state whatever its motives. And there were men of
quite a different reform mind, who saw the combination movement as a natural feature of modern industrial life and were
eager to control it through a vigorous government with both
regulatory and welfare responsibilities. It is of no great importance that the labels do not entirely fit either Woodrow
Wilson or Theodore Roosevelt, or that the parties they led under
those labels were even more than the candidates' minds a mixture of creeds. Many progressives held views of the New Freedom or the New Nationalism variety with considerable tenacity,
and whatever party they favored, the categories mark off and
help us to speak about large areas of consistent attitudes and
behavior. The New Freedom had reactionary tendencies, which
became evident later on (T.R. and others perceived this at the

Otis L. Graham, Jr., *The Great Campaigns: Reform and War in America,
1900–1928*, © 1971, pp. 126–169. Reprinted by permission of the author
and Prentice-Hall, Inc., Englewood Cliffs, N.J.

time, calling it "rural toryism"), but it kept alive a healthy distrust of private economic power. The New Nationalism had affinities for a government that knew what was best and would put an end to the squabbling of groups, a government preferring unity to justice. In this respect it bore a few slight resemblances to the theories and practice later to be strutted about by Mussolini. But it understood industrial civilization better than the New Freedom, and it tried to teach the American mind to accept the necessity for constant management in the public interest by public officials.

These categories, as useful as they are, do not contain all the important styles among reformers. Another pair of typologies might be designated the moralists and the scientists. The moralists were those men and women who thought the answer to the "social problem" lay in a return to the values that had served the nineteenth century—honesty, abstinence, continence, individual effort, fiduciary integrity. They filled the prohibition ranks, tried to abolish prostitution, hounded men from office if they were stained with a bit of graft. Because they did all of these things with an air of righteousness (and because they did some of them at all) we do not remember the progressive moralists with nostalgia. Today we like neither their moral code nor the aggressive way in which they held it.

Quite in contrast were men who had rejected the Victorian code in their personal lives and had no thought of applying it to America's social problems. They preferred to apply science, or at the very least, rationality, rather than the Bible or tradition. Lincoln Steffens is perhaps best remembered (because of his *Autobiography*) for such attitudes, although he had little knowledge of science. He was uncomfortable with the upright reformers he encountered in his observation of American cities, dubious of the efficacy of mere honesty in office, and irresistibly drawn to the flexible, affable, worldly bosses who had a sense of humor he missed in the Goo Goos. To Steffens and men like him neither the moralistic reformer nor the political boss could bring America out of her crisis; the answer lay in science, in technically trained people, in "trained intelligence." If Steffens was the popularizer of a reform type uncomfortable with moral certitudes and full of confidence in the critical intelligence, John Dewey was its preeminent philosopher. This preference for science over received moral absolutes appealed to engineers, public health officials, economists, statisticians, architects, physicians, and even some businessmen, social types who had learned orderly and critical processes of thought and who were eager to bring their expertise to bear upon an unruly society in need of reorganization.

It is clear to us now that the reformers who were pragmatic and had a respect for science understood better the America of their time and the America in the making than did the moralists. They seemed to perceive the need for mental flexibility in a society so caught up in change, and they understood that progress would come only to the nation that trained and utilized its scientists and social scientists. They sensed that modern society required social control guided by a constant flow of data and that it could not proceed on the rigid truths of dated sermons. The saloon was not the prime menace to the well-being of Americans, nor was the political boss. An unregulated economy holds that honor, crashing on toward profits and blind to the social consequences. But while the scientific progressives were best equipped temperamentally and occasionally also intellectually to cope with modern problems, in retrospect we have been unable to commend them wholeheartedly.

In the first place, talk as they might about critical intelligence, technique, and urbane sophistication, most of them had not traveled very far from the fervid style that marked their entire generation. A scientist like Harvey Wiley might ground his crusade in figures and experimental data, but in ways he was as moralistic as the heavyset ladies of the WCTU. This was simply not a cool generation, and those in it who spoke admiringly of trained intelligence never managed to spring their own intelligences loose from service to some unexamined values. This inconsistency, however, is not what we chiefly regret in the scientific school. A consequence of their thought and activity seems to have been the impersonal, bureaucratic world that envelops us, crushing out spontaneity, disrupting community, and in general robbing us of some of the finer byproducts of a premodern social order.

Every student may be allowed a third category, those reformers who had just the right vision and balance, who took from the moralists their passion for risky, worthy causes, and from the scientists their mental flexibility and their respect for technical expertise in the service of the public. But for anyone this is a small list, since so few men and women then or now avoided the excesses of dogmatism or manipulative urges. My own list includes Jane Addams and Lillian Wald, Benjamin Marsh, John B. Andrews, George Norris, Paul U. Kellogg, Judge Ben Lindsey, Mary White Ovington, and that "unwearied hoper," Florence Kelley.

One could go on noting these efforts at a taxonomy of progressive reform, but we are perhaps in a position to see the main outlines of what we wish to summarize. The progressive era was a compound of these elements: (1) attempts to impose order and modern procedures upon an archaic nineteenth-century society; (2) attempts to come to the aid of the casualties of industrialism—the ghetto dweller, the female factory laborer, the working child; and (3) attempts to impose nineteenth-century moral codes on a twentieth-century world. Each of these major objectives enlisted different social types, drew strength from different social classes, and more often than complementing each other, contradicted each other. Some overlap in leadership, and the usual confusion of legislative struggles and their inevitable blend of impulses and interest groups, have naturally blurred the outlines of these three types of reform effort. So also has the fog of self-justifying and generally sincere rhetoric. The common use of phrases such as *The People, Justice, restoration of American ideals,* helped obscure what was distinct about the components of progressivism. Yet even if these categories reflect the reality of what contemporaries saw as one undifferentiated movement for greater democracy, important and difficult tasks remain. How may these various objectives be ranked so that we understand with reasonable accuracy how that generation was apportioning its corrective energies? And what results were achieved in each area?

On the question of which objective predominated at the time, we have only impressions, uncorrected by any methodology capable of measuring the intensity of commitment of reformers in prewar America. The urge to submit social processes and governmental institutions to the discipline of technology and

industrialism seems in retrospect to have been the most significant motivation of the period and one that met with the most
far-reaching results. America at the beginning of this century
was a modernizing society, shifting from agriculture to industry,
from crude and small-scale industry to larger units, becoming
daily more urbanized, technological, rationally and specially
organized for specialized tasks. Efficiency, the hope of efficiency,
and the sheer desire to expand meant that broad commercial
interests would impinge upon narrow, local ones with mounting
success. Ambitious entrepreneurs followed a vision of nationwide and predictable operations, and it was shared by experts
who longed to manage large projects. Expanding enterprise
confronted localized jurisdictions and habits, irresistibly pressing them toward subordination or obliteration. The bureaucratic
habits of orderliness and regularity were prized, eccentricity and
lack of planning discouraged. The initiative rested with the
forces of centralization, integration of systems, rationalization,
coordination, and efficiency, even though these were slowed by
tradition and other impediments.

What has all this to do with reform? The rationalization of
systems meant the internal reform of those large business enterprises that meant to participate in the future, and this required
men with a respect for the methods of science, a passion for
order, an expansionist psychology, and a sense of mission. Such
men, and women, arose in business and the professions, and
they may be called reformers as readily as we have used the
word for public servants like Roosevelt, LaFollette, Pinchot.
Samuel Haber's book *Efficiency and Uplift,* tells of the Taylor
movement to bring efficiency to industry with stopwatches and
efficiency studies, and the moral fervor and guiding principles
of Taylorism mark it as a cousin to the well-known political
aspects of progressivism. In the medical profession, the Flexner
Report of 1910 should be equally recognizable as an event in
reform history. The report exposed the chaotic manner of preparing and certifying physicians in the United States, and led
to the rationalization of medical education through common
standards and effective examination of aspirants. Another example from the private sector would be Seaman A. Knapp's
pioneering efforts to establish demonstration farms and to
educate adults in rural areas in the practices of scientific
farming.

It was inevitable that this aggressive, modern spirit moving in the larger capitalist institutions and the professions would discover that it also had a calling to the reformation of public life. Indeed, the challenge here was even greater, since the world of business had forged ahead with modern methods and left public institutions stagnant and backward by contrast. Modern corporations were increasingly in command of their environments—gathering data, anticipating the future, eliminating uncertainty and waste. But the cities were fragmented, ignorant, leaderless, directionless. Roy Lubove's *Twentieth Century Pittsburgh* (1969) provides a good example of the shocking contrast between growing private order and public disorder. The steel industry was planned and poised for the future, while the city in which it sat was fragmented by class, ethnic, and residential divisions, unable to respond to its desperate problems. Not unnaturally, the coalition that emerged to attack the problems of Pittsburgh and other cities not only borrowed the methods of modern business, but enlisted the businessmen themselves. Those whose operations were citywide (or greater) wished a city government that answered to the data generated by experts rather than the haphazard appetites of a welter of wards with their local and parochial preoccupations and their tendency toward drift. For them, reform meant a strong, routinized government they could control or influence, with well-staffed regulatory agencies at all levels—public health, finance, police, public utilities, city planning, and the like. The ranks of urban reform were filled with people of lesser economic stake but a similar determination to have a modern, orderly city. They were often individuals of small-town background, lawyers, and other educated citizens ready for new professions, people who brought to the city the evangelical style of the Protestant countryside, which disguised urban progressivism with the rhetoric of moralism when its inner dynamic was really rationalization.

Men with similar outlook but with broader investments or professional horizons came to see the need for reform at the federal level—and reform meant new and enlarged functions performed by trained and properly oriented men. The regulatory measures at the federal level that form the best-known part of the progressive record—regulatory commissions in railroading, banking, special industries from meat-packing to pharmaceuti-

cals, and a commission for all large industry—were largely
created by a special type of businessman and a special type of
young professional. We have earlier reviewed the sources of
regulatory statutes: disgruntled shippers demanded railroad
regulation and enlightened owners and managers concurred; a
coalition of noneastern bankers and small businessmen demanded banking reform and were joined in the idea if not all
the details by the Wall Street financial leaders; meat-packers
wanted a meat-packing inspection act; food processors and
retail druggists pressed for a food and drug administration.
And in all these struggles to reform business practices the
pressure came not only from business interests but also from
professional men, many already in the federal service, who had
caught a glimpse of the public and personal advantages of
bureaucratic control over the existing chaos.

This type of progressivism might occasionally talk of democracy, but it was elitist rather than democratic, efficiency-
minded rather than justice-minded. Where it was successful,
power was not diffused among The People but was concentrated
in a knowledge-elite without whom no modern mayor or industrialist would dream of proceeding. While the opposition
was fierce and often lumped this sort of reformer with the
do-gooders who worried about the urban poor, poverty was no
prime concern of theirs. They were out to end the diffusion of
power and the randomness of social processes; they wished to
vest social control in safe hands, and fewer hands.

Because of this conservative potential, and because they
were in tune with the logic of industrialism, the exponents of
efficiency and orderly procedures lost little momentum after the
war. The effort to bring the advantages of centralized, bureau-
cratized government to the cities continued in the 1920s, with
303 cities turning to the commission-manager plan (only 31
cities had adopted the plan from 1905 to 1915). This was an
innovation that centralized responsibility, with a few men
elected on a citywide vote in place of the old unwieldy council
elected on a ward basis. Reformers promised that the result
would be lower taxes even as services were strengthened and
expanded. These changes had the strong support of most businessmen, who thought the old mayor and council system cumber-
some and wasteful and deplored the strength (or at least,

autonomy) it gave to working-class wards that would be under-represented under a system of citywide elections.

The bulk of the postwar activity of this sort came at the state level, where a series of reform administrations wrote a reform history that has received insufficient attention. New York under Al Smith (1920–28), Pennsylvania under Gifford Pinchot (1924–28), California under Clement Young (1926–30), North Carolina under Cameron Morrison (1921–25), Alabama under Bibb Graves (1926–30), Louisiana under John W. Parker (1920–24), these and other states were the scenes of legislative activity and administrative reorganization that George Tindall has described as "business progressivism." Businessmen may have supported the new policies of the 1920s, since part of what was involved was a series of subsidies in the form of increased expenditure on transportation improvements and state agencies for promotion and research. But the central idea was not subsidies, but efficiency. By 1931 at least forty-one states had followed the lead of Indiana, which had in 1909 established an agency to coordinate other state agencies (in Indiana, the Department of Inspection and Supervision of Public Offices). In 1912 no state operated with a budget; by 1930, all but one had adopted that prerequisite to financial planning. No state in 1910 had a central purchasing agency; by 1930, thirty-five had centralized their purchasing. The 1920s in state government was a time of the integration and rational-ization, as well as the expansion, of modern governmental bureaucracies.

After the war there were also continued efforts at the federal level to bring order to the economy through a scientific and technical bureaucracy. Federal government spending in 1930 was 350 percent greater than in 1915, and while much of this was war-related, the functions of government expanded yearly through the 1920s as bureaucrats and constituencies agreed to let fewer things alone in America. Spending on health and welfare did not keep pace with population increase, but the government became very active in the promotion and regulation of commerce and agriculture. The largest increases came in expenditures on transportation, the postal system, aid to shipping, the data-gathering functions of the Bureau of Foreign and Domestic Commerce and the Bureau of Agricultural Economics. The Commerce Department under Herbert Hoover, an engineer who was impressed with the success of the War Industries Board at bringing rationality to sectors of industry (the WIB, for example, had standardized the shape of auto tires and bricks), became an agency with a mission—to foster efficiency and coordination in American business. Under Hoover's guidance (1920–28) the department gathered information on trade conditions, prices, and markets, and distributed it (free) to competing firms to allow them to eliminate wasteful competition. Agricultural economists like Mordekai Ezekiel and Louis Bean were doing the same things for farmers from their offices in the Department of Agriculture. The goal was predictability and control, the reduction of the bad guesses and wasteful duplications—in a word, the inefficiency—of American producing and selling. There were similar opportunities in the agencies involved in resource management for those bureaucrats who were ambitious to bring their expertise to bear upon decisions affecting irreplaceable natural resources. "Pinchot-type conservation did not deteriorate in the 1920s," historian Donald Swain tells us, "but expanded and matured" as agencies such as the Forest Service enlarged their operations.

The same thrust toward rationalization was apparent in the streamlined public administration at the federal level. The Budget and Accounting Act of 1921 carried out many of the recommendations of the Taft Commission on Economy and Efficiency (1911–13), most importantly establishing a Bureau of the Budget to coordinate not only federal spending plans but its bureaucratic procedures. Outside government one finds the same tendencies. City comptrollers, police and fire chiefs, state auditors, even mayors and governors organized in the 1920s, if they had not done so just before the war, and began to share information and standardize procedures. World Convention Dates for 1920 shows forty-five annual conventions of national organizations of public officials, and by 1930 the figure was ninety. President Hoover's Commission on Recent Social Trends reported that the 1920s had been a time of great change in American public administration, and the words the commission used over and over again were centralization, simplification, supervision, research, efficiency. There were no dramatic victories—this sort of reform rarely provided them. But the gains for social control progressivism were measurable and permanent.

Progressive speechmakers, our fathers who read the older textbooks, and our children now frowning their way through the social studies curriculum in junior high schools would all fail to recognize the foregoing account as a description of the real core of the progressive movement. We see social control where older histories described liberation, we attribute reform measures to professional and commercial elites rather than the indignant rhetoricians of Congress, pulpit, and magazines, and we describe the goal as the rationalization and centralization, not the democratization, of American society. What jars most in all the new writing on progressivism, if one had been reared on more traditional accounts, is the discovery of businessmen swarming throughout the domain of reform, originating, shaping, modifying, and in general lobbying—unassimilable notion—for regulation. One may wonder what took us so long to discover them, and the answer seems to be a compound of the beguiling rhetoric of the reformers themselves, the advent of better sampling procedures, the intensification of monographic studies, and the congeniality of the discovery to the radicalized intellectuals of the 1960s. There is some reason to wonder if, under the latter influence, the younger historians are discovering too many of them. The most important task now is to try to learn the precise extent of the influence of commercial groups in the various sectors of that wave of deliberate social change we call progressivism. It is sufficiently clear that many of those working to impose rational processes upon the mass of individual liberties that made up the pretwentieth-century American economy and social order were in fact businessmen, and that the old Beard and Parrington theory that reform meant the common man was thrashing the predatory interests was no good at all in explaining progressivism—or what appeared to be the main or most significant part of progressivism. Two new theories have recently been offered to explain the emergence of a broad drive, at many levels across an entire nation, to achieve greater social control. Gabriel Kolko, in *The Triumph of Conservatism* (1965), and James Weinstein, in *The Corporate Ideal in the Liberal State, 1900–1918* (1968), see progressivism, at least at the federal level, as a businessman's drive to use the state to stabilize the large-scale capitalist system, which was threatened both by the uncertainties of vigorous competition and by a rising tide of political radicalism.

These are brilliant, challenging books, but they are not entirely persuasive. Data formerly ignored are now being overemphasized. Businessmen were reforming, but they were also being reformed. The scene is not at all tidy. A more convincing and conceptually much broader interpretive framework has been offered by Samuel P. Hays and by Robert Wiebe. In this view the nineteenth-century social structure, characterized by a local focus, small-scale operations, and personal, face-to-face relations (in Frederick Tonnies's encompassing term, *community*, or *Gemeinschaft*), was giving way at the turn of the century to a social order based on a cosmopolitan and national focus, large-scale operations, and impersonal, bureaucratic procedures (*society*, or *Gesellschaft*). Social groups who had a stake in hastening this transition—this would-be large businessmen and their professional allies in law, engineering, city planning, and the like—turned to the state to build a bureaucratic environment conducive of stability and congenial to greater social control. Their rhetoric obscured their real purposes, but this was not because they dissimulated but because in an exciting time when the young and enlightened were reordering society they turned to the only moving rhetoric they knew, the language of the Protestant Reformation, the Old Testament prophets, the Declaration of Independence, the great national vision of Lincoln. In any event they hardly understood the historic function they were performing. They were reformers, but in this view what was being reformed in the progressive years was not only or even primarily graft or poverty, but disorderly, inefficient, and unsystematic ways of doing things.

The conceptual scheme of Hays and Wiebe is an invaluable contribution to our understanding of the progressive era, preferable to the view of Kolko and Weinstein in that it accounts for the extensive role of business groups in various reform areas without ignoring the professionals, and without overemphasizing elements of conspiracy and naked self-interest. Wiebe's *The Search for Order* is the only systematic effort to place the diverse facts of the progressive era into this conceptual framework. The book clarifies so many things that one must make a decided effort to remember that in Wiebe's hands the community-society framework has not yet comfortably been made to contain all the data. Wiebe, intent on demonstrating the transcendent importance of the reformers who represent industrial and governmental rationalization, did not devote sufficient attention to the continuing counterattack of another set of reformers, the spokesmen of community. But if this is a flaw, it is a flaw of proportion, not a flaw of his framework, which accommodates nicely the prohibitionists along with the apostles of scientific management. A more serious problem is the tendency of this framework to squeeze out the element of conscience in progressivism, i.e., the social welfare volunteers, the ladies of the settlements, the Social Gospel ministers and novelists, and every other contemporary whose Christian or Emersonian principles brought him, however briefly, into the orbit of progressive activism. Hence, in this study I have tried to devise categories that allow us to utilize the community-society concept, but that also provide a framework for understanding contradictory evidence. But that reform was to a great extent a drive to stabilize large-scale industrial society by centralization of decision-making and rationalization of social processes can no longer be seriously doubted.

Because the principal beneficiaries of this side of progressivism were the owners and managers of corporations and the experts who staffed the powerful new governmental and educational bureaucracies, progressivism is on its way, especially among younger scholars, to becoming a much resented social movement. It accelerated the demise of small, neighborly communities, about which we are nostalgic, and brought the domination of a bureaucratic, scientized, depersonalizing world, which feeds our bellies so well and our souls so badly. It talked of coercion and the imposition of restraints more effectively than it talked of freedom. It educated leading capitalists in how to use the state to prevent real change, and the mental lock-step and high profits of wartime America further revealed to them the conservative possibilities of large government.

But there were both liberating and radical possibilities in the urge to coordinate and plan for greater efficiency. In the minds of Croly and Veblen and T.R. himself efficiency led away from a profit standard toward standards of social usefulness, with efficiency only a way station. Engineers who harkened to Veblen, intellectuals who read Croly, were likely to find their minds permanently occupied by the subversive idea that profit was not the point. Admittedly, neither the coordination and cooperative practices of the war nor the 1920s much resembled the radicals' social vision or followed their priorities. But the social control strain of progressive thought need not have been put to reactionary and repressive uses. Its leading thinkers sought freedom through order, not order for its own sake. They did not intend for the liberating possibilities of social discipline to be lost sight of. Croly sought to restrict certain economic liberties, but only because he knew there was no real freedom in a disorderly and uncontrolled economy. Margaret Sanger and the progressives of the eugenics movement proposed to submit the "right" to procreate to certain social controls; and while Adolf Hitler succeeded in putting such proposals under suspicion, Margaret Sanger was unquestionably right that real freedom in the future depended upon greater control over the production of human beings. The path that history actually took should not obscure the fact that the social control movement was at least in the beginning a liberal movement. Its leading theorists, people like Thorstein Veblen, Herbert Croly and John Dewey, assumed a basic conflict with the profit motive and saw in more cooperative forms of social organization a great step toward freedom. This legacy of progressive thought was reactivated in the 1930s as men like Adolf Berle and Rexford Tugwell took from that tradition their dream of an integrated economy run by social engineers responsible to the public. Ingrained individualism and jealous interest groups swept them aside as it had their progressive forerunners, but as the planet fills up with humanity the management of freedom will bring men back to the philosophers of social control.

Another distinctive type of reformer was the social justice progressive. *Justice* was a word frequently used in progressive circles. Some defined justice as equal economic opportunity (equal access to resources and markets, not to jobs or housing), others as the right to exercise meaningful political power. But by *social* justice the progressive understood all those efforts to give assistance, usually but not always through an agency of the state, to groups that had for any reason fallen into an intolerable arrears in the "natural" social arrangements of modernizing America. Conservatives argued that what social justice progressives sought was neither just nor socially desirable; but whether it was justice or generosity, it was impossible to ignore. Had pressure for humanitarian legislation come only from directly affected groups it would have made little headway, for such groups were unorganized and apolitical. But support came from middle and upper classss—the professional altruists of the social work-social settlement movement, and their allies in law, journalism, and even politics. When these progressives were added to the groups who would be the beneficiaries and who happened to be organized or at least aroused—railway labor, retail clerks, seamen, certain groups of farmers—it became a coalition to be reckoned with. While a coalition of altruists and beneficiaries was still not wealthy or numerically very strong, under fortunate circumstances it proved able to manipulate the political machinery with tangible effect.

Writers have been attracted to the social justice progressives, and for good reasons. On the whole these were attractive, humane people. But such writers have often implied that social justice was the central concern of the era, which it was not. Recently it has been implied by young scholars that the social justice component was either nonexistent or unimportant; but it was not that either. Compile a brief list of the men and women, the organizations, and the accomplishments of this effort, and the list has a famiilar ring and a not inconsiderable bulk: Jane Addams, John B. Andrews, Roger Baldwin, Louis Brandeis, Paul Kellogg, Florence Kelley, Benjamin Marsh, Owen Lovejoy, Margaret Dreier Robins, Mary Simkhovitch, Graham Taylor, John A. Ryan, Stephen S. Wise, Lillian Wald; organizations so well known that their initials are enough, such as the NCL, WTUL, AALL, NCLC, NAACP, ACLU; institutions like Hull House, Greenwich House, University Settlement, Denison House, Chicago Commons, and all the Charities Organizations in the major cities; The Pittsburgh Survey of 1906; the Industrial Relations Commission Report of 1915; the New York Tenement Law of 1901; the child labor laws in the various states, and the long national campaign; thirty-nine maximum-hour laws for women by 1917, and fifteen minimum wage laws for women by 1923; factory safety laws in most industrial states; workmen's compensation in forty-two states by 1920—the list could easily be extended, but the outlines are clear.

Does such a list not sketch the outline of a kind of revolution, a shift from the heartless, devil-take-the-hindmost indus-

trialism of the nineteenth century to a humanized, early version
of the welfare state? Unfortunately, a close, skeptical look at
the record does not sustain such optimism. Paper victories,
though hard enough to win, had a way of melting away in the
mazes of administration and judicial interpretation. Despite the
child labor laws passed by the states after the founding of the
National Child Labor Committee in 1904 (southern anti-child
labor groups had operated earlier) the census of 1910 showed
more children at work than in 1900. State laws were notoriously
weak, levying minimum penalties or none at all, providing for
elaborate court review, excluding many industries, and—in
nineteen of the thirty-one states passing child labor laws, providing no funds at all for even one inspector to enforce the law.
Among other reasons for such inadequacies, state legislators
complained that strict laws drove industry to relocate in friend-
lier states and argued that child labor regulation was properly
a federal matter. When the NCLC overcame its Constitutional
scruples and restored to a federal law (the Keating-Owen law
was passed in 1916 after Woodrow Wilson overcame *his* Constitutional scruples), it was declared unconstitutional in *Hammer* v. *Dagenhart* (1918). A differently phrased law of 1919 met
the same fate, and the despairing reformers turned to a Constitutional amendment (passed finally by Congress in 1924)
only to see it smothered in the tangle of state legislatures. A
national ban on child labor came only in 1938 with the passage
of the Fair Labor Standards Act, and it came then not so much
because of four decades of agitation by reformers as because
the most radical force of all, the dynamic American economy,
had undermined the institution. State child labor and compulsory education laws had cut the proportion of working children
from 18 percent in 1890 to 15 percent in 1910. The decline of
the family farm and the farm labor force in general, along with
the automation of the more repetitious jobs, brought a rapid
postwar drop to a figure of 4 percent by 1930.

But victory over child labor, whatever the share of credit
between reformers and impersonal economic forces, actually
produced additional evidence of the superficiality of so many
progressive remedies. Even had the child labor reformers taken
the children out of the mills, their home environments would
have remained in many cases as brutalizing as the work environment. Industrial labor was hard on children, but the home

lives of most such children were unrelieved by adequate recreational or educational opportunities. The child-labor reformers, like most progressives inclined toward simple, negative solutions, gave little thought to the total environment of the child. At the passage of the Fair Labor Standards Act, NCLC leader George Alger, ignoring the problem of school dropouts, delinquency, and the like, closed the books on their crusade with the remark that he "knew of no further legislation to suggest." The historian of child labor in New York State was forced to conclude that "child labor reform was purely surface in nature and failed to reach the basic problems of New York's youth," leaving them after the victory of 1938 worse off than when the reformers started thirty-five or forty years before.

The failure of child-labor reform was widely admitted and broke the hearts of many social justice progressives, as well it might. But it was not an ayptical case. State labor legislation proved equally porous when it was enacted. Fifteen states passed minimum wage laws for women, but when the Supreme Court ruled the law for the District of Columbia unconstitutional in the *Adkins* case (1923), six of the state laws were nullified along with it. Yet while the *Adkins* case "killed all enforcement," as Elizabeth Brandeis wrote, the laws had never amounted to much in the first place. Of the fifteen laws only five were enforceable at all, the others being so badly drafted that they either failed to set up a minimum wage or established one beneath the prevailing minimum. Of the fifteen states willing to take even these shaky steps toward the protection of women workers, only two, Massachusetts and Wisconsin, were important industrial states. The others found the laws palatable because they had little industrial labor to regulate.

In the area of housing, it must be remembered that the legislative reforms that enhanced the record of progressives in cities like New York and Chicago built no new housing units but only purported to regulate the existing ones, or some of them. Leading housing reformer Lawrence Veiller was typical in his concentration on restrictive legislation to make existing tenements more livable; he explicitly rejected the idea of public housing. So long as such attitudes characterized progressive housing reformers, even had funds for tenement inspection and enforcement of restrictive laws been sufficient (which they never were), there would still have been no new units as the result of reformers' efforts, and no racial integration in the old ones.

The progressives' experience with housing reform well illustrates not only the intractability of modern social problems but also the occasional intellectual deficiencies that restricted the progressives from making much headway against the social evils they bravely attacked. Sweep away the slums with one clean legislative stroke, progressives like Veiller believed, and the cities will bustle with happy people. Their analysis in this instance was shallow and their remedy simplistic. Of course they were too optimistic and the law would be evaded; but even had the hallways been cleaned and lighted, the increased costs to tenement owners raised the whole question of who would build more urban housing, where would they build it, and how would it be designed? This was left to take care of itself. When the profit motive did not produce the right sort of housing for urban human beings, the New Dealers, feeling somewhat superior, took the next necessary step into public housing. They then learned how little both they and the progressives before them had known about what the "right" sort of housing was. People lived in neighborhoods, in a total environment; it was not enough to pile clean, well-lit apartments on top of one another in towers. We gave the slum-dwellers new buildings with modern elevators and kitchens, one New Dealer complained, "and they're still the same bunch of bastards they always were." The urban environment was not corrected to insure human happiness by the progressives—or by the New Dealers—not only because the scale of the job went far beyond both their awareness and their resources but also because they had no positive conception of what that environment ought to be. Yet it must be said for them that they at least launched the scientific study of housing and city planning, the ultimate source of better ideas than their own.

Social justice progressives are credited with bringing to America the idea and inaugurating in a modest way the practice of social insurance—the public assumption of responsibility to compensate victims of industrial accident, illness, old age, and unemployment. The unbearable private cost of industrial accidents generated a drive for workmen's compensation laws, pressed initially by "altruistic" organizations like the AALL and the NCL, which provided skilled lobbyists and careful studies based

on the available data. Forty-three states had enacted workmen's compensation legislation by 1920. But we know from
recent studies by Roy Lubove and James Weinstein that the
workmen's compensation movement drew its main support from
the employers, who preferred the predictable costs of such
systems to the uncertainties of legal proceedings. The National
Association of Manufacturers proved more important in the
workmen's compensation drive than the tiny AALL. Businessmen adopted the workmen's compensation movement and saw
to it that the system covered only about one-fourth of actual
medical costs, and that (in most states) private insurance companies held and administered the funds rather than the government.

Whatever its defects, workmen's compensation was the only
compulsory social insurance program operating in the United
States before the 1930s. Conservatives often frightened themselves with the theory that any concession to reform would open
the floodgates to socialism, but in practice the reverse was
often the case. Roy Lubove writes: "Social insurance experts
mistakenly assumed that the rapid spread of compensation
legislation after 1911 would lead to other compulsory programs . . . [but] far from providing an entering wedge, it solidi-
fied the opposition of private interests to any further extension
of social insurance." A small group of progressives began to
agitate for health, old age, and unemployment insurance in
1915, calling health insurance "the next step." The step was
likely to be a small one in any case, but the war killed whatever
chance health insurance had, as opponents were able to condemn the idea as "Germanic." Absolutely nothing was accomplished along any of these lines at any level until the 1930s.

Thus, progressive social justice legislation brought very
meager gains to the intended beneficiaries. The central statistical indicator that illuminates the social justice record is income
distribution. Progressives were quite conscious that income
redistribution was crucial to social reform, both as a matter of
equity and to preserve the society from dangerous social extremes. Herbert Croly in his *The Promise of American Life*
(1909), for example, argued that the decision to pursue "constructive national purpose" meant that "the American state will
in effect be making itself responsible for a morally and socially
desirable distribution of wealth." Many other reformers gave
redistribution high priority. While the data on income and

it appears that the distribution of income became, if anything,
wealth leave much to be desired for the years before the 1930s,
slightly *more* unequal over the period from 1896 to 1929, the
period when reformers thought themselves to be diminishing
such inequalities both through taxation and through regulatory
laws that shifted more of the costs of production onto the
employer. Walter Spahr estimated in 1896 that 2 percent of
the people owned 50 to 60 percent of the wealth, but Willford
I. King in 1917 judged that the intervening years had seen "a
marked concentration of income in the hands of the very rich."
King's studies of income distribution showed the top 5 percent
of families receiving 28 percent of the national income in 1910,
a slight increase (so far as he could tell) over 1896; ten years
later, in 1920, the war had apparently caused some leveling,
with the top 5 percent of families claiming 22 percent of the
national income (according to Simon Kuznets); by the mid
1930s, the share of the top 5 percent had risen to 29 percent.
Of course, income is much less concentrated than "static"
wealth. King found that in 1910 the top 1 percent of families
claimed 15 percent of the national income but 47 percent of the
national wealth, a figure roughly comparable to that for socially
reactionary Prussia. All such estimates are rough, and unquestionably underestimate the maldistribution, as they do not cover
capital gains, gifts, and other forms of untaxed compensation,
which are substantial in the higher and negligible in the lower
income brackets. The main outlines of income distribution are
clear: the first thirty years of this century saw a gradually
increasing concentration of income in the hands of the top
income tenth, generally at the expense of the middle rather than
the lower-income receivers. "Reform" made no impact on this
trend; only the war interrupted it, and after the war the concentration commenced again. Despite the lowering of the tariff
in 1913, the pathbreaking little income tax of the same year,
and the other measures that the wealthy claimed were tanta-
mount to socialism, income distribution at the very best remained about where it was when the fiddles of reform tuned
up in the 1890s.

While the actual results deriving from a few legislative victories
were often discouraging to social justice progressives, in some
areas of glaring inequality they achieved no victories at all,

symbolic or otherwise, because they never made the effort. Solicitous toward white women and children, the social justice progressive was typically uninterested in the plight of two groups in the most serious economic difficulties in those years (as now), the Negro and the rural poor.

To some extent these were overlapping categories, but most farm laborers and tenants were white, and they had a strong claim on the middle-class conscience if the degree of poverty established such a claim. But while progressives were often shocked by the state of life among the urban lower classes and addressed themselves to their improvement, they gave little time to the hidden agricultural lower class. There was a modest awakening to the problems of country life before the war, but the attention of men like the educational reformer Liberty Hyde Bailey or the founder of agricultural demonstration work, Seaman A. Knapp, was directed toward modernizing the middle-class, commercial farmer. Theodore Roosevelt's Country Life Commission studied the problems of rural life, but its report of 1909 neglected the landless farmer almost entirely. Considering the state of public and Congressional opinion, the flaws in their vision made little difference. Congress ignored even the slim recommendations of the Commission—better conservation, investigation of middleman profits, the banishment of the saloon, and similar measures of middle-class appeal. Progressivism came and went, leaving rural poverty untouched. Tenancy, the condition of 36 percent of American farmers in 1880, was up to 49 percent in 1920 and rising. Progressives, with very rare exceptions, were too busy to notice.

Also largely unnoticed was the Afro-American. The facts show that blacks were in a condition of sustained emergency. They were confined to the menial trades and the more brutal levels of agriculture, poorly paid, intellectually isolated, socially ostracized, and physically intimidated. The black illiteracy rate in the South approached 50 percent, as against a rate of 12 percent for whites. The life expectancy for blacks at birth was 32 years in 1900, while for whites it was 47. Blacks were harder hit by most diseases because their environment was harsher; yet they were also less likely to find or afford medical care. But, incredible enough, worse was yet to come. As the progressive era opened, the condition of blacks was in important respects deteriorating.

The last years of the nineteenth century produced a powerful tide of racism, more virulent and dangerous than had ever before marked American race relations. There had been earlier cycles of xenophobia that excited native Americans to abandon their uneasy tolerance and find ways to persecute alien peoples. But the nativism of the 1890s and after was not only more intense, but it now bore upon the blacks, who before had been somewhat protected by their status as chattel property. As the 1880s gave way to the 1890s one could notice the changing signs: rumors of the inundation of native Americans by hordes of unassimilable immigrants (these, in northern cities, included blacks), a torrent of speeches and books elaborating on the theme of white supremacy, talk of racial world conflict just ahead. To the Catholic and the Jew this spelled intolerance, suspicion, political and social discrimination. To the black it meant all these things, and also a degree of physical danger, which brought him in these years to the point Rayford Logan calls "the nadir of the Negro's status in American society."

C. Vann Woodward in *The Strange Career of Jim Crow* has described the legal expression of the new racism. A system of enforced segregation, unevenly developed before the 1890s, was perfected in the early progressive era, with the black everywhere confined to inferior civil rights and public facilities, or denied them altogether. The Negro had suffered economically perhaps more than any other group from the depression of the 1890s, but when prosperity returned the hurricane of racial intolerance made sure that the blacks would not fully participate in the recovery that other groups would experience. The agricultural black may have shared slightly in the rising farm prices after 1898, but the small black middle class was deliberately decimated. The rigid caste system of separate railroad cars and toilets was extended to jobs as well. The black began to disappear from trades he had formerly monopolized—tailoring, painting, smithing, carpentering. The depression initiated this downward pressure, and the intense nativist emotions after the turn of the century caused further displacement from reasonably attractive jobs. There were occasional pockets where blacks held out, such as coal mining, but for the most part they were the losers in a bitter struggle with whites for jobs that permitted an urban existence and something better than a marginal standard of life.

More dramatic than his economic difficulties was the increase in racial violence. Lynching in America had always had a strong class incidence—the rate was high among the poor and the transient—but it had been relatively color-blind before the 1890s. From 1882 to 1888 some 595 whites were lynched, and 440 blacks (this, of course, is a higher rate for blacks); by 1892 lynching was becoming racialized, with 169 blacks and 69 whites lynched that year. At the peak of the progressive period, 1906 to 1915, ten times as many blacks (620) as whites (61) were burned, beaten, or hanged to death. Inevitably the racial feelings behind these acts against individuals found occasion to shift to entire communities. Savage race riots broke out in New York and New Orleans in 1900, in Atlanta in 1906, in Springfield, Illinois in 1908. Between the reports of such incidents in the history of American race relations one could observe in the press and even in the best journals such as *Harper's, Scribner's,* and *Century,* the white mind at work reinforcing its racial streotypes: the black man was subhuman, childlike, docile, comic, lazy, criminal, superstitious, oversexed, lying, and stupid, a nigger, a spade, a pickaninny, a coon. This view of the black, we now suspect, was more damaging to the black and his aspirations for the future than the economic deprivation and physical danger that burdened his body.

Surely this exploitation and suffering would not go unnoticed in the progressive era, when sentiment for the underdog ran high and the ideals of the Declaration of Independence were being revived. And in fact the conscience of the white community began to stir. A few journals, such as *The Independent, The Arena,* and *Charities,* spoke out editorially against lynching. *McClure's* displeased its southern readers by printing a mild denunciation of race relations by Carl Shurz in 1904, and a splendid series of articles in *The American Magazine* by Ray Stannard Baker gained further circulation when bound into the book *Following the Color Line* (1908). Baker's book was widely noticed, and, along with more detailed investigations such as Mary White Ovington's *Half a Man: The Status of the Negro in New York* (1911), Louis D. Bowen's *The Colored People of Chicago* (1913), and John Daniel's *In Freedom's Birthplace: A History of the Boston Negro* (1914), took at least the first, fact-gathering step toward intervention. Several Negro settlement houses were established, and one or two settlements mixed the black and white poor. The philanthropic urge was quickened in the progressive era generally, and some attention was paid to the educational needs of blacks in the establishment of the General Education Board by the Rockefeller Foundation in 1902, the Anna T. Jeanes Fund in 1905, the Julius Rosenwald Fund in 1913. And it was a group of white progressives and socialists, among them Miss Ovington, William English Walling, Charles Edward Russell, Henry Moskowitz, and Oswald Garrison Villard, who took the organizational steps that led to the founding of the National Association for the Advancement of Colored People in 1909.

But these efforts do not add up to serious attention to the condition of blacks. The progressives had more pressing business than the welfare of the Negro, and the handful of reformers who concerned themselves with racial issues was unrepresentative and essentially ineffective. Progressivism at the local level discovered graft, captive political systems, inadequate public services; it never discovered the almost total lack of educational, medical, and eleemosynary institutions available to blacks. There were praiseworthy efforts in the South to abolish the infamous convict-lease system (six southern states had done so by 1917), but the southern jails and prison farms remained, as Frank Tannenbaum's *The Darker Phases of the South* reported in 1924, inhumanly brutal. Race relations being what they were, the penal institutions of the South were the places where blacks had their most sustained, damaging contact with white power and where reform was both most urgent and least likely.

At the national level, progressivism disappointed the few articulate blacks and whites who heard the language of humanitarianism from presidential campaigners and misjudged the limits that would be set by the pervasive racism of the American public. Theodore Roosevelt showed an initial independence in the matter of black civil service appointees and dared to invite Booker T. Washington to dinner at the White House. But when there was criticism of his appointment and dining policies he not only abandoned them but further reassured his white critics by his handling of the Brownsville affair. The white citizens of Brownsville, Texas, had worked themselves into an ugly mood over the presence of black troops stationed at the edge of town, and a controverted shooting incident on the night of August 13, 1906, was at least partially and perhaps entirely their fault. But T.R. accepted the questionable evidence of black culpability and dishonorably discharged three companies of black infantry, thereby holding black soldiers to standards of docility, discipline, and collective guilt that would have been unthinkable in the case of whites. After Brownsville, T.R. neither harmed nor helped the American black, and the Republican Party through 1912 continued to collect black votes and ignore the platform remnants of its Lincolnian heritage.

Despite the racial conservatism of the Democratic Party, Woodrow Wilson hinted strongly that blacks would be included among those aggrieved groups the New Freedom would help. But the humanitarian strain in Democratic progressivism was no match for its deep-seated racial attitudes. The Treasury and Post Office Departments segregated lunchrooms and bathrooms shortly after Wilson's cabinet took over, and, with Wilson refusing to intervene, black-held jobs dropped from 6 percent in 1913 to 5 percent in 1918. Despite repeated entreaties the President would not denounce lynching, never visited a black picnic or school. Booker T. Washington admitted in 1913 that he had "never seen the colored people so discouraged and bitter as they are at the present time." Wilson was personally no bigot, mixed with blacks when the occasion demanded it, and in fact had Washington to dinner at Princeton. But as President he would take absolutely no risks on the issue of race relations. Oswald Garrison Villard finally gained an interview with Wilson in October, 1913, and presented him with a plan for a national race commission to study the question. Wilson admitted that he would not endanger his program or administration by even that degree of involvement with the delicate racial issue: "I say it with shame and humiliation," he told Villard, "but I have thought about this thing for twenty years and I see no way out. It will take a very big man to solve this thing."

Why had progressivism made such an infinitesimal difference in the racial attitudes and customs of Americans? The failure to place this issue higher on the agenda ought to be seen in historical perspective, or it will appear merely as a monumental and inexplicable display of callousness. At that time *all* white Americans were raised in an atmosphere of sustained racism. They were convinced of Negro inferiority and armed against reality by separate institutions and racial stereotypes. White Americans learned how to see (and not to see) the black from casual comments of parents and peers, from "Uncle Remus" stories, from novels such as the trilogy of Thomas Dixon, *The Leopard's Spots* (1902), *The Clansman* (1905), *The Traitor* (1907). A United States Senator (Benjamin Tillman, Dem., South Carolina) condemned Roosevelt's dinner with Booker T. Washington with the comment that "entertaining that nigger will necessitate our killing a thousand niggers in the South before they learn their place." To some that remark seemed proper; to the rest, understandable. Roosevelt himself thought blacks inferior and admitted the dinner was a mistake.

In such a climate, whites did not "think" about the black. Their notions were fixed; their armor against aberrant thoughts was impenetrable. Progressives were white Americans and their culture equipped them wtih these attitudes. And in those rare instances when an individual, through some combination of perhaps an abolitionist heritage and an unusual personal encounter with black refugees in the northern cities, broke free of the old attitudes and began to sympathize and seek reform, the state of public opinion made the race issue the most unpromising subject a reformer could raise.

But to credit their ineffectiveness on this issue to the racist climate of opinion is to miss an insight into the progressive mentality. The black was overlooked because the entire culture overlooked him, but he was overlooked by a reform movement that made a specialty of uncovering neglected social evils because that reform movement had built-in blinders when it came to the desperate troubles of society's lowest classes. Progressivism was a middle-class movement, and only in a few instances, such as the social welfare movement in New York City or the state movement in Oklahoma, did progressivism take up the grievances of really submerged people. Its faith in political democracy was in conflict with, and often overruled by, the instinctive elitism of the confident, educated people who were the backbone of reform. In the end progressivism was better at directing than at listening.

Progressivism was also associated with the rising group self-assertiveness and solidarity of the native white American. Reform was not only contemporaneous with nativism but seemed to have a symbiotic relationship with it. While there were reformers who were free of the fever of a Nordic mission, there was a tendency for people who became excited about progressive causes also to be excited about the duty of "the race" to preserve and extend its dominion. Recall the careers of Roosevelt, Albert Beveridge, William E. Borah, Hiram Johnson, or Woodrow Wilson, with their happy union of Nordic nationalism and progressivism. Reform required a bold, crusading, self-assertive temper and aggressive moral certainty. As subversive as it may have sounded to smug conservatives, reform did not encourage doubt or tolerance. Such qualities were dysfunctional in a war, which is the analogy the reformers most often drew upon in describing what they were doing. Reform drew its strength from the unquestioned moralities of the white Protestant American. From such an impulse the descendants of slaves could expect at best occasional paternalistic advice and charity, at worst the disfranchisement associated with southern progressivism and the harassments against Orientals common in Hiram Johnson's California.

These qualities of the reform mind help to explain its insensitivity to a social problem more serious, both in terms of fundamental human morality and of social efficiency, than the trusts, or political corruption, or child labor, or alcohol. White progressivism offered little aid to blacks. Yet the expectation that a time of idealism and social introspection would bring some breakthrough for the black American was not in error. Currents of thought found in white progressivism had their parallels among blacks. These were the years when Booker T. Washington's program of black self-effacement and industrial education began to lose its grip on the younger blacks, and men like W. E. B. Du Bois and William Monroe Trotter revolted against white assumptions and social arrangements. Their speaking and writing expressed and encouraged a heightened group consciousness not unlike that which swept the white community. In the Niagra movement of 1905, and in the NAACP, this awakening of black professional and white-collar elites found organizational form. There were also several black organizations aimed, like their white counterparts, at rescuing the victims of urbanization—Victoria Earle Matthews's White Rose Industrial Organization founded in 1897 in New York, for example, or the Committee for Improving the Industrial Coalition of Negroes in New York, founded by the black educator William Lewis Bulkley in 1906. Rejection of the status quo, the conviction that something could be done, organization, political pressure for state intervention, racial self-assertion, and the rhetoric of liberal humanitarianism—all these phenomena were found on a small scale among blacks at the same time that they appeared on a larger scale among whites.

We slight these beginnings because they were too little and too late. Yet from this distance it does in fact appear that a corner was turned in this period for this most exploited of America's oppressed groups. When real change in American race relations finally came, it would build upon the awakened conscience bequeathed by white progressivism, and the organization and self-discovery stimulated among blacks in this same era. If the social justice movement for blacks later took on a radical, even violent aspect, it was not because these early black reformers willed it so, but because the few hesitant steps of white progressives proved so ineffectual against the misery of blacks or the racial attitudes of the mass of whites.

So this problem was postponed. It was the progressive generation's most conspicuous failure, and yet, in view of the social realities in which they moved, their most understandable one. And it did not go entirely unnoticed. Walter Weyl, for example, wedged an important insight into his *The New Democracy* (1912) in one lapidary sentence: "The Negro problem is the mortal spot of the New Democracy."

Reform had a third major thrust, toward restoring the economic arrangements of small-scale capitalism and the social values of small-town America. To this cause rallied businessmen from the South and Midwest, and from small towns in all parts of the country where New England memories were strong. The most effective exponents of economic individualism were articulate young lawyers like George Record, William Borah, and Woodrow Wilson, who thought they were defending liberty rather than the interests of a dwindling entrepreneurial class. In its most intelligent forms, as in the thought of Louis D. Brandeis, this antitrust, and, at least covertly, antiurban school did have something to contribute to a dialogue about freedom and made a useful critique of the dominant tendencies toward centralization. In less intelligent hands its psychology was defensive and negative to a fault, and its social vision neither generous nor—since immigration was shut off so late—plausible.

The achievement of the economic individualists is hard to estimate, but the word *failure* suggests itself, despite its rough sound. The courts, the war, and a deep public ambivalence about economic concentration, all kept the progressive antitrust efforts from anything like a restoration of the conditions of nineteenth-century littleness. The worst fears of the economic individualists have come true: most Americans *have* slipped from self-employment to employee status. What is more, they seem to be adjusting to it. That was the main disaster these progressives feared, and they could not avert it. It is true that a few of their campaigns produced apparent victories. There was great vitality in the drive to break the stranglehold of eastern interests upon credit and transportation advantages, and some legislative successes were secured. But in the end small interests were usually outmaneuvered. The Federal Reserve Act set up a system of twelve decentralized districts so that New York could not dictate to Main Street or Market Street, but Wall Street actually emerged stronger than before, dominating the New York branch, which in turn dominated the system. The ICC gave southerners no satisfaction in their efforts to eliminate the long and short haul differentials in freight rates. Some have argued that the antitrust efforts of progressives at least humanized big business and taught it a sense of public responsibility, even if no real dissolution was achieved. Perhaps so. At least beginning in the 1920s, most corporations had sufficient concern for the public to hire public relations assistance.

This defensive component of progressivism had a cultural as well as an economic side. Its aim was restoration of the nineteenth century community—classless, neighborly, hard at work, devout, morally disciplined. The threat came from the moral loosening of urban life, and from the sheer number and fecundity of the immigrant. The remedies they devised constitute a subcategory of the progressive uprising: exhortations to unity, the prohibition movement, the Americanization movement, the drive on prostitution, the eugenics movement. Return progressivism fought a reasonably successful rearguard action against the cultural challenge of urban America, but unfortunately it coerced an urban milieu that won out in the end, especially among the intellectuals. Since urbanized intellectuals write the histories, this sort of reform is treated with a conspicuous lack of sympathy. Some criticism is deserved. If the excess of progressivism identified with social control was to abandon under stress its democratic sympathies and to set an elite to dispensing national discipline, the excess of the school seeking to return to nineteenth-century values was to reduce reform to a drive for enforced conformity to a compromised moral code that was no longer held by a majority. What was valuable in that moral code has unfortunately not received its due, since the moral reformers were unable to make distinctions between lasting and outmoded virtues. Much can be said for small communities (including those found in large cities), for stable, small-family agriculture, and for "Victorian" virtues such as sobriety, self-discipline, and honesty—all, of course, in moderation. They were not much advanced by progressives, since they chose to identify the nineteenth-century moral inheritance with such obviously defunct ideas as the notion that drinking beer was an evil. We are in great need of some of the virtues of the premodern generation, but if we are to recover them we must ignore their public crusades and turn to biography, to the lives of splendid and untiring men and women like Louis Brandeis, Jane Addams, or the rabbi Stephen S. Wise.

Only a few perceptive contemporaries sensed that the goal of returning to nineteenth-century virtues was an odd bedfellow for the impulse to aid the underprivileged of the cities, or the impulse to enlarge the sway of trained intelligence in American life. Crusades to keep America a place where the Yankee culture was dominant were a part of progressivism by every test— chronology, fervor, middle class base, pressure for legislation, interlocking personnel with other reforms—but one. They were not liberal. At the core they expressed a reactionary spirit— hostile to change, suspicious of the cities, fearful of the future. They preferred faith and tradition to reason and were wedded to narrow racial, regional, and national loyalties just at the moment in history when basic forces urged broader perspectives. Some have been uneasy that the term *progressivism* has been arched to spread over illiberal social movements as well as those of a generous, tolerant, and rational cast. These irregu-

larities should not drive us from the term. Parts of progressivism
blended nicely with what later came to be known as liberalism,
and parts did not. There is no need to define certain activities
out of the movement simply because they contradicted other
activities, reform values, or subsequent preoccupations. Internal
contradictions existed at the time, but contemporary journalists,
not blessed with the analytical and taxonomical skills of college
professors, perceived the common elements in the uproar
around them, and they were right to speak of a progressive
movement. Prohibition, immigration restriction, and the anti-
prostitution drive were different in spirit—and usually attracted
different types of reformers—from the scientific management
effort, or conservation, or housing reform, but they were all
middle-class, aroused, marching Americans, vintage 1910, and
they shared a core of intellectual traits: they were activists,
they had an unshakable confidence in intervention, they were
equally optimistic that social practices could be changed by
exhortation, scientific study, the police power of the state, or
some combination. Abraham Flexner, writing in 1914, used
the sort of language they used whether they were Social
Gospelers, engineers, social workers, or young lawyers running
for city council:

> Civilization has stripped for a life-and-death wrestle with tu-
> berculosis, alcohol and other plagues. It is on the verge of a
> similar struggle with the crasser forms of commercialized vice.
> Sooner or later, it must fling down the gauntlet to the whole
> horrible thing. This will be the real contest—a contest that will
> tax the courage, the self-denial, the faith, the resources of
> humanity to their utmost.

Rhetorical similarities among the various sectors of reform
went beyond an exhortative, crusading style. The word *efficiency*
was a kind of litmus of reformism. All the renovators and inno-
vators believed in efficiency, counted on its strong appeal to a
generation impressed with the promise of science, and used it
to justify the most diverse activities. The municipal Goo Goos
wanted to make city government more efficient, not a difficult
argument to follow, but we also find social worker Crystal East-
man justifying workmen's compensation on the grounds of
efficiency, Louis Brandeis justifying railroad regulation and a
complete social insurance system on the grounds of efficiency,

Charles Edward Russell arguing that urban poverty was an inefficient use of human resources, and Irving Fisher appealing for prohibition on the grounds that it would so increase the national efficiency as to produce a 10–20 percent addition to the GNP. If nothing else tied together these various and occasionally contradictory crusades—and much else did—their common resort to the ideal of efficiency would be enough to suggest some sort of fundamental identity. Frederick W. Taylor, the father of scientific management (a synonym for efficiency), wrote in *The Principles of Scientific Management* (1911) that his principles "applied with equal force to all our social activities; to the management of our homes; the management of our farms; the management of the business of our tradesmen, . . . of our churches, our philanthropic institutions, our universities, and our governmental departments." His generation was in agreement. Each in his own way, the member of a civic voter's group, the city planner, the settlement worker, the prohibitionist, all had caught a common vision of a society happier because social engineers had brought an end to wastefulness and irrationality in all its various activities. So to a large extent they spoke a common tongue.

But the most compelling reason for spreading the word progressivism over somewhat contradictory social objectives is that one often finds some single reform or campaign that unites quite dissimilar values beyond any effort to factor them out. The most objectionable strain in Return progressivism was its racism, but it is possible to find even this harnessed with concern for some part of exploited and suffering humanity. Aileen Kraditor tells us, in *The Ideas of the Woman Suffrage Movement 1890–1920* (1965), how often anti-immigrant and anti-Negro sentiments appeared alongside the noble ideals of the Declaration of Independence in the inspirational literature of the movement. An equally good but less well-known example of a reform born of mixed impulses is the LaFollette Seaman's Act of 1915. The act improved the pay and working conditions of an historically exploited group and strengthened their hand in contractual arrangements with shipowners; it enlisted the support of progressive altruists who responded to Andrew Furseth's pleas for justice. But the act had strong southern support in the Congress because it was openly racist. In Jerold Auerbach's words, it was frankly designed "to drive

Asiatics from American vessels" by eliminating the economic advantage in hiring orientals who either depressed "white" standards or drove occidentals from the merchant marine.

Another such combination appears in the drive against prostitution. It was often pressed by people who did not like sex, and who appear to modern eyes as not only prudish and coercive, but ethically misguided and probably no real friends of the American female. At the same time prostitution did involve exploitation and a threat to the public health, and the fight against it attracted nonprudish and thoroughly admirable people like Lillian Wald and Jane Addams who urged a scientific rather than a moralistic approach to the matter and who were primarily interested in the protection of virtually helpless individuals (females) from overpowering environmental pressures against their dignity and freedom. Some reformers spoke of the evils of prostitution and thought of how much they disliked not only the sex act but Jewish immigrant girls who were probably producting ethnically undesirable bastards; others spoke of the evils of prostitution and wished to stamp out disease and economic exploitation, not non-WASP breeding and nonconjugal love. Many reforms had this same schizophrenic composition, and virtually every campaign was laced with contradiction. Hiram Johnson's progressives in California found time and motivation to work on conservation, workmen's compensation, and laws excluding Japanese from landholding and citizenship. James K. Vardaman's progressive admiration in Mississippi (1903–7) raised teacher's salaries, increased expenditures on mental and tuberculosis hospitals, attacked the convict-lease system, advocated the reduction of interest rates and higher taxes upon corporations, and at the same time cut appropriations for Negro education and set new lows in the rhetoric of bigotry. These and other progressive campaigns brought together impulses one might have thought incompatible until observing them in some dynamic blend. But the world of the progressive was confusing, and many emotions combined in their sense of social crisis. They sacrificed logic to action, and made reform a house of many mansions.

Where in this scheme does one place the friends of political democracy? Most progressives of whatever type thought of themselves as advocating changes that were widely popular and would instantly prevail if the people were awakened by the written and spoken word. When this did not happen they suspected defective political machinery rather than the accuracy of their estimate of the state of public opinion. Blaming the political machinery for immobilizing ther latent majority, they pressed for procedural reforms widening the suffrage and extending the popular influence. But the Direct Democracy aspects of reform do not constitute a distinct category, for they were usually not ends in themselves but means to other ends. The grant of federal suffrage to women was presented as a concession to the idea of individual worth, done because it was right for men to do so if they claimed to be democrats. But Alan P. Grimes shows, in *The Puritan Ethic and Woman Suffrage*, that in the western states where woman suffrage was strongest it drew strength not so much from egalitarian sentiment—there was some of that, mostly among women—as from the expectation that enfranchised women would further the drives to enact prohibition and immigration restriction laws. There were usually similar substantive hopes behind all the campaigns for procedural democratization. The Oregon reformer William ·S. U'Ren worked for years to democratize Oregon politics, but he was not primarily interested in Direct Democracy. "All the work we have done, for Direct Legislation," he wrote late in life, "has been done with the Single Tax in view." U'Ren was, in this respect at least, typical of reformers interested in Direct Democracy measures. Progress depended not merely on enlarging the political community, but on pursuing certain ends with the newly acquired power. There was hardly a distinct Direct Democracy component of progressivism since invigorated electoral procedures were almost invariably pressed as preliminary to and valued subsidiary to substantive changes. Jane Addams, in an article "Why Women Should Vote" published in 1909, justified their enfranchisement on the ground that they might then extend to the entire city the cleanliness they maintained in their own homes. Woman suffrage was a reform, but it was also a means to reform.

It is worth noting that disappointments in this area were the rule rather than the exception. Enlarged electorates showed a stubborn tendency to continue to vote for machine politicians (Boss Boise Penrose, astonished that he was still in the Senate after the first Pennsylvania election in which Senators ran before the people, was supposed to have said, "give me the people every time"). The females enfranchised in the Rocky Mountain states did in fact help the prohibition forces, but the enfranchisement of women generally disappointed its supporters. As John Gordon Ross wrote in 1936: "After a fair trial of 16 years, it seems just to appraise women's suffrage as one of those reforms which, like the secret ballot, the corrupt-practices acts, the popular election of senators, and the direct primary, promised almost everything and accomplished almost nothing." And, much to his disappointment, U'Ren and the single taxers in Oregon wore themselves out on their procedural reforms only to find that the broader electorate had as little interest in the single tax as the smaller electorate of the late nineteenth century.

The general ineffectiveness of Direct Democracy measures to accomplish the fine things promised by overexcited reformers has been noticed many times, almost invariably with a touch of scorn that men could believe such tripe about "the people." "A man that'd expict to thrain lobsters to fly in a year is called a loonytic," said Mr. Dooley, "but a man that thinks men can be tur-rned into angels be an iliction is called a rayformer an' remains at large." It is hard to see why observers of the progressive faith in democracy are so pleased at discovering such gullibility; if the reformers were wrong, and it appears that they were, the implications are not at all pleasant. Their simple faith in the efficacy of drawing more and more people into the voting booths reveals them—in view of the record—as hopeless innocents. But men who remark the proven invalidity of that faith are hardly realists if they do so smugly. We may know man better, after army intelligence tests, the analysis of dreams, pogroms, and a procession of regicides, but the last emotion this justifies is a sense of superiority.

Surveying this record of dreams of justice and promises of uplift in the moral and physical life of the people, and finding that it all came to so much less than the progressives had wanted, one wonders what meaning to draw from the gap. Some would say that capitalism was not substantially reformed because it cannot be, others because it need not be. Every person must decide whether such modest gains are the best a citizen can wish, or whether he prefers one of those twins who offer themselves as substitutes for reform—apathy and revolution. But a number of lesser inquiries are equally enlightening.

Notice the advantages held by the conservatives. The American character, individualistic, sanguine, and suspicious of the state, fought on the conservative side, resisting a movement that relied upon the irritations of criticism and the exertions of collective action. The holders of priviliged positions were united by economic interest, by social outlook, and usually by intermarriage. The potential allies in any uprising were largely unorganized or at best poorly organized on the eve of the struggles of the progressive era. Of American workers, only 7 percent were in unions in 1904, and these were largely in the Gompers-led American Federation of Labor, emasculated politically by his doctrine that nothing could be expected from political action. Consumers were unorganized until Florence Kelley and others started the consumers' leagues in the late 1890s, but even after this their real power was negligible. The same is true of other social groups who might have joined any crusade to redistribute the good things of earth—Negroes, farmers, and the more recent and less advantaged immigrants. Of course the progressive era was the era of organization, and such gains as they made were made largely by organization, but it was slow work.

After men had been brought to see the necessity of organizing, either around their own interest or around a shared concern for the exploited and unfortunate, the job of actually redistributing advantages and burdens was staggering. It required endless patience, sustained pressure, and luck. An acceptable and talented leader had to be found, campaigns had to be pressed beyond the initial defeats and delays, public opinion had to be mobilized or at least neutralized, political and legislative machinery mastered, bureaucracies shouldered aside and new bureaucrats recruited, mistakes unraveled and the game begun again. As the months and years went by, both tedious and breathless, the Social Justice coalition tended to fragment, its components to return piece by piece to that apathetic impotence from which they had with such difficulty been aroused.

Even when some angry coalition forced its will through a legislative body, the courts could always be counted upon to defend property, and corporation counsel could always be counted upon to bring each reform enactment to judicial attention. Note the list of toppled regulatory, labor, or social insurance laws: in *E. C. Knight* (1895) it was learned that Congress had no control over manufacturing; in *Pollack* (1895), that Congress could not directly tax individuals; in *Lochner* (1905), that the legislature of New York could not set maximum hours for bakers; in *Hammer* v. *Dagenhart* (1918), that Congress could not outlaw child labor (although the Court had earlier decided that the memory of the Founders would not be outraged if Congress prohibited lotteries and the white slave trade; apparently property losses in the shady areas of capitalism were tolerable to the Constitution); in *Adkins* (1923) that Congress could not fix minimum wages for women who lived in the District of Columbia; and so on. When the Federal Trade Commission gave signs just after the war that it might construe broadly its mandate to investigate and indict practices in restraint of trade, the Court ruled the FTC findings of fact would not be accepted as prima facie evidence, but must pass through the filter of nine more reliable men than the commissioners. In all, American judges understood that their most sacred trust was to use the Constitution, with its wonderfully ambiguous language and varied precedent, to safeguard property rights. It must be said that they shouldered their responsibilities to civilization with that combination of determination and a passion for duty that has long marked the American patrician class. Wrote Chief Justice William Howard Taft as he held the conservative majority together in the 1920s: "I am older and slower and less acute and more confused. However, as long as things continue as they are, and I am able to answer in my place, I must stay on the Court in order to prevent the Bolsheviki from getting control. . . . The only hope we have of keeping a consistent declaration of Constitutional law is for us to live as long as we can."

The People, admittedly, *could* ultimately override the judiciary if they blocked the popular will; they *could* alter constitutions through the prescribed, laborious processes and bring the courts to heel. A number of progressives, among them Roosevelt in 1912, talked openly of the need for action against constitutional barriers and even against judges themselves. But constitutional alterations required the most sustained political effort, and curbing individual judges was an idea that made slow headway against the deep popular respect for the robe and the bench.

So conservatives—those who wanted wealth, economic and political authority, and social status to be held tomorrow and forever where they were held today—could throw up a formidable defense against meddling levelers. They were barricaded behind public and interest-group apathy, unrepresentative political systems, a conservative judiciary drawn from their class, conservative and intellectually stagnant universities, a genteel and irrelevant literature, a folklore that insisted that complete social mobility was a reality, and mass media owned by men who could be counted on (or if necessary forced by advertising cancellations) to mesmerize the public with trivia and either ignore or smear the radicals. It was a deep, complex maze through which few redistributionist proposals could pass at all, and none without crippling concessions. But this is to speak only of the defenses of conservatives. The progressive years saw them take the offensive, at first haltingly, and then with mounting success. Conservatives learned that their greatest advantage lay not in their defenses against government, but in their ability to manipulate it.

While the state had always been used by dominant groups to protect or extend their economic advantages, it is nonetheless true that the American ruling classes had not had a sustained and comprehensive resort to governmental power until the twentieth century. Admittedly there had always been a tariff, there had been railroad grants, and as the nation industrialized the upper classes saw to it that their government shouldered the task of repressing, through force or injunction, the restless laboring masses. Yet Barry Goldwater learned it to be a fact in 1964 that the dominant economic interests now demand a use of governmental power that is not sporadic and punitive but continuous and positive. The change did not come overnight, but we can state that if it did not exactly begin it at least accelerated sharply in the progressive era.

Prior to this century, those whom the industrial system (and the land) had made rich and comfortable used the state only infrequently, despised politics, counted upon conservative politicians to keep things quiet, and beat off the occasional inept attempts of radicals to actually use the state for other than police purposes. Basically the ruling classes were Sumnerians, or social Darwinists. They had no real vision of what the state might do for them beyond hiring policemen and judges and delivering the mail.

The progressive period was apparently a very educational period for them. Obviously, they learned that the state could be used against them, as waves of angry "little" businessmen from the South and West (shippers, commercial farmers, small bankers), as well as smaller waves of assorted do-gooders, assaulted the sleepy halls of legislatures and the Congress with coercive and confiscatory programs. The first impulse of the conservatives was to fight the very conception of the state as an active force in the economy, and because some of the less intelligent and imaginative among them still follow that impulse, it has come down to us that the business community has always been negatively oriented toward government. Actually, those few historians who have turned from the political life of intellectuals to the political life of American businessmen have found that a more positive conception of the state took hold in certain sectors of the American upper class in the years before the war. The more sophisticated members of the upper classes overcame their doctrinaire Jeffersonian suspicion of state power and moved from obstruction to a position resembling that of the reformers—demanding sustained governmental intervention in the nation's economic life. There was no reason, they saw, why the regulatory agencies of the modernized state must serve the purposes of the radicals. In the words of such an enlightened conservative, Richard Olney, at the opening of the modern era:

> The Commission (ICC), as its functions have now been limited by the courts, is, or can be made of great use to the railroads. It satisfied the popular clamor for governmental supervision of railroads at the same time that the supervision is almost entirely nominal. Further, the older such a commission gets to be, the more inclined it will be found to be to take the business and railroad view of things. It thus becomes a sort of barrier between the railroad corporations and the people and a sort of protection against hasty and crude legislation hostile to railroad interests.

Olney spoke for a small minority of businessmen in 1892, but his view made headway among men of his class. There was every reason for his confidence that a government of new and useful but potentially dangerous powers could be controlled by the owners of industry rather than the dispossessed. The only disadvantage of the entrenched classes was numerical inferiority. But they had instant access not only to legal talent for persuasive testimony before congressional committees but also to the sympathetic ear of politicians of a common ethnic and social background who respected wealth and breeding, sometimes despite themselves. If the politicians on infrequent occasions were pressed so hard by angry groups that a regulatory agency was set up under a law at least potentially dangerous, the corporations on the commanding heights still held numerous advantages. The agencies were kept on miserly appropriations and were never large enough for the research, field, and legal work required to survey a national economy. The FTC, in a rare mood, investigated the meat packing industry in 1919 on suspicion of fixing prices, and in that year the advertising budget of Swift and Co. was six times the total budget of the agency. But there was more to the matter than size. Governmental bureaucracies were composed of men who were cautious, basically conservative, and—largely because of the meager salaries the public was willing to pay—likely to be men who in intellect and energy were quite inferior to their legal and technical adversaries from industry. There is a revealing passage in Secretary of the Treasury William G. McAdoo's autobiography where McAdoo, whose $12,000 yearly salary was the highest in the American government excepting only the president's, set out to hire into the federal service the presidents of the railroads he had just seized (1918) in the wartime emergency. To men with salaries ranging upward from $100,000 yearly, government employment with its rewards ranging steeply down from $12,000 was a virtual disaster and an insult. McAdoo was embarrassed, and the government hired its railroad directors at $40,000–$50,000, depending upon the region. Any contest between such men with their New York lawyers against the civil servants of the Interstate Commerce Commission was likely to be, as it had been since 1887, an unequal contest.

These advantages of the dominant interests were not necessarily permanent. Time brought changes that tended to make the governmental bureaucracy more independent—slightly larger appropriations for staff and research, the enhanced attractiveness of federal service to talented people, the gradual organization of more interest groups, the gradual improvement of public understanding of the stakes involved in public policy decisions. But these trends had not developed very far by the end of the progressive era. As a result, using government to reduce the economic advantage of those who *have* the economic advantage was uphill work. As the entrenched interests accepted the inevitability of enlarged government, they found themselves in a post position in the race for its favors.

This gloomy account derives largely from contemplation of the record of social justice progressivism. Progressive attempts to rationalize habits and institutions must be accounted partially successful and in the end irresistible. Progressive efforts to restore the moral consensus of the nineteenth century were moderately successful in the short run and served their therapeutic purpose. But while social justice progressivism was demonstrably the least successful component of reform, the preceding review of the advantages of conservatives in frustrating it gives us a perspective from which to estimate social justice accomplishments as a bit higher than nothing at all. Progressives of this sort had done a substantial damage to the conservative outworks, and although beaten back, their sappers' trenches were still at the wall for another day of siege.

Think of the advantages of conservatives that, while proving enough in the defense against social justice progressives, had been eliminated or weakened. For its defense the status quo counts heavily on abstract modes of thought—a legalistic constitutionalism, a fixation upon natural law or the divine order, and in the realm of education a curriculum firmly limited to the "classic," i.e., resolutely nonrelevant studies. But progressive thinkers riveted the attention of their era upon the current and the real. Realism was the most pervasive intellectual quality of the leading thought of their day, whether political theory, law, literature, or the arts. There is an obvious kinship between muckraking and oil paintings of ashcans and alleys, between social investigations like the Pittsburgh Survey or the Industrial Relations Commission of 1911, and short stories about denizens of saloons. That kinship resides in a common preference for the real, which to the progressive generation usually meant the hard and sordid side of existence, as against what William

Dean Howells called "the smiling aspects of life." As perceptive
conservatives suspected, such morbid and unswerving attention
to social reality often led to the most subversive consequences.
For the world to remain at rest, it is best that it not be thought
about too much, certainly not studied with any rigor. This is
not to ignore the importance of abstraction in reform thought
itself. It is important that the progressives also served abstractions and that they were new ones—justice rather than the
Constitution or property rights. But what gave progressive
ideals an upper hand so often was the progressive mastery of
the facts and relations of actual life. With these in hand their
ideals—which were after all ancient ideals, but not heretofore
much threat to the going arrangement of things—could no
longer be domesticated to the primers of school children and
the Sunday school lessons of Victorian ladies. True, conservatives were able to block most of the agitation arising out of
realist thought, but they were not able to exorcise realism
itself, which went on working its corrosive way through the
fabric of received ideas and habits.

Things-as-they-are were also protected at the turn of the
century by the notion that freedom was a condition of being
let alone, and especially let alone by the state, the form of power
most suspected despite its relative puniness. Progressive intellectuals argued that freedom had a positive dimension and
that the prerequisites for freedom included at the very least the
presence of public institutions strong enough to intervene to
secure economic opportunity. Some even went so far as to
suggest that there was no freedom without good housing,
health, and economic security in illness and old age. Such
notions as these suggested that the way to freedom might
lie in a measure of coercion—a complicated, paradoxical,
troubling thought destined to grow in influence because it
was increasingly true.

Equally disturbing was the redefinition of justice that certain progressive thinkers accomplished. Herbert Croly, for instance, went so far as to argue that merely seeing that all men
started with the same political rights and the same economic
opportunities (access to credit, markets, transportation, and
inventions), as hard as they might be to achieve, would still
constitute no guarantee of an even start. Even if equal access
to profit-making opportunities were realized, only certain individuals could take advantage of it. "Those who have enjoyed

the benefits of wealth and thorough education," Croly wrote in
The Promise of American Life, "start with an advantage which
can be overcome only by very exceptional men . . . ; the average
competitor without such benefits feels himself disqualified for
the contest." The social environment from birth to age twenty-
one had filtered out some who were deserving. If we may
think of social justice for a moment as, among other things,
careers open to talent, Croly saw that it would not be so cheaply
bought as his contemporaries hoped. It would require some
positive intervention to provide the sort of social environment
in which no one of talent was stultified or deprived of the
requisite stimulation. Croly did not see how radical such a
thought might be. It was not only too radical for his time, but
goes down hard in our own. It led to the conclusion that for
careers to be truly open to talent there could be no real difference, around the nation and from class to class and race to
race, in the factors that awaken and nurture talent from birth—
nutrition, health care, exposure to intellectual and aesthetic
stimulation, formal education, peer group aspirations. This
suggests stunning alterations in our institutions and habits,
and one can hardly claim the progressives had this fully in
mind. Men such as Wilson aimed at justice only for young
white males of good family, but there were men and women
of his generation who saw that real justice would require more
than he thought in the way of reforms and had in mind a
broader range of social groups to whom it might reasonably
be owed—to women, for example, and to recent immigrants.
Yet if no one of that era followed the idea of social justice as
far as it led, did not in any numbers and in any serious way
extend it to Negroes and American Indians, for example, it
is still to them we owe the reactivation—after a lapse of forty
years and the death of men like Lincoln and Wendell Phillips—
of one of the most disruptive, creative ideas of our time.

Another requirement of conservatism was that the existing
legal and moral definitions of crime and good conduct remain
unchallenged, since fortunes had been made and deviants had
been jailed by men working on these assumptions. Some civic
reformers thought it earthshaking to enforce rigorously the
existing standards, punishing public officials for familiar crimes
such as graft, and the outcry from threatened people encouraged
the Goo Goo's image of himself as an advanced thinker. But

what was really radical were ideas such as that popularized by
E. A. Ross in *Sin and Society* (1907), that the modern age of
social interdependence requires a new, social definition of sin.
This meant less concentration on behavior affecting only oneself (drunkenness, reading pornography, lack of ambition), and
identified as sinful any act that had deleterious social consequences (watering of stock or strip mining). Such a shift in
values could not be accomplished in one generation no matter
how many books were written, but it began to work its way
into the leading minds, and today we see its growing influence.
While some among us would still enforce the moral code of
Anthony Comstock, many are coming to condemn more severely
the man who drives "his" car with oily exhaust, operates "his"
transistor radio on a bus, or carelessly lumbers "his" forest
than we do the users of alcohol or hallucinogens or the com-
mitters of fornication.

Thought and practice in the realm of crime and punishment was vital to conservatives, whose lives had been built upon
scrupulous moral rectitude in the familiar moral categories
(in most cases), but whose fortunes had been built upon environmental pollution, exhaustion of resources, and health-
breaking working conditions. And if it were not enough to
suggest that the "best people" might in fact be criminals, some
leading progressive thinkers were beginning to argue that the
worst people were not at fault for their behavior. Reformer
after reformer began by wishing to jail the municipal bosses.
"Their motto," said Mr. Dooley, "was—'Arrest that man!'." These
reformers ended up convinced that "the system" corrupted men
and that it was neither humanly defensible nor socially effica-
cious to pillory the criminal. One sees Lincoln Steffens come
to this in his autobiography, and Fred Howe in his *Confessions
of a Reformer*. But the best example is surely California's crusading editor Fremont Older, who helped jail San Francisco's
Boss Ruef; then, after reflecting upon the real sources of municipal corruption, Older worked as hard to get Ruef out of jail
as he had to put him in. What was most significant in Older's
action was not his sympathy for Ruef but the fact that he had
shifted the blame from Ruef's character to the existing social
arrangements.

These were some of the ideas let loose by progressive
thinkers to discredit and disturb the status quo. The net effect

of their thinking was to strengthen the social as against the private focus in American life. After the First World War the individualistic orientation reasserted itself, and the country (and many reformers) shrugged off such collectivist patterns of thought and action as had been foisted on it. As in the days when progressives began their uprising, the dominant current after the war was again toward those uncoordinated, egoistic strivings that had "built this country." But no postwar reaction could entirely erase the collectivized perspective. When the individualistic culture botched its best and in some ways its final opportunity, it would be somewhat easier to move toward collective solutions because of progressivism.

In rating the few intellectual steps toward collectivism as the most substantial accomplishment of progressivism, one would not wish to dismiss the institutional framework progressives erected. Through progressive reform there was established effective supervision of railroad rates, a central bank to begin mastering the art and science of monetary manipulation, innumerable well-staffed bureaus at all governmental levels where the public's interest in insurance funds, securities issues, sewage disposal, patent medicine, and public health might conceivably be protected. Progressivism revitalized the presidency. Progressivism spurred the organization of hundreds of interest groups, from architects to mayors to teachers, and even a few general interest groups for the few altruists and consumers who wished to work for broad public goals. These institutions and organizations are the scaffolding of a more rational, efficient, and possibly even a more liberal social order. We must not confuse this scaffolding with the actual achievement of such a social order, for it was far from that. But it was a beginning.

Impatient men in the troubled 1970s will not highly estimate this accomplishment—a few dangerous ideas, a few organizations, a few governmental agencies that might or might not serve their best implied ends. The study of progressivism does to some extent support the crushing judgment of some contemporaries, but those who incline to such a critical stance might gain a useful perspective by attempting to name the generation that accomplished more.

Fortunately for a movement with so much unfinished business, progressivism in all its forms would be given other chances.

After 1929 the country would stand in especial need of the best qualities of those earlier reformers—an activist and hopeful spirit, a faith in human reason, a resourceful humanitarianism. It would need more than these qualities, but they were something, and they were vital. It would need above all their conviction that the forces loose in the "private" world must somehow be brought to public account, so that America could preserve her society in its precious, fragile inheritance: neighborliness, security, moral purpose, meaningful freedom.

No man better embodies all that was generous and sane in progressivism, along with much that was narrow and parochial, than William Jennings Bryan. Surely he spoke for progressivism at its best when, in 1912 with the movement at its apogee and another man selected to lead, he reaffirmed their commitment to an unwearying struggle for a better democracy with a ringing quotation from Byron:

> The dead have been awakened—shall I sleep?
> The World's at war with Tyrants—shall I crouch?
> The Harvest's ripe and shall I pause to reap?
> I slumber not; the thorn is in my couch.
> Each day a trumpet soundeth in mine ear—
> It's echo in my heart.

INTRODUCTORY NOTE

The history of how historians have interpreted their past is called historiography, which is one of those dry and abstract terms that, like epistemology, attract students who are fascinated by abstractions but repel the rest. This is understandable, but it is also very unfortunate because each generation must reinterpret its past in terms of its felt needs, and this continuous process is marvellously revealing. Now, the Progressive era has many champions, but it must be acknowledged that World War I sapped its energies, that during the 1920s the weary nation turned its back on most of what progressivism signified, and that the depression of the 1930s invited a repeat performance, but of reform with more teeth and staying power.

Most students are familiar in broad outline with the accomplishments of Franklin Roosevelt's New Deal. The first generation of historians to interpret the New Deal saw it as a two-part program. They tended to be highly partisan in support of its liberal legacy and to fear that a post-World War II surge of conservatism might dismantle it. They saw in the first New Deal (1933–1935)— an emergency attempt at recovery, similar in spirit to Theodore Roosevelt's New Nationalism in business-government cooperation —through an alphabet soup of new agencies: NIRA, AAA, CCC, TVA. Similarly, they likened the second New Deal (1935–1938) in spirit to Woodrow Wilson's New Freedom, and applauded its reformist thrust: antitrust, social security, fair labor standards, an attack upon the conservative Supreme Court. But whatever the merit of these somewhat simplistic analogies, they celebrated and defended the New Deal's extension of federal authority, unprecedented in peacetime, over banking, agriculture, social security and public welfare; they defended the Hamiltonian muscle with which it pressed forward toward Jeffersonian goals, the abandonment of conservative Darwinism and laissez-faire, and the adoption by the modern corporate state of social responsibility.

But in the 1950s, when the conservative Republican administration under Eisenhower declined to dismantle the basic structure of the Roosevelt reforms, the New Deal seemed safe—safe, even, for a more reflective criticism. Then in the 1960s came the rediscovery of massive poverty, the increasing realization that the New Deal had never seriously even attempted to come to grips with the nation's tenacious race problem, and mounting criticism of a military-industrial complex that had thrived on the New Deal's structural legacy. In response, a younger generation of more radical historians, often identified as the New Left, attacked the New Deal as a typical liberal failure. It had not achieved recovery; by 1940 8 million people, or 15 percent of the labor force, were still unemployed. Nor had it achieved fundamental reform, in that an analysis of the distribution of income as a basic barometer of social equity revealed that by the mid-1960s income was distributed no more equitably than in 1910, and that the bottom fifth of American income earners had actually lost ground during the past half-century, the 1930s included.

We cannot resolve the question here. Our central concern is less to pass firm judgments on the success or failure of specific American reform movements than to understand, in the context of our political process, the complex relationship between opportunities and obstacles. Historians of American political life have been excessively inclined to focus on the achievements of reform movements at the expense of a consideration of the structural impediments to reform, the latent inertia as well as the active opposition. In the following essay, Otis L. Graham, Jr. presents an analytical overview of the balance of achievement for the New Deal, focusing on the complex matrix of personal, ideological, and institutional constraints that are implied in the definition of politics as "the art of the possible."

The New Deal

OTIS L. GRAHAM, JR.

Are the radical historians correct about the New Deal? If this means their argument that the New Deal did not bring either much recovery or reform, even those who think the argument overstated must find it basically persuasive. Significant political changes did occur in the 1930s, along with increased security for some American workers, improvement in the economic level of many farmers, and a better conservation record than any previous administration. But these examples of movement did not touch the fundamentals. Social power and wealth were basically in the same hands at the end of the New Deal as they had been at the beginning. Even so, are the radical historians right when they say that the New Deal performance could and should have been better, and that the principal reason it was not better lay in intellectual deficiencies within liberalism? The answer must be: Not yet. We do not have much radical history written on the New Deal, and what has been written has not conclusively defined how much more was possible and where lies the responsibility for the remarkable persistence of the old habits and social arrangements.

Edward Freeman is supposed to have said that history is "past politics." Certainly that is one variety of history, but a poor variety, even though it has sold rather well over the years. Another popular but poor variety of history is history as present politics: a scholar is so influenced by contemporary political pressures, including those within himself, that he distorts the past for present purposes. None of us escapes these pressures entirely. In elementary and high schools they are intense. History is expected to glorify the nation, reinforce patriotism and national pride. Professional historians have struggled to free themselves from the utilitarian standards forced on writers of elementary textbooks, but they nonetheless have serious problems contending with contemporary pressures, despite their relative institutional freedom. Pressure is especially acute in writing recent history, where there is much continuity with current problems, issues, even personalities. Historians with the rarest exceptions deplore the deliberate use of the past to serve contemporary ends, especially when it is done by academics from the socialist bloc. We are right to condemn it everywhere. Presentism is a vice.

Those historians interested in the New Deal must give this problem especially thoughtful attention. The simplest solution, to refuse to allow the present to influence us, is apparently not available. New Deal issues still agitate the contemporary mind. Baptism, the doctrine of the real presence, and the Immaculate Conception may be discussed without passion, but men display emotion at the first mention of federal economic policy, agricultural subsidies, public housing, conservation—even, still, at the name Franklin Delano Roosevelt. What scholar could be so ascetic as to have no opinions on such issues, so cloistered as to be unaware of their bearing upon his future and his society's future? Further, even if the issues of the 1930s were not so dangerously charged with contemporary significance, philosophers of history such as Charles Beard, Carl Becker, and Benedetto Croce tell us that the ideal of objectivity is unattainable.

Resourceful historians, recognizing all of this, have argued that some virtue may be distilled from our subjectivity. The present sharpens our sensitivity to new issues in what we thought was a familiar past and reveals new perspectives when the older ones are no longer productive. The present also will often tell us which men, groups, and tendencies won and lost in the long run; this too is possibly of some help. In this view, if we try to eliminate contemporary concerns from our minds we not only fail to do so, but we block ourselves from the invigoration of new perspectives and narrow the range of our probing of the past.

These reflections have much to recommend them, but they can lull us into forgetting how much truth there was in the fear of present-mindedness. The present is, after all, more important than the past, and will have a tendency to dominate it in any healthy mind. Men will entertain the hope, as they struggle as citizens with urgent private and public problems, that the past may be forced to yield up the lessons required for our immediate salvation. In this understandable frame of mind it is not long before the needs of the present become stronger than respect for the past, and we begin to manipulate the past, hearing some of its voices and dimming out others, carrying confidently out of its confusions the clear lessons we wish our peers and political leaders to adopt. This tendency caused men to devise the ideal of objectivity. Too many scholars go to the past as a Hanging Judge, in Acton's phrase, and flawed history is almost invariably the result. The concerns of the present, while they may make us receptive to more data, often wind up making us receptive to less.

The damaging effects of contemporary concerns mark the history of New Deal scholarship. Conservative writers, more interested in repealing the New Deal than in understanding it, credited the public policies of the 1930s with having accomplished a centralization of power in Washington that stifled capitalist initiative and granted political and economic power to obscure intellectuals and the indolent masses. This was nonsense. Power in the country did shift slightly toward Washington, yet long after the New Deal it was being used for the same general purposes as before. But this conservative view of what American government had become, however distorted, did seem to threaten the welfare measures of the 1930s and did influence liberal writers after the war. Their writing was adversely affected. They responded to the political environment by describing the public policies of the 1930s as having instituted a massive federal intervention, right enough, but one with the most benign purpose and beneficial effects. This view was not much closer to the truth than the exaggerations of the conservatives. The New Deal had been a short-term political success, but many nonliberal constituencies shared in its favors; its long-range political goals had been at least half-frustrated; and its economic goals, from recovery through security to a more equitable distribution of wealth and income, were substantially defeated. When this became clear in the 1960s it tended to discredite all earlier interpretive writing, even though both conservatives and liberals had occasionally written with insight and narrative skill.

Conservative hostility and liberal indulgence resulted from a virulent combination of ideological commitments and situational political pressures. These influences led them to write history that had less lasting value than their native talents, especially those of the liberals (the conservative writers had been politicians and journalists for the most part, with little scholarly potential to spoil), might have otherwise produced. The conservatives and liberals too frequently argued over whether the vast changes brought by the New Deal were good or bad for America. They put off addressing themselves to a more productive question: why have we had such stability in our basic social arrangements and institutions, even during the deepest economic crisis in our history?

Interestingly enough, those suspect influences, contemporary sociopolitical pressures and the ideology of the author himself, provided the perspective in the 1960s that undercut the emphasis upon "revolutionary" change. The writing of younger, radical historians has helped clarify how much more modest than we thought were New Deal attainments in income redistribution, in power restructuring—industrial and even political—and in relief of suffering. It is largely their writing that has alerted us to the considerable gains of the "business community," supposedly routed by Roosevelt's government. All these things had been pointed out by leftist critics in the 1930s, but the New Left critics of the 1960s supported these views with more and better evidence.

Having conferred its advantage, the present delivered its nemesis. It led the New Left interpreters, despite their valuable insights, to tell as one-sided, selective, and probably dated a story as did earlier politicized historians who wrote in the shadow of FDR's divisive memory.

Today's radical criticizes the American political economy and is convinced that liberalism not only helped produce the social crisis in which we find ourselves but cannot possibly lead us out of it. He believes that the state in a capitalist society cannot really respond to noncapitalistic groups, cannot really bring sufficient justice and rationality to capitalism to make it economically viable and ethically acceptable. He sees continuing liberalism in the 1970s as the conservatives' formula for co-optation, designed to deflect the forces of genuine change by a combination of idealistic rhetoric and minimal economic concessions.

Whether such views of contemporary America are valid is not the issue here. The issue is how they affect the scholarship of men who hold them. I have earlier paid my respects to the insights produced by the radical perspective. Now let us consider its potential defects. How would one prove, to advance today's struggle against a discredited liberalism, that the liberalism of the 1930s was defective? First, one would demonstrate that New Deal achievements for the poor and the general public were disappointing, even to some candid New Dealers themselves. This has been done, or is largely accomplished. But readers with unusual logical powers will see that the New Deal achievement, scanty as it was, may have been the most that was possible. So the radical scholar who is determined to employ his scholarship to save his country in the 1960s and 1970s must, for those readers, argue that opportunities were squandered, and he must lay the blame for that squandering on the ideology he strives to discredit. The liberals of the 1930s must be made to appear indefensibly cautious, insensitive to misery and injustice, in fact just another variety of conservative.

This interpretation would be greatly strengthened by a selective handling of the evidence. The forces of movement would be maximized in number and in resolution—and here one thinks of Huey Long, Father Coughlin, Governor Floyd Olson, Upton Sinclair, and other mass leaders with angry constituencies; the progressive bloc in Congress; the third party movement in Wisconsin; the pervasive radicalism of the intellectual classes. The forces of resistance would be minimized—the Supreme Court; southern congressional leadership and antiquated congressional rules; the national media with its subserviency to large advertisers; the lack of trained people and adequate statistics for economic management; the public ignorance; the depth of the commitment to individualism; the political apathy and impotence of the under classes. This is fundamental. The possibilities of the situation may be manipulated like an accordion, narrowed or expanded by the relative emphasis given to the forces of movement and the forces of resistance. If one wished to write antiliberal history, the forces of movement would come to the foreground, and the only obstacle worth extensive mention would be liberal ideology, with its fatal cautions and blind spots.

Withdrawing any suggestion that they were consciously adopted, these are the perspectives that characterize New Left writing on the New Deal. The New Left conclusion, that in the 1930s opportunities for extensive change were inexcusably lost, that New Dealers always compromised too soon, may conceivably be valid. But one must question the route taken to that conclusion. To know where there was room for greater change, we must scrupulously reconstruct the full circumstances. We must make clear what ideas were heretical and what ideas were intelligible and acceptable to men of power, what institutions blocked reform and which ones could have been bent to its service, what was the weight of the past, what was the position and magnitude of revolutionary sentiment and the confidence and resolve of the moneyed classes.

Actually, few general interpreters of the New Deal have studied the relation between opportunities and obstacles in the 1930s with any real dedication. Every author forms his own impressions in this matter, believing it to be crucial. But few consider the pressures with meticulous care. One good reason for this is that a reasonably complete account of what happened does not compress easily into one volume (or even three, as with Schlesinger). To explore what could have happened as well as what did happen has been more than authors attempting synthesis could manage. So authors have relied upon quick calculations and instinct, the conservatives seeing Roosevelt pushing where there was no mandate or need, the liberals seeing barriers of exonerating dimensions, the radicals describing inviting vistas to the left.

The evidence suggests that an indignant tone toward the small steps taken by the New Dealers is not quite appropriate. To be sure, there seem to be occasions when the forces of movement had the advantage and failed to exploit it even reasonably well. To take one example, in their recent books on the Social Security Act, Dan Nelson and Roy Lubove strongly imply that concessions were made to conservative opinion in financing and in standards that were not politically necessary. Other instances may exist where even the most diligent research fails to discover any substantial reasons why the President or his administration settled for less than they asked for. But one usually discovers formidable institutional and intellectual difficulties.

The New Deal story is heavy with barriers, resistance, dilution of the reform purpose. Recent studies reaffirm this impression. One learns in Robert Lekachman's *The Age of Keynes* (1967) and in Herbert Stein's recent *The Fiscal Revolution in America* (1969) how little economists of the 1930s understood the forces they sought to control, and how they lacked reliable statistical evidence on which to base their primitive prescriptions. Ellis Hawley's *The New Deal and the Problem of Monopoly* (1966) offers a most persuasive description of America's deep commitment to the mutually contradictory goals of economic individualism and of concentration and argues that in such a setting the New Deal could not have escaped the economic incoherence that helped defer recovery. Those who sense unlimited reform opportunities in the Hundred Days would receive some chastening in Raymond Moley's *The First New Deal* (1967), for example, where he makes a strong case that a more radical banking policy during the March collapse was completely ruled out by the absence of competent personnel who might have framed a nationalization measure. More significantly, William E. Leuchtenburg's essay "The New Deal and the Analogue of War" (1964) helps to explain the general atmosphere of "cooperation" with business that blunted the measures of the Hundred Days. The only relevant past, in the crisis of 1933, was the World War I planning experiment, and under the heavy influence of that memory with its stress on cooperation and unity the New Dealers understandably frittered away the golden months of conservative demoralization with schemes based on the cooperative ideal, which actually involved no fundamental reforms. Leuchtenburg, in another essay, "The Constitutional Revolution of 1937" (1969), explains very clearly the dampening influence on legislative draftsmanship and tactics exerted by the omnipresent threat of unconstitutionality. James T. Patterson has stretched out before us for the first time, in *The New Deal and The States* (1969), one of the most formidable labyrinths of all—the reactionary and unrepresentative state governments, where more New Deal measures were obstructed than even in Congress.

One could easily continue listing studies that enlarge our

awareness of the defenses of existing arrangements in the 1930s. Those noted already appeared in the 1960s, and the shelves were full of such studies long before the 1960s arrived. Any interpretation of the New Deal must meet this evidence squarely. The writers on the left, old and new, have not done so. Just as the liberal centrist historians have had a tendency to lack a strong interest in the spaces to the left of Roosevelt, the New Left historians have systematically, even brilliantly, underrated the obstacles—with one important exception.

To speak in particular about the essays by Barton Bernstein and Howard Zinn that have attracted so much attention, radical historians focused on one major obstacle, an internal rather than an external one: the "ideology" of the liberals themselves. In Bernstein's words:

> The boundaries of New Deal experimentalism, as Howard Zinn has emphasized, could extend far beyond Roosevelt's cautious ventures. Operating within very safe channels, Roosevelt not only avoided Marxism and the socialization of property, but he also stopped far short of other possibilities—communal direction of production or the organized distribution of surplus. . . .Usually opportunistic and frequently shifting, the New Deal was restricted by its ideology. It ran out of fuel not because of the conservative opposition, but because it ran out of ideas.

Here is the heart of the New Left argument. There were possibilities for really radical change; a conservative set of New Deal liberals failed to explore them and blocked access to power for those who would.

Any student of the New Deal will sympathize initially with this argument. While no one has satisfactorily studied the ideas of the New Dealers (whatever may be meant by that label), we are familiar with many of their ideas, and who has not been exasperated by Morgenthau's fiscal conservatism, Hopkins' breezy superficiality, Moley's stubborn faith in businessmen, Wallace's confusing mysticism, Lilienthal's naive assumption that the Farm Bureau-Extension Service bureaucracy represented "grassroots democracy," Eleanor's unflagging innocence. They did not understand Keynes, they did not insist upon uncompromising racial justice, they actually believed that the federal regulatory bureaucracies could be made independent of business power. As for the President, commenta-

tors from Walter Lippmann through Richard Hofstadter and
James M. Burns and Rex Tugwell to Paul Conkin have exposed
the deficiencies of his simple, confused ideas and the many
timidities of his leadership. With a little selective memory, they
may be made to sound incredibly conservative and cautious.
Recall and recite the occasions when they held back, remember
their confusions; hold up their speeches against the brilliant
essays of John Dewey and others with time to think and no
political responsibilities; hold them up against our generation's
broader social vision, three decades wiser and sadder. The
result may be good contemporary politics, but as history it has
serious drawbacks.

The full context has not been supplied. Let us add the
total range of social and political ideas in America in the 1930s
and before, and the New Dealers appear well toward the in-
novative and daring end of the spectrum, with stronger democratic instincts and a stronger commitment to racial justice and
a more steady humanitarianism than all but a scant minority of
their contemporaries. Then add the institutional barriers against
which they worked. When these obstacles are restored to the
picture in fair proportion to their contemporary massiveness,
some defeats are going to be explained less by intellectual
failings than by the sheer inertia of the existing network of
social relations. Finally, restore to the picture the war, agent
of the unravelling of so many liberal plans and the fortuitous
strengthening of corporate capitalism. To those who know
how many reformist initiatives and institutions were crippled
by the war, only the most detailed and powerful argument will
convince them that the America of 1945–1970 was designed
and constructed by the New Dealers.

With these considerations in mind, it is not simple to
answer the question: Why was there not more reform in the
1930s? How important in the final summation will be the inadequacies, preventable and inexcusable, of liberalism as an
ideology? A safe guess is: not nearly as important as the New
Left historians have said. Certainly there were times when
Roosevelt and his lieutenants either failed to press an advantage
or actually restrained more ardent champions of change. But I
would judge that these occasions, if exploited, add up only to
marginal gains and would not have made substantial inroads
on the core of white, upper-class power. The answer to the

question about social change in the 1930s is mostly structural, not ideological; the advantages of the defense, not the errors of the offense; a story justifying sadness more than indignation.

Some of my students, of well-matured radical views, are distressed by this argument. They do not like the sympathy it implies for liberals who held power and left so many unsolved problems. If we argue that the stress ought to be on the external rather than the internal impediments in the 1930s, are we not adopting a determinism that has its own ideological thrust—protecting American political leadership from serious criticism, when many of those leaders have been liberals? But I concede that there are periods in human affairs when men appear to have room to act, have the necessary ideas and power, and mismanage. Such periods would naturally be critically interpreted. Perhaps the New Deal was such a time. I have not insisted that it was not, but only expressed strong doubts that the inadequacies of American liberalism may be decisively demonstrated from the evidence of the 1930s. Too much evidence from that era testifies to inertia and resistance to reorganization, and the radical historians have not adequately argued for a more open situation. Conceivably, books rather than essays would secure Zinn's dream of a discredited liberalism based on a study of the New Deal. My unsolicited opinion is that this will be easier to manage for the postwar period, when the inadequacies of liberal policies gradually became more glaring.

But the 1930s should still attract the friends of a radically different, democratized America. History may not always allow us to condemn those we wish, since it is filled with mighty currents and confusions, and produces sympathy on occasion even for soldiers, hangmen, industrialists, and liberals. But good history seeks, among other things, to specify what it is that holds men back from realizing their best ideals. If it is man's nature that defeats him, this will not encourage the radical. But if, as I believe, men are held back by institutions and the superstructure of ideas they foster, to specify them and describe their deadening drag is to write the most radical history of all.

CONCLUSION: THE IMPACT OF PARTY AND IDEOLOGY ON REFORM

*O*ne cannot draw definitive conclusions from a volume such as this, for its scope of inquiry is extraordinarily broad. Because both the primary and secondary evidence is selective and illustrative, this book is more useful in suggesting fundamental tendencies and raising broad questions than in providing conclusive answers. We began with the present, presenting two highly critical analyses of the American party system. In sustaining their indictments, both Burnham and Burns turned instinctively to historical analysis, and we followed them back to the revolutionary founding, particularly in an attempt to come to grips with the origins of the ideological boundaries within which the American political system has functioned. Surely it is here that we find the greatest of continuities linking the present to the past—a national political character that abhors political extremes. Louis Hartz and others have argued that the absence of a feudal tradition in America and the commanding presence of a Jeffersonian liberal consensus have meant that the American political spectrum has been severely truncated. A comparative judgment is implicit here: in Europe and, by colonial extension, in many of the societies of what we have come to call the Third World, great masses of citizens have held political beliefs tending toward the extreme left and right, and as a consequence both facism and communism have been possible. But in America the great mass has clustered tightly around the political center; there are very few potential recruits on the revolutionary left and the counterrevolutionary right.

It is ironical that the chief celebrants of this historic liberal consensus have been conservatives; for, as Gunnar Myrdal once observed, "America is . . . conservative. . . . But the principles conserved are liberal." The contradiction, however, is more apparent than real, because as we have seen, the American liberal faith that was enshrined at the founding harbored a central fear of governmental power, and the Madisonian structure of government that flowed from this doctrine has ill served those who would use the muscle of government to affect fundamental changes in the status quo. Conservatives have always thrived on stability, and the governmental structure that has sustained the oldest constitutional democracy among the major nations of the world, the oldest currency, and the oldest modern party system has generally served the conservatives well.

At the level of party competition and reform, the consequences of this broad ideological consensus have been profound. First, the Americans instinctively evolved a basic two-party model of partisan competition that the theorists subsequently rationalized as approaching a political ideal (Americans being a much more pragmatic than theoretical people). According to the theory, a two-party system is superior to a one-party system because it offers a viable alternative for democratic choice of governance. It is superior to a multiparty system because the out-party offers a single locus for attracting the allegiance of popular discontent, and hence functions both as a democratic barometer and a potential source of leverage for "throwing the rascals out." In practice, the system has accommodated this function remarkably well, with the out-party ousting the in-party at the presidential apex seventeen times in the United States' first two centuries. This suggests a tendency toward equilibrium in the system, one that is reflected in the party-systems theory of critical realignment.

Another important attribute of the American two-party system that flowed in large part from ideological consensus has been its historic tendency to so broadly structure the two parties that their constituencies have considerably overlapped—that is, both parties have harbored a variety of ideological, class, religious, social, occupational, racial-ethnic, and sectional interests. The great advantage of this arrangement has been that the strains on the political system as a whole have been minimized, and relative governmental stability has been the norm. The chief disadvantage has been that each party has been expected internally to mediate these conflicting interests, and consequently the strains have, at times, been disruptive of party itself. The classic case is the fragmentation of the second party system on the eve of the Civil War. On that occasion, the opposite tendency prevailed, and the basic ideological, sectional, racial, religious, and class cleavages rapidly sorted themselves into a multiplicity of parties that enjoyed an unusual degree of internal cohesiveness, but at the expense of transferring the disruptive strains to the level of government itself. Such a multiparty system, rare in America, has been closer to the norm in Europe, where so many of the modern nation-states have harbored a congeries of mutually hostile factions—socialist, monarchist, communist, republican, fascist, Catholic, Protestant, labor—that have tended to produce infrequent majorities, volatile coalitions, often chronic instability of government, and a great deal of electoral confusion. In modern France, for instance, in the words of a recent comparative study,

> a group unenthusiastic about the Republic was called the Republican Federation. Almost every group which included the word "left" in its title . . . sat in the center or toward the right. . . . Socialist meant democratic, radical meant center, left meant right, right meant reactionary, and independent might mean fascist.[1]

This two-party versus multiparty paradigm of course greatly oversimplifies reality in both cases. In Europe, recent history has witnessed a substantial amount of two-party dominance, and in the United States, the apparent two-party continuity obscures as much as it reveals. For in the light of recent research,[2] we can no longer afford to embrace the simplistic dualism of the Progressive historians. Since the New Deal particularly, this dualism has linked the Democratic Party to the interests of the lower social strata and crusades for liberal reform, and it has projected this linkage from Franklin Roosevelt back through Wilson, Bryan, and Jackson to Jefferson. On the other hand, the Republican Party was linked to the upper social strata and conservative de-

---

[1]Gwendolen M. Carter, John H. Hory, and John C. Ranney, *Major Foreign Powers: The Governments of Great Britain, France, Germany, and the Soviet Union*, New York: Harcourt Brace Jovanovich, 1957, p. 243.

[2]The economic analysis that dominates American Progressive historiography has been more useful in illuminating the politics of the late eighteenth century and the twentieth century, wherein secular and class patterns of politics have been more salient, than for the nineteenth century, wherein religious and ethnic concerns appear to have transcended economic conflict as organizing principles for partisan political life. See, for instance, Lee Benson, *The Concept of Jacksonian Democracy: New York as a Test Case*, Princeton, N.J.: Princeton University Press, 1961; Ronald P. Formisano, *The Birth of Mass Political Parties: Michigan, 1827–1861*, Princeton, N.J.: Princeton University Press, 1971; Michael F. Holt, *Forging A Majority: The Formation of the Republican Party in Pittsburgh, 1848–1860*, New Haven, Conn.: Yale University Press, 1969; Paul Kleppner, *The Cross of Culture: A Social Analysis of Midwestern Politics, 1850–1900*, New York: The Free Press, 1970; and Richard Jensen, *Winning of the Midwest: Social and Political Conflict, 1885–1896*, Chicago: University of Chicago Press, 1971. All of these recent analyses rely heavily on quantitative techniques.

fense of the status quo, and this linkage was projected from Hoover back through McKinley, Grant, and the Whigs to Hamilton and the High Federalists. This is not to say that this socio-economic dualism is dead wrong. Indeed, it has been employed as a useful ordering device throughout this volume because it is helpful in understanding the dynamics of party and politics in our own era, which has inherited the New Deal legacy, in which the socioeconomic dualism makes sense, especially in the light of survey research. Yet in the United States, the dualism has not led to the polarization that has occurred elsewhere.

In Europe, the disruptive strains of the industrial revolution tended to polarize politics in the direction of the socialist left and the tory right, but this did not occur in America. We have discussed the principal reason for this: given a broad ideological consensus that was almost equivalent to no ideology at all, the slightly left-leaning Democrats and right-leaning Republicans still clung to the centrist tradition where the mass of voters were located (witness the recent fates of presidential candidates Goldwater and McGovern). But there is another reason why party polarization has been resisted in America, especially in recent history: the dynamics of socioeconomic stratification, which attracted the allegiance of the lower social strata toward the Democrats and of the upper strata toward the Republicans, has contained a built-in ambiguity.[3] Generally, the white-collar class has been more conservative than the blue-collar class on most economic issues (such as the graduated income tax), but the blue-collar class has been more conservative on a variety of social issues relating to civil liberties and civil rights, international involvement, patriotism, law enforcement, and the like. A more liberal position on such issues correlates highly with the greater education that the upper social strata have traditionally enjoyed. Hence, white-collar Republicans who approve of conservative Republican economic policies (such as regressive taxation) might disapprove of consistently conservative social policies (such as requiring loyalty oaths of public employees). Similarly, but in reverse, blue-collar Democrats approving of liberal Democratic economic policies (such as a high minimum wage) might look

[3]We know this more from relatively recent survey research than from traditional historical evidence, and historians should be cautious in projecting such generalizations backward in time. But the ambivalence with which status stratification has endowed partisan identification is important to understanding contemporary political life, especially its ideological inconsistency.

askance at consistently liberal Democratic social policies (such as amnesty for draft resisters). Contemporary liberalism and conservatism, in this sense, can be highly issue-specific, depending upon one's class status. To the degree that this has been historically true, at least in the twentieth century, critics of the American two-party system who have denounced the two parties for not really differing in any fundamental way have in part misperceived the parties' function. And many of the same critics, who have called for all the liberals to join one party and all the conservatives to join the other, have purchased ideological consistency at the price of misunderstanding (as distinct from disapproving of) reality, because the great mass of the citizens do not seem to have regarded themselves as either liberals or conservatives in any consistent ideological sense. Rather, the more recent evidence suggests that the masses have tended simply to inherit their partisan identity from their parents through the normal socialization of the child, and to have supported positions on specific issues that could be categorized by more sophisticated observers as either liberal or conservative stances, but rarely has there seemed to have been much consistency involved.[4] Given this pronounced tendency of citizen responses to be issue-specific rather than ideologically consistent, the salience of the dominant issue has often determined the success or failure of American reform movements. For instance, as we have seen, during the Civil War the dominant issue in the North was union, and Lincoln was able to keep intact his coalition of conservative unionists and radical antislavery men. But when the war was won and the Union was assured, the dominant issue reverted to the question of race relations, and Lincoln's coalition fell apart. Similarly, during the New Deal the dominant issue was economic deprivation, and Roosevelt was able to keep his polyglot coalition intact. But by the 1960s the increasing salience of the "social issue" (e.g., welfare, crime and violence, race relations) largely shattered the New Deal coalition.

Given these dynamics and constraints of ideology and of

[4]The experience of the pioneer survey researchers is especially revealing here. Initially they included in their questionnaires a standard query whether the respondent regarded himself as liberal or conservative. But internal checks among specific issue-related items revealed such generalized inconsistency that the pollsters concluded that such questions were meaningless, and they threw them out. The modern American, at least, has not been a very ideologically self-aware creature.

party structure and function, we clearly cannot sensibly talk about reform, as did too many of the Progressive historians, by talking about it as exclusively a liberalizing function of the Democratic party. For a nation making a two-century transition from the status of a small agrarian republic to that of an urban-industrial giant, the entire system was continually caught up in the process of reform; and in examining that complicated process we are less interested in the morality play of reform—of who was *for* and who was *against* the public weal—than in the basic direction it took and the degree to which its machinery achieved its stated goals.

Historically the major thrust of the American reform impulse through party competition has been in a basically leftward direction, *if* by leftward we mean the attempt to restructure society's institutions so as to minimize the unfair advantages inherited from a more elitist concept of society and government, and to maximize both the diffusion of society's rewards and the responsiveness of public institutions to majority demands without sacrificing minority rights. This is a very loose definition, but it must be, because the history of American reform is extraordinarily complex. Certainly not all reformist drives have been leftward; few modern liberals would approve, for instance, the campaigns for immigration restriction through national origins quotas, prohibition and blue laws, or eugenics and disfranchisement of the lower social orders, yet these proposals were regarded by their proponents as reforms designed to improve the quality of American life.

But let us consider a selected list of those major American reforms that modern liberals would likely approve—reforms that were successfully embedded in the Constitution or placed in the statute books—and generally ask what happened to them. Several must be regarded by today's standards as universally desirable and largely achieved: the abolition first of the slave trade, then of slavery itself, and eventually, of peonage and the conflict lease system; the gradual extension of suffrage to include all adults regardless of sex and race; the evolution of a commitment to public education, to industrial safety standards, and workers' compensation; and, much more recently, a commitment to minimum standards of public sanitation and health maintenance. Structurally, we should also include the direct election of the president (leaving aside the potential time bomb of the electoral college) and of senators, and the much more recent equal apportionment of legislative representation. We should also include the destruction of the *de jure* system of racial caste.

Such a list is illustrative rather than inclusive, but it suffices to indicate the justly proud achievements of American reform. But let us consider another list of reforms, one that is equally selective and that also includes social goals that are widely regarded as desirable, and reflect on their unintended and often contradictory consequences. Consider, for instance, the campaign against corrupt politics during the Progressive era. The Progressives made war on the city machines and ultimately crippled many of them. But in the process they destroyed, without replacing, an organic and symbiotic network of human relationships that traded jobs and favors for votes—more often than not corruptly—but that nevertheless linked the suffering urban masses to the governing structure in an almost intimate relationship that provokes nostalgia in an age of alienation and faceless bureaucracy. Similarly, the progressive drive for the initiative, referendum and recall, and the election of judges was designed to democratize politics. But the election of judges often compromised the independence of the judiciary and enmeshed it in partisan political snarls, and the initiative, referendum and recall has lent itself too frequently to slick and simplistic or disingenuous public relations appeals directly to "the people" in efforts that avoided the deliberative and fact-finding machinery of law making, and has produced long ballots of bewildering complexity even to the most sophisticated voters. At the national level, the Progressives' successful achievement of the direct election of senators indubitably improved the representative quality of the Senate. But the Progressives' almost equally successful war on the authoritarian power of the Speaker of the House greatly reinforced the centrifugal tendency that was to diffuse power into the hands of senior committee chairmen who were usually elected by "safe" unrepresentative districts. The structural changes in government that so fascinated the Progressives were as often boomerangs as panaceas. But let us turn to a major category of reform activity that involves less structural changes in government, which we associate primarily with the Progressives, than the kind of liberal social legislation that is more readily associated with the New Deal.

Such a list would certainly include the regulatory agencies and the graduated income tax, commitments that the New Dealers inherited from the Progressives and then expanded. Also prominent on such a list would be such staples of the New Deal mold of welfare capitalism as social security, the minimum wage, prolabor legislation, corporate taxation, and TVA. I do not seek to deny the broad public benefits that have flowed from such notable reforms as these. Rather, I wish heartily to acknowledge them, but also to point out how readily the targets of the reforms have absorbed their impact, transferred their costs, and often co-opted their machinery. As cases in point, American corporations have easily transferred taxation costs to consumers and employees, so that the theory of a shared employer-employee burden, as in social security, has been honored largely in the breach. Employers have frequently responded to increases in the minimum wage by eliminating marginal jobs—less out of a punitive perverseness than in response to economic imperatives. The legitimization of organized labor has provided a useful countervailing power to balance industry, but it has also produced conservative unions that were insensitive to the needs of the unorganized. Frequently we have witnessed a punishing and self-fueling inflationary scenario in which labor demanded large increases in wages and benefits, industry balked, labor struck, and industry soon conceded, then promptly passed on to the consumer more than the additional cost in the form of higher prices. The graduated income tax was designed to distribute wealth more equitably, but only the wealthy have been able to afford the loopholes and tax shelters.

The most dramatic example of the tendency of our system of political economy to blunt and absorb the thrust of reform is the history of the federal regulatory agencies. Their very beginning was dramatically revealing in this regard. In 1892, when railroad lawyer Richard Olney left Chicago to become attorney general in Cleveland's second administration, a client asked him to do his best to abolish the five-year-old Interstate Commerce Commission. Olney's shrewd response to the Chicago Burlington & Quincy Railroad (quoted in part in Otis Graham's essay, "Progressive Reform") is a classic:

> My impression would be that looking at the matter from a railroad point of view exclusively it would not be a wise thing to undertake.
> . . . The attempt would not be likely to suceed; if it did not succeed, and were made on the ground of the inefficiency and uselessness of the commission the result would very probably be giving it the power it now lacks. The commission, as its functions have been limited by the courts, is, or can be made, of great use to the railroads. It satisfies the popular clamor for a government supervision of rail-

roads, at the same time that that supervision is almost entirely nominal. Further, the older a commission gets to be, the more inclined it will be found to take the business and railroad view of things. It thus becomes a sort of barrier between the railroad corporations and the people and a sort of protection against hasty and crude legislation hostile to railroad interests. . . . The part of wisdom is not to destroy the commission, but to utilize it.[5]

Clearly, the passage of reform-labeled legislation should not simply be equated with effective reform, as the standard textbooks have too often done—as, for example, in celebrating the passage of the Pure Food and Drug Act of 1906, and then promptly moving on to the next item on the Progressives' agenda of reform. For Congress has not been generous in appropriating funds for its regulatory agencies, and the combination of inadequate staffs, weak fines, and extensive court review has often made a mockery of the agencies' regulatory charge. The first case brought by the government under the Pure Food and Drug Act is a splendid example. The Bureau of Chemistry indicted one Mr. Harper, who was producer of a highly questionable patent medicine with the improbable name of Cuforhedake Brane-Fude. After extensive litigation the bureau eventually won and levied upon Mr. Harper a fine of $700, which he promptly subtracted from his estimated $2 million profits as a kind of licensing fee for blessing the public with the miraculous Brane-Fude. Now, most of the history of American regulatory agencies is not so ludicrous or pathetic, but it does reveal a common pattern wherein the regulators of commerce, trade, power, aviation, broadcasting, banking and securities, the maritime, atomic energy, and space have tended to become adjuncts of the enterprise they were supposed to regulate. This has occurred less through corruption than through a mutual convergence of interests and a mutual circulation of staff, with the vastly superior pay of the corporate executive and attorney not surprisingly besting the federal civil service in commanding ultimate allegiances.

The ultimate litmus test of the efficacy of American reform, particularly in the twentieth century, for which the statistical evidence is most abundant, is the distribution of income. That is, if American reform has generally produced the results that its proponents claimed to pursue, then certainly the American pattern

[5]Quoted in Joseph C. Goulden, *The Superlawyers*, New York: Dell, 1971, p. 185.

of distribution of income should gradually reflect a more equitable trend. But this has not occurred.[6] The most damning radical indictment of liberal reform is that in spite of the successive waves of square deals, new deals, fair deals, new frontiers, and great societies, the maldistribution of income has not fundamentally changed. Critical realignments occur and fundamentally change our political patterns, but these changes do not seem to be reflected in our society's distribution of its basic rewards.

The major point of this brief digression into the frustrations and achievements of American reform is the same point that underpinned the earlier discussion of ideology and party: the need to discard the too-easy dualisms that have characterized the interpretation of American political history in the recent past. This is not to deny that dualisms can be useful and real if kept in perspective—such as the New World versus the Old, Jefferson versus Hamilton, Democrat versus Republican, left versus right. The problem is that they tend so quickly to sort themselves into that ultimate dualism: good versus bad. The point is not that history must be neutral and irrelevant, it is that good historical analysis is both difficult and inevitably value-laden and that it is extremely important in understanding the troubled present. A useful way to illustrate this by analogy, if not pressed too far, is to compare historical with psychological analysis by equating historical ignorance with amnesia. Amnesia is regarded as an extremely severe malady because if one has forgotten who one was, one cannot possibly understand who one is or where one is going. A less pathological example is repression, whereby extremely painful memories are either distorted or are forced from consciousness. Such a mechanism as repression or highly selective recollection is recognizable at the historical level, for example, in the inability of the Allies to locate many Nazi Germans after the fall of the Third Reich, or in the persistence of Americans in regarding General Custer as a glorious hero. All nations harbor ugly recollections, and most attempt to paint their national traditions in rosy colors. It is interesting to note, however, that after so many generations of patriotic history, a tendency recently has surfaced in radical quarters to equate the American national experience with little more than three and one-half centuries of rape

[6]See Herman P. Miller, *Rich Man, Poor Man*, New York: Crowell, 1970.

and genocide. Apparently the masochism of self-flagellation plays its psychological role collectively as well as individually.

But our assessment of the light that historical analysis throws on our present concerns, emphasizing, as it has, fundamental continuities with our past, would be dishonest and self-serving if it failed to acknowledge the discontinuities that distinguish our time from its predecessors. By far the greatest of these is the velocity of change itself, the exponential acceleration in the rate of change that has flowed primarily from science and technology. In *The Meaning of the 20th Century*, Kenneth Boulding dramatically demonstrated this by surveying a number of statistical time series with an eye to locating the date that divides all of human history into two equal parts in regard to the activity surveyed. Mankind of sorts has been around for 2 or 3 million years, but the midpoint for metals extracted from the earth is around 1910, and for chemical publications it is 1950. Indeed, 25 percent of all human beings who have ever lived, and 90 percent of all scientists, are alive today! Should one conclude, then, that with every passing day historical analysis grows less and less useful? Or should one conclude the opposite, that it is precisely those who are hurtling through a storm of change who most desperately need a sense of their origin?

At a less cosmic level, consider the dramatic political changes that surfaced so tumultuously in the 1960s with three phenomena that must be judged as historical firsts in America in terms of their purpose and magnitude: students were rioting for political reasons on the campuses, blacks were rioting in the cities, and a majority coalition forced the government to pull out of an overseas war. Furthermore, the Madisonian government of checks and balances was suddenly dominated by a leviathan Presidency. Also, as Burnham complained, the party system as we had known it seemed to be disintegrating (a 1974 Gallup poll revealed that Republican identifiers had fallen to an all-time low of 24 percent, the Democrats held steady at 42 percent, and the independents had zoomed to 34 percent).

Yet America wasn't quite so topsy-turvy, so severed from her past as it seemed. Polls revealed that most students were not radical activists, most blacks preferred integration and disapproved of rioting, and the antiwar coalition was a curious alliance between left-wing opponents of the war and traditional conservative isolationists. The leviathan Presidency blundered egregiously at Watergate and thereby invited the belated reassertion of congressional and judicial authority. The parties may indeed have been disintegrating, but reputable authorities had circulated decidedly premature rumors about the death of the Republican Party in the wake of Goldwater's disaster in 1964, and similar greatly exaggerated rumors had doomed the Democrats following McGovern's fiasco in 1972.

We shall see. But the point of this contemporary discussion is not to minimize alarm by pointing to reassuring continuities, for that would reflect a conservative bias that continuity was preferable to change, and imply a thralldom of history to conservatism. The essence of historical analysis is not a quest for continuity; rather, it is to assess the balance between continuity and change over time. In calling attention to the remarkable persistence of historical forces, however perverse some of them may be judged, we certainly should not seek to enshrine them, nor to deny that they should be recognized and therefore more effectively fought. To ignore or deny the inertia of history is to shackle the forces that would consciously change its direction. Otherwise we abdicate to the powerful but too cynical French epigram: *plus ça change, plus c'est la même chose.*

SUGGESTIONS FOR
FURTHER READING

$\mathcal{T}$he literature is so vast in the area of American political history that I will suggest here only recent collections that survey the literature and are very helpful in grasping its dimension, complexity, and interpretive thrust. Two anthologies published in the early 1960s provide a comprehensive analysis of the historiographical transition from the "progressive" to the "consensus" school of interpretation: William H. Cartwright and Richard L. Watson, Jr., eds., *Interpreting and Teaching American History,* Washington, D.C.: National Council for the Social Studies, 1961; and John Higham, ed., *The Reconstruction of American History,* New York: Hutchinson, 1962. A third collection, also edited by Cartwright and Watson and published by the National Council for the Social Studies, *The Reinterpretation of American History and Culture* (1973), is a broader sequel to the 1961 volume and assesses by both topical and chronological category the light that a dozen years of research has thrown on the interpretive debate between the progressive, consensus, and new left schools. Also, we are fortunate to have two recently published collections that reflect the latest historical scholarship, much of it quantitative, in American political history: Joel H. Silbey and Samuel T. McSeveney, eds., *Voters, Parties and Elections,* Lexington, Mass: Xerox, 1972, and Lee Benson, Allan Bogue, J. Rogers Hollingsworth, Thomas Pressly, and Joel H. Silbey, eds., *American Political Behavior: Historical Essays and Readings,* New York: Harper & Row, 1974. Enough important publications are cited and assessed in these volumes to capture the interest of students of American political history, not for weeks or semesters, but for years.